LET THE TEXT TALK

Preaching that Treats the Text on its Own Terms

An Update and Revision of Jeff Ray's
Expository Preaching

C. Kyle Walker

Let the Text Talk: Preaching that Treats the Text on its Own Terms
By C. Kyle Walker
Copyright © 2018 by Seminary Hill Press

Seminary Hill Press (SHP) is the publishing arm of Southwestern Baptist Theological Seminary, 2001 West Seminary Drive, Fort Worth, Texas 76115.

All rights reserved. No part of this book may be used or reproduced in any manner whatsoever without written permission from SHP except in the case of brief quotations embodied in critical articles and reviews. For more information, visit seminaryhillpress.com/licensing/permissions.

All Scripture quotations, unless otherwise indicated, are from the New American Standard Bible® (NASB), Copyright © 1960, 1962, 1963, 1968, 1971, 1972, 1973, 1975, 1977, 1995 by The Lockman Foundation. Used by permission. (www.Lockman.org)

Scripture quotations marked ESV are from the ESV® Bible (The Holy Bible, English Standard Version®), copyright © 2001 by Crossway, a publishing ministry of Good News Publishers. Used by permission. All rights reserved.

Scripture quotations marked KJV are taken from the King James Version, public domain.

ISBN-10: 0-9994119-9-3
ISBN-13: 978-0-9994119-9-5

To Mickey Dalrymple:
A pastor who raised up "preacher boys."
He was the first expositor I ever heard.

Table of Contents

Preface ... 1

Part I: The Practice of Text-Driven Preaching

Chapter 1
The Importance of Preaching ... 11

Chapter 2
The Steps of Text-Driven Preaching -
Part I: Interpreting the Text ... 29

Chapter 3
The Steps of Text-Driven Preaching -
Part II: Communicating the Text ... 63

Chapter 4
The Advantages of Text-Driven Preaching ... 99

Chapter 5
The Public Reading of Scripture as a Method
of Exposition ... 115

Part II: A History of Text-Driven Preaching

Chapter 6
Jeff Ray and the History of Preaching ... 129

Chapter 7
Jeff Ray's Influence on Expository Preaching
among Southern Baptists ... 177

Bibliography ... 201

Appendix ... 221

PREFACE

In 1940, Jefferson Davis Ray (1860-1951), the first homiletics professor of Southwestern Baptist Theological Seminary, published *Expository Preaching*.[1] Ray wrote it not for the scholar, but for the common man—the man who had been denied educational advantages. By 1940, Ray was approaching the end of his 37-year tenure (1908-1944) as a preaching professor at Southwestern. He had trained almost 5,000 men to preach, including men such as T.A. Patterson, Paige Patterson's father; Charles Koller, past president of Northern Baptist Seminary and author of *Expository Preaching without Notes*[2]; and Jesse Northcutt, who perhaps taught more men to preach than any other man in Christendom.[3] After 33 years of teaching homiletics, Ray decided to publish his instruction on expository preaching for the men who could not sit in his classroom.

Ray was candid concerning the scarcity of expository preaching in his day. He argued that one was as unlikely to encounter a buffalo on the Texas prairie as he was to hear an expository sermon.[4] Ray's lamentation emerged among a host of others. In fact, the author of every major volume on expository preaching published within 10 years of Ray's work also expressed chagrin at the lack of exposition in the

---

[1] See Jeff D. Ray, *Expository Preaching* (Grand Rapids: Zondervan, 1940).
[2] See Charles W. Koller, *Expository Preaching without Notes* (Grand Rapids: Baker, 1962).
[3] Scott L. Tatum, "The Contribution of Jesse James Northcutt to Southern Baptist Preaching," *Southwestern Journal of Theology* 27 (Spring 1985): 46. Tatum estimates that Northcutt taught approximately 10,000 men to preach during his tenure at Southwestern Seminary from 1939-1987.
[4] Ray, *Expository Preaching*, 81.

pulpit.⁵ Furthermore, the year after Ray's death, Douglas M. White published *He Expounded: A Guide to Expository Preaching*, within which he claims that, between 1910 and 1940, there were "only five books written dealing exclusively with expository preaching" and that "there is a great dearth of expository preaching in the pulpits of today is apparent to all."⁶

Therefore, when Ray penned *Expository Preaching*, he produced one of only a few pieces of literature available on this theme. More significantly, Ray authored the very first volume by a Southern Baptist that exclusively advocated for expository preaching. As an advocate for expository preaching in the first half of the 20th century, Ray found himself in an extreme minority. No other element establishes this truth more than the fact that in the history of Southern Baptists, Ray appears to be one of only two to publish a work advocating exclusively for expository preaching until Jerry Vines published *A Practical Guide to Sermon Preparation* in 1985.⁷

So why have you most likely never heard of Ray's book, *Expository Preaching*? Several reasons deserve attention. First, the book originated

---

⁵See Harold E. Knott, *How to Prepare an Expository Sermon* (Cincinnati: The Standard Publishing Company, 1930); Andrew W. Blackwood, *The Preparation of Sermons* (New York: Abingdon-Cokesbury Press, 1948); G. Campbell Morgan, *Preaching* (New York: Fleming H. Revell, 1937); Faris D. Whitesell, *The Art of Biblical Preaching* (Grand Rapids: Zondervan, 1950); Josiah Blake Tidwell, *Concerning Preachers* (New York: Fleming H. Revell, 1936); James S. Stewart, *Heralds of God* (London: Hodder & Stoughton, 1946); and R. Ames Montgomery, *Expository Preaching* (London: Fleming H. Revell, 1939).
⁶Douglas M. White, *He Expounded: A Guide to Expository Preaching* (Chicago: Moody Press, 1952), 147 and 7. The five books White references include: *The Art of Exposition* by Harry Jeffs, 1910; *Expository Preaching, Plans and Methods* by F.B. Meyer, 1910; *How to Prepare an Expository Sermon* by Harold E. Knott, 1930; *Expository Preaching* by Ames Montgomery, 1939; and *Expository Preaching* by Jefferson D. Ray, 1940.
⁷Jerry Vines, *A Practical Guide to Sermon Preparation* (Chicago: Moody Press, 1985). The following year, Jerry Vines published a companion volume, *A Guide to Effective Sermon Delivery* (Chicago: Moody Press, 1986). The second author is Douglas M. White, who, in 1952, published *He Expounded: A Guide to Expository Preaching*, which was later published as *The Excellence of Exposition* (Neptune, NJ: Loizeaux Brothers, 1977). Although White ministered all over the United States and in various countries, he served most prominently as pastor of First Baptist Church, Bassett, Virginia, for more than 25 years.

Preface

during a time when expository preaching was neither popular nor widely practiced. Second, *Expository Preaching* was not primarily written for the classroom, and, therefore, it was not utilized in the classroom at Southwestern beyond Ray's tenure. Third, Ray himself was not a particularly powerful or popular preacher. Ray pastored small, rural churches, and upon coming to the seminary, he found himself chained to a desk grading the sermons of immature preachers at a young and struggling school.

When Ray retired from Southwestern Seminary in 1944, he wrote in an article for The Fort Worth Star-Telegram that he hoped his brethren would not regard him as the "forgotten man in the matter of preaching."[8] Ray had given his life to the task of training preachers, and he apparently wanted no other endeavor he undertook to overshadow his life's calling. His role of training preachers at Southwestern, however, was obscure.[9] Ray claimed that "he wouldn't change jobs with any man on this earth," but "he didn't want to come to the Seminary as a teacher at first," as he knew he would be trading the prestige of a prominent pastorate for a place of obscure service training young preachers at a newborn seminary.[10] Ray expressed his perspective on the role in a letter to George Truett as follows:

> But I am writing this primarily to congratulate you on your tact in the choice of your last theme. I am not conscious of the need of it myself for, though by nature loving the glamour and charm of the battle field, I have long since, after a pretty hard fight, reconciled myself to staying by the stuff—buckling down over a desk grading the immature sermon outlines of embryonic great preachers … while my

---

[8] Jeff D. Ray, "Hat Still In the Ring," Jeff D. Ray Collection, Archives, A. Webb Roberts Library, Southwestern Baptist Theological Seminary, Fort Worth, Box 4, Folder 155.
[9] Joel Gregory suggested that Ray remained obscure because of Southwestern's tenuous existence during the course of his tenure. Events such as the Depression and World War I greatly threatened the school's future (Joel Gregory, Interview with Author, Waco, February 5, 2014).
[10] Mike Elliott, "Uncle Jeff," Ray Collection, Box 7, Folder 615.

> fellow soldiers are reaping worthy and deserved applause out on the firing line. However, while through the text you used and other scriptures I long ago thoroughly reconciled myself to a life of non-spectacular drudgery and do not chafe under it but rejoice in its opportunity of service.[11]

Finally, Ray's *Expository Preaching* received scant attention within the academy because Ray wrote for the public. In fact, writing for the public versus the academy seems to have cost Ray a place in *The Legacy of Southwestern: Writings That Shaped a Tradition*.[12] According to James Leo Garrett, during the presidency of Ken Hemphill, a proposal was made that the faculty of the School of Theology construct a book to highlight the literary contributions of Southwestern faculty.[13] Garrett served as chairman of the committee nominated to produce the book. The criteria for each chapter highlighting a professor required that professor to possess two things: a substantial corpus of literature to discuss and an extended tenure at Southwestern. Ray met both of these criteria.

As the committee began the process of selecting professors for each chapter, Ray was nominated. The current homiletics professor at Southwestern was then asked to author the chapter on Ray. He responded, however, that he had come to the conclusion that Ray had not produced a substantial portion of literature to constitute a chapter. According to the professor, the committee desired only scholarly writing, and although Ray's writings were voluminous, they were not scholarly. Therefore, the professor proposed that the committee should not include a chapter on Ray. According to Garrett, this was the only case like this that the committee faced. The committee accepted the recommendation without further investigation, and Ray was not included in the book.

---

[11]Jeff D. Ray to George W. Truett, 5 February 1940, Ray Collection.
[12]James Leo Garrett Jr., ed., *The Legacy of Southwestern: Writings That Shaped a Tradition* (North Richland Hills, TX: Smithfield Press, 2002).
[13]James Leo Garrett Jr., Interview with Author, Fort Worth, February 18, 2014. Garrett served as a faculty member at Southwestern in the School of Theology between 1949-1959 and 1979-1997. He continued to do some post-retirement teaching until 2003.

Preface

Garrett admits that the committee did make some mistakes concerning whom they omitted; perhaps Jeff Ray was among them.

Ray indeed became a forgotten man in the matter of preaching. His position and place of service were obscure. Ray was also forgotten because he left so few sermons in print, and writing for the public versus the academy cost him a place in the literary sector of the field of preaching. As a result, Ray was omitted from *Southern Baptist Preaching Yesterday*[14] and *The Legacy of Southwestern*. Furthermore, due to its intended audience, Ray's *Expository Preaching* was never used in the homiletical classrooms of Southwestern Seminary beyond Ray's tenure. It was not even included on the additional reading lists offered on preaching class syllabi. In fact, the book was not listed on Southwestern's Ph.D. comprehensive preaching bibliography until revisions were made in 2010.

Why update and revise Ray's *Expository Preaching*? Within Southern Baptist preaching, Ray was the first to write a volume advocating exclusively for exposition, and he perhaps became the first Southern Baptist professor to champion the singular philosophy of exposition in the classroom. As a result, Ray made a lasting contribution to the legacy of expository preaching among Southern Baptists by establishing a homiletical foundation upon which Southwestern Seminary stands as an advocate for text-driven preaching today. Ray established this foundation by authoring *Expository Preaching* and by instructing approximately 5,000 men in the philosophy of exposition over 37 years.

Historically, Southern Baptists have not been an expository people. Rather, the majority of Southern Baptist preaching has been textual/topical in nature and rhetorically driven in structure. The homiletical methodologies producing such preaching trace back to Jean Claude and the 16th century, and Ray was not exempt from their influence. Ray advocated for expository preaching by instructing students in these methods that both helped and hindered true biblical exposition. However, Ray distinguished himself among Southern Baptist preachers

---

[14] See R. Earl Allen and Joel Gregory, eds., *Southern Baptist Preaching Yesterday* (Nashville: Broadman Press, 1991).

by allowing the authority of Scripture to dictate his philosophy of preaching. Despite his methodological inconsistencies, Ray established the philosophical foundation required for text-driven preaching to be taught at Southwestern today.

Ray preserved and nurtured expository preaching at Southwestern Seminary by ingraining into 5,000-plus men both why they should embrace exposition theologically and how they should perform exposition practically. These men embodied the trajectory of Southwestern's preaching legacy and became the foundation upon which students at Southwestern learn text-driven preaching today. Young preachers at Southwestern deserve to know in whose footsteps they walk, upon whose shoulders they stand, and whose homiletical blood courses through their veins.

The difference between the expository preaching taught by Ray and the text-driven preaching taught by Southwestern's School of Preaching today is not theological but methodological in nature. Text-driven preaching seeks to supply the most faithful methodology for the preacher to honor the nature and authority of Scripture by allowing the text to drive the sermon's substance, structure, and spirit. The trajectory of Southwestern's homiletical instruction has not always been consistent with the direction Ray established. Yet, by returning exclusively to the philosophy of expository preaching and the advocacy of text-driven preaching as a methodology, Southwestern now stands upon the homiletical foundation Ray built.

Text-driven preaching is expository preaching in its purest form.[15] Expository preaching, however, "at its core is more a philosophy than a method."[16] Though Ray wrote *Expository Preaching* with the philosophy of expository preaching in mind, he primarily intended the book to be a guide regarding the methods of performing expository preaching. The problem, however, is that Ray's expository methods did not always align as appropriate expressions of his homiletical convictions. Homiletical

---

[15] The terminology of text-driven preaching and expository preaching will be used interchangeably throughout this work.
[16] Haddon W. Robinson, *Biblical Preaching: The Development and Delivery of Expository Messages*, 3rd ed. (Grand Rapids: Baker Academic, 2014), 5.

Preface

history swayed his expositional ways. Hence, the need stands today for an updated guide to text-driven preaching that appropriately weds the philosophy behind expository preaching and the practice of expository preaching in its purest form. This volume offers that guide.

Although revised and updated, the intent and purpose of Ray's *Expository Preaching* will be retained. The original layout and structure will be followed but reorganized. The content will be updated while highlighting Ray's original convictions and emphases. The result will be a current introductory guide to text-driven preaching. Text-driven preaching will not only be defined and described but also distinguished within the context of the history of preaching as well as of Southern Baptist preaching. This book is intended for any preacher, regardless of his educational level, who desires to preach God's Word faithfully.

C. Kyle Walker
Fort Worth, Texas
October 2018

PART I:

THE PRACTICE OF

TEXT-DRIVEN PREACHING

CHAPTER 1

THE IMPORTANCE OF PREACHING

"The act of preaching is not only the most sacred, but the most important task ever assigned to man." – Jeff Ray

The Word of God

What is more important on planet earth until Jesus returns than preaching? In its most basic form, preaching is speaking God's Word. Out of nothing, all creation came forth the moment God spoke the word! God created the heavens and the earth by speaking. To be more specific, Jesus Christ, the living Word of God, created all things "in the heavens and on earth, visible and invisible, whether thrones or dominions or rulers or authorities—all things have been created through Him and for Him ... and in Him all things hold together" (Colossians 1:16-17.) Who but the one called "The Word of God" will return wearing a robe dipped in blood, leading the armies of heaven, striking down the nations with the sword of the words He will proclaim from His mouth (Revelation 19:13-15)? All of life is sovereignly created, sustained, and governed by the Word of God.

For the people of God, the Word of God comprises a great and granular role in our lives. When God brought the Israelites out of Egypt as a people for Himself through whom He would bring the Messiah, He gave them 10 "words" known as the Decalogue, or Ten Commandments (Exodus 20.) These words reveal God's character and the way of life as

God intended His people to live it. God's people could not live as He intended them to live without His Word.

The words of the Decalogue and the Law were the words the Israelites were to internalize in their hearts and teach to their sons and daughters, that they might fear the Lord and walk in His righteousness. When Moses' mantle passed to Joshua, the Lord commanded Joshua not to let the Book of the Law depart from his mouth so that he would meditate on it and "be careful to do according to all that is written in it" (Joshua 1:8). Joshua could not lead God's people to live as God intended them to live without the Word of God.

The people of God floundered during the days of the Judges because a generation arose who did not know the Lord because they did not know His Word (Judges 2:10). God tore the kingdom from Saul, Israel's first king, because he did not obey the Lord (1 Samuel 28:18). When Saul disobeyed God's voice, God stopped speaking to Saul, and Saul eventually fell on his own sword. David, however, was a man after God's own heart because he was willing to do God's will. He was willing to obey God's Word (Acts 13:22, 1 Samuel 13:14). In fact, David penned these words concerning God's Word:

> How can a young man keep his way pure?
> By keeping it according to Your word.
> With all my heart I have sought You;
> Do not let me wander from Your commandments.
> Your word I have treasured in my heart,
> That I may not sin against You.
> Blessed are You, O Lord;
> Teach me Your statutes.
> With my lips I have told of
> All the ordinances of Your mouth.
> I have rejoiced in the way of Your testimonies,
> As much as in all riches.
> I will meditate on Your precepts
> And regard Your ways.

> I shall delight in Your statutes;
> I shall not forget Your word.[17]

Although David's heart hungered for God's Word, unfortunately, the hearts of the people he led did not. God sent prophet after prophet to remind His people of His word, but they refused to listen. Hence, God's message through Jeremiah: "This wicked people, who refuse to listen to My words, who walk in the stubbornness of their hearts and have gone after other gods to serve them and to bow down to them, let them be just like this waistband which is totally worthless" (Jeremiah 13:10). When God first spoke creation into existence by His Word, it was good. Yet, God's people become good for nothing when they heed not God's Word.

But praise be to God, who, in His mercy and grace, unveiled His plan to take His Word and write it on the hearts of His people (Jeremiah 31:31-34). The second person of the Trinity, who acted as the agent of creation, would be the one to take on human flesh and inaugurate this new covenant. The Word become flesh. His life made the perfect substitutionary sacrifice. His blood paid the penalty. His resurrection from the grave defeated death. His ascension prompted the sending of the Holy Spirit to seal the people of God and write God's Word on our hearts (Hebrews 8:10).

Jesus commissioned His disciples to make disciples of all nations by taking the Word of God to the world—baptizing and teaching (Matthew 28:19-20). Empowered by the power of the Holy Spirit, the apostles where charged with the duty to witness—to speak of what they had seen and heard (Acts 1:8). As they spoke the Word of God concerning what they had seen and heard, "the Lord was adding to their number day by day those who were being saved" (Acts 2:47). The apostles continued "to speak the word of God with boldness," and "the word of the Lord continued to grow and to be multiplied" (Acts 4:31; 12:24).

Paul explained the operation of the supernatural power of the Word of God according to the plan and purpose of God when he wrote:

---

[17] Psalm 119:9-16.

> How then will they call on Him in whom they have not believed? How will they believe in Him whom they have not heard? And how will they hear without a preacher? … So faith comes from hearing, and hearing by the word of Christ.[18]

The Word of God heard and received by faith causes one to be born again:

> For you have been born again not of seed which is perishable but imperishable, that is, through the living and enduring word of God. For, "All flesh is like grass, and all its glory like the flower of grass. The grass withers, and the flower falls off, but the word of the Lord endures forever." And this is the word which was preached to you.[19]

If "man does not live by bread alone, but man lives by everything that proceeds out of the mouth of the Lord,"[20] then what on planet earth is more important until Jesus returns than preaching the Word of God? The answer is nothing other than hearing and heeding the Word of God. Jeff Ray was right: "The act of preaching is not only the most sacred, but the most important task ever assigned to man."[21]

The Word of God and Preaching

The importance of preaching proceeds from the power and authority of the Word of God. Preaching, therefore, can be stripped of its value in two ways. First, preaching is plucked of its power when it attempts to communicate anything other than the Word of God. As water to an engine engineered for gasoline produces instant malfunction, so, too, does a substitute for the homiletical fuel of the Word of God.

---

[18]Romans 10:14, 17.
[19]1 Peter 1:23-25.
[20]Deuteronomy 8:3.
[21]Ray, *Expository Preaching*, 16.

Second, preaching suffers when its source of power, the Word of God, is not fully relied upon and trusted to accomplish its intended goal and purpose. Unfortunately, many preachers claim to preach the Word of God but betray their distrust in its ability by extracting portions of the text that appear relevant, only to discard the rest. When textual meaning is intentionally omitted, preachers jettison much of the Word they claim to trust. Dangers such as these call for clarifying the homiletical implications of the nature and authority of Scripture.

To clarify the nature and authority of Scripture for preaching, let us peer through the eyes of the original author of *Expository Preaching*. When conveying Ray's view of the Bible and its implications for preaching, it is difficult to overlook the role played by two specific men—B.H. Carroll and John A. Broadus. Both men walked as giants in Ray's life, wielding extraordinary influence on him personally and homiletically. Therefore, in order to articulate the truth about the Bible through Ray's eyes, it is appropriate to highlight the convictions of the men upon whose spiritual shoulders Ray and hosts of Baptist preachers stood and still stand.

B.H. Carroll on the Bible

Carroll in particular made a great effort to express his view of Scripture in his work *Inspiration of the Bible*.[22] He begins the volume with Article I of the New Hampshire Confession of Faith, which states:

> We believe that the Holy Bible was written by men divinely inspired, and is a perfect treasure of heavenly instruction; that it has God for its author, salvation for its end, and truth without any mixture of error for its matter; that it reveals the principles by which God will judge us; and therefore is, and shall remain to the end of the world, the true centre of Christian union, and the

---

[22] B.H. Carroll, *Inspiration of the Bible* (New York: Fleming H. Revell, 1930).

supreme standard by which all human conduct, creeds, and opinions shall be tried.[23]

In his own words, Carroll goes on to write, "When you hear the silly talk that the Bible 'contains' the word of God and is not the word of God, you hear fool's talk."[24] For Carroll, the bottom line concerning the Bible is that "when these inspired declarations were written, they were absolutely infallible."[25]

Carroll's convictions certainly cannot be transferred directly to Ray. However, it seems difficult to discount the theological lineage Ray entered from the time he first encountered Carroll at First Baptist, Waco. This lineage was strengthened as Ray sat at Carroll's feet as a student in the embryonic seminary in Carroll's back bedroom. The lineage culminated as Carroll entrusted the seminary of his dreams to Ray and a few other faithful and like-minded men. In fact, no man could acquire a teaching position at Southwestern Baptist Theological Seminary without fully endorsing the first article of the confession mentioned above.[26] According to J.B. Gambrell, the Scriptures were to Carroll "the voice of God speaking to his soul and to humanity with divine authority."[27]

Ray provides confirmation of the continuity of his convictions with Carroll through his own words. He argues that the Bible is "the source of religious information … the vehicle of God's will and … the ultimate authority in religion."[28] It comes as no surprise then for Ray to include among his suggestions for finding a pastor that a church should seek "a man who accepts the Bible as the authoritative word of God and daily studies it and humbly tries to practice and enforce its teachings."[29]

---

[23]Ibid., 15.
[24]Ibid., 20.
[25]Ibid., 25.
[26]Ibid., 35. Ray was among the first faculty of Southwestern Seminary. See Ray, *The First Faculty of the Seminary.*
[27]Jeff D. Ray, *B.H. Carroll* (Nashville: Baptist Sunday School Board, 1927), 61.
[28]Jeff D. Ray, *The Highest Office* (New York: Fleming H. Revell, 1923), 159.
[29]Jeff D. Ray, Ray Collection, Box 5, Folder 209.

Ray's most revealing thoughts pertaining to the Bible come from a page in the back of one of his personal copies of God's Word. On this page are Ray's sermon notes for a message he entitled "The Word of God."[30] Through seven points, each supported by three textual references, Ray expresses his doctrine of Scripture as follows:

I. We are begotten by it.
    a. James 1:18
    b. 1 Peter 1:23
    c. John 6:63

II. We are nourished by it.
    a. 1 Cor 3:2
    b. Heb 5:12-14
    c. 1 Pet 2:2

III. We are built by it.
    a. Acts 20:32
    b. John 17:17
    c. 1 Thess 2:13

IV. We are kept by it.
    a. Ps 17:4
    b. Ps 119:11
    c. John 17:14-15

V. We are made clean by it.
    a. Ps 119:9
    b. Eph 5:26
    c. John 15:3

VI. We are furnished for work by it.
    a. 2 Tim 2:15

---

[30] Jeff D. Ray, Ray Collection, Box 2, Folder 28.

      b. 2 Tim 3:16-17
      c. Acts 17:11-12

VII. We are overcome by it.
      a. Jer 23:29
      b. Heb 4:12
      c. Eph 6:7[31]

In the sermon's conclusion, Ray summarizes the Bible as "God's message," "the law of life," and "the story of the Church."[32]

John Broadus on the Bible

In addition to B.H. Carroll, John Broadus made an unmistakable theological and homiletical mark on Ray's life. Ray never knew Broadus to the same degree he did Carroll. Furthermore, Ray missed the opportunity to study directly under Broadus at Southern Seminary. However, the evidence of Broadus' influence on Ray's theology and practice of preaching runs deep, beginning with a common conviction concerning the Scriptures.

Broadus established the foundation of his scholarship on "the divine inspiration of the Bible" and expressed his doctrine of Scripture most clearly in *Paramount and Permanent Authority of the Bible*, a sermon preached before the American Baptist Publication Society in 1887.[33] In this sermon, Broadus declares "that the Bible is the word of God; not merely that it contains the word of God," and that "the Bible is to us the highest authority of religious truth" in "whatever it intends to teach."[34] In his pastoral ministry textbook, *The Highest Office*, Ray provides further evidence of Broadus' perspective on the Bible and simultaneously adds his personal endorsement. Ray writes:

---

[31] Ibid.
[32] Ibid.
[33] Russ L. Bush and Tom J. Nettles, *Baptists and the Bible* (Nashville: Broadman and Holman, 1999), 205-06. See also John A. Broadus, *Paramount and Permanent Authority of the Bible* (Philadelphia: American Baptist Publication Society, 1887).
[34] Broadus, *Paramount and Permanent Authority of the Bible*, 3-4.

The last address that Dr. John A. Broadus ever made to his students was about Apollos, where it is said of him that he was "mighty in the Scriptures." In this last address, his swan song, this man of many books, this man familiar with the world's literature as few men have been, with a pathos, a fervor and an evident sincerity that no man who heard him will ever forget, insisted that the Bible must be the preacher's preeminent book. To the preacher, if other books shine as the stars, the Bible must blaze as the sun.

What higher encomium could the Holy Spirit give a man than to say of him that he is "Mighty in the Scripture"? What price would be too great to pay that the preacher might become "Mighty in the Scripture"? What increased stability, efficiency and spiritual joy would come to our churches if it could be truthfully said of them all that their pastors were men "Mighty in the Scriptures"?[35]

Furthermore, Broadus connects his beliefs about the Bible with preaching in his famous homiletical text *On the Preparation and Delivery of Sermons*. Based on the permanent and paramount authority of the Bible, Broadus argues that the primary purpose of a sermon "is the development of a (biblical) text, an explanation, illustration, application of its teachings," and that the preacher's primary business "is to teach God's word."[36] Ray not only endorsed such ideas but also instilled them in thousands of preachers at Southwestern Seminary as he utilized Broadus' textbook for all 37 years of his teaching tenure.[37]

Grasping the nature of Scripture and its implications is crucial to an accurate understanding of the nature and importance of preaching. Ray's view of the Bible laid the slab upon which he built his belief that preachers must study the Bible as the "source of authoritative preaching

---

[35]Ray, *The Highest Office*, 159-60.
[36]John A. Broadus, *A Treatise on the Preparation and Delivery of Sermons*, 18th ed. (New York: A.C. Armstrong & Son, 1892), 39.
[37]Jeff D. Ray, "Homiletics," Ray Collection, Box 5, Folder 206.

material."[38] Ultimately, a high view of Scripture demands a high view of preaching.

Implications for Preaching

The Nature of Preaching

Again, Ray championed the conviction that "the act of preaching is at once the most sacred and the most important task ever committed to any man."[39] His reasoning for such a conviction is simple: "Other things may and certainly do help, but public preaching, with its intensity of thought and its impassioned emotion, has always been and doubtless always will be the major note in winning men to Christ."[40] He also argues that "five things give public, vocal preaching an immeasurable advantage over any other method: magnetism, aggressiveness, compassion, adaptability, responsiveness."[41] When addressing the topic "If I were a Young Preacher," Ray notes:

> If I were a young preacher I should concerning my preaching task say with Paul 'this one thing I do'; I should not allow myself to get tangled up in business, politics, social reform or athletic sports; I should lay myself out to be a preacher, just a preacher, nothing but a preacher, all a preacher.[42]

---

[38]Jeff D. Ray, "Do Preachers Think?" in *Meant for Men* (Nashville: Broadman Press, 1939), 19.
[39]Jeff D. Ray, "The Place of Preaching," Ray Collection, Box 5, Folder 212. Here, Ray continues this affirmation by writing, "An act so high and sacred in its importance rebukes the slovenly, disorderly, superficial way in which, many times, we discharge its holy functions."
[40]Ray, *Expository Preaching*, 16.
[41]Ibid. Ray admitted that not every preacher will possess all five of these qualities to the fullest degree. However, he did believe that "any man called of God with an atom of preaching gift ... will find himself possessed to a surprising degree of all five of these soul-moving oratorical qualifications."
[42]Jeff D. Ray, "If I Were a Young Preacher," Ray Collection, Box 5, Folder 164.

According to Ray, preaching truly is the most noble and "virile task on earth" because it involves communicating the inerrant and authoritative Word of God by which men are saved.[43] The intimate bond between God's Word, preaching, and salvation grounds and justifies the connection between the authority of the Scriptures and Ray's stance on the nature of preaching. A conviction concerning the importance of preaching also theologically determines Ray's next move from the nature of preaching to its proper priority in the life of a local church.

The Priority of Preaching

Ray fundamentally believed that "great churches stem from great pulpits."[44] His warrant behind this aphorism was the reality that "the right sort of church is not built by managerial skill—by diplomacy and engineering and wire-pulling and gum-shoeing and pussy-footing," but only "by an open, frank, outright, thorough, impartial feeding of the people out of the Holy Scriptures—rightly dividing the Word of God."[45] In the eyes of Jeff Ray, the pulpit was sacred, and he lamented the languishing status of many pulpits in his day.[46] Here, another case arises where the blood of B.H. Carroll courses through Ray's veins, for Carroll proposed, "As water will not rise above its level, so no church will ever rise permanently above its pulpit."[47] Therefore, Ray vigorously sought to defend the priority of the pulpit from anything that might detract from its preeminent position, including the wrong sort of man to fill it.

Ray not only viewed preaching as the highest task given to man, he also viewed the position of pastor as the highest office. His high view of preaching coupled with his regard for the pastor's position as the highest

---

[43]Ray, "Do Preachers Think?" in *Meant for Men*, 19. The DNA for such a conviction appears traceable to B.H. Carroll, as Ray wrote that preaching was for Carroll "the knightliest, most chivalrous, most appealing, most romantic task to which man ever set his hand" (*B.H. Carroll*, 63).
[44]Ray, "The Place of Preaching," Ray Collection.
[45]Ray, *The Highest Office*, 54.
[46]Scott L. Tatum, Interview with Author, Telephone Interview, Fort Worth, February 15, 2013.
[47]Ray, *B.H. Carroll*, 84.

office crystalizes in the context of the local church. He writes, "The public preaching of the gospel is the preeminent task of the church."[48] According to Ray, no activity on earth transcends the priority of this responsibility. In his own words, he writes:

> Whatever may be said of the value of other pastoral functions the careful preparation and effective delivery of sermons is the preacher's preeminent task. If he majors on any other duty at the cost of preaching he sacrifices the best on the altar of the merely good. Effective preaching is a quality essential in the growing of an effective church. There never has been and there never will be a long continued, mutually congenial, eminently useful pastorate with a weak man in the pulpit. There never has been an all-around perminently [sic] preeminent church that was not blessed with a strong preacher permanently in the pulpit.[49]

Ray unashamedly believed the most important position on planet earth is the office of pastor, the most important place is the pulpit, and the most important task is preaching. The nature of Scripture ultimately lands Ray at this position, with all its practical implications that he never took for granted.

Based on his theology of the Bible and preaching, Ray recognized that "the greatest human need of our churches today is strong, unfettered gospel preaching in the pulpit," so he commanded, "Untie your preacher's hands and tell him to preach the gospel or get out of the way for somebody who can."[50] In his article entitled "Preachers Urged to Give Full Hour to Worship, Not Pep Rallies, Funds Drives," Ray asserts:

---

[48] Jeff D. Ray, *The Country Preacher* (Nashville: Sunday School Board of the Southern Baptist Convention, 1925), 120.
[49] Ray, "The Place of Preaching," Ray Collection.
[50] Jeff D. Ray, "A Columnist at Church," Ray Collection, Box 4, Folder 105.

The Importance Of Preaching

> My first word is about the Sunday morning hour set aside, theoretically, as an hour of worship and prayerful meditation on the Holy Scriptures. Not even one minute of this 11 o'clock hour on Sunday should be given over to promotional activities of any sort—neither for an increase of numbers, nor the advertisement of a banquet, nor a pep announcement about the winners in a basketball game, nor even a boost for the young people's meetings in the evening. ... Are there not other occasions when you can tinker with and oil up the machinery and thus avoid robbing that strategic 11 o'clock 60 minutes of its spiritual fervor?[51]

Ray explains how the preeminent place of preaching should be realized by a local church. First, he argues that the physical structure and equipment of the meeting house should be designed "for the most effective preaching of the word."[52] Second, a church must realize the preeminence of preaching "in the call of the preacher," thereby "untying his hands that he may make preparing and delivering sermons his chief business in his pastorate."[53] Finally, the preacher's attitude toward preaching should communicate its preeminence. This attitude for Ray means the preacher giving careful attention to the "multiform demands" of preaching, including "its doctrines, its homiletical order, its vigorous English, its grammatical correctness, its proper pronunciation of words," and "its winsome delivery."[54]

Perhaps the most disregarded implication today that concerns the preeminence of preaching according to Ray involves the activities that should or should not occur from behind the pulpit. Ray acknowledges that a physical pulpit is no more sacred than any other piece of furniture in a church meeting house. Yet, he laments the passing of a bygone day

---

[51]Jeff D. Ray, "Preachers Urged to Give Full Hour to Worship, not Pep Rallies, Funds Drives," Ray Collection, Box 1, Folder 19.
[52]Ray, "The Place of Preaching," Ray Collection.
[53]Ibid.
[54]Ibid.

when "the brethren of a previous generation … had such an exalted opinion of the sacred quality of the act of preaching the Word that by an association of ideas it sanctified the very place where it was done."[55] Such an opinion carried the following implication:

> In that day, if a layman addressed the church, he never did it from the pulpit because he believed that in that place none but God's anointed prophet must stand to deliver to the people the holy oracles of the Lord. The present day democratizing of the pulpit is dangerous only as it indicates in the life of the church a recession from the former preeminent place of preaching. Whatever may be the temptation to the contrary, your pulpit and especially your Sunday morning pulpit, is to be a place and time when you should follow the example of Jesus (Luke 24:27): "And beginning at Moses and all the prophets, he expounded unto them in all the Scriptures the things concerning himself." In that solemn hour, so charged with spiritual possibilities, the true preacher, turning away from little topical talks about current events, will so expound a portion of God's Word that his congregation going out will be saying, like the two on their way to Emmaus, "Did not our heart burn within us…."[56]

A Philosophy of Preaching

Ray's stance on the authority of Scripture not only determined his position on the nature and priority of preaching but also his philosophy of preaching. According to Ray, the inspiration and infallibility of Scripture necessitates a singular philosophy of preaching. Ray refers to this philosophy as expository preaching.[57]

---

[55] Ray, *Expository Preaching*, 19.
[56] Ibid., 19-20.
[57] Ibid., 46. Ray argues, "If the primary idea of preaching is the expounding of God's Word, does it not follow that exposition would be its

The Importance Of Preaching

Ray defined expository preaching as "that which accurately interprets, intelligently amplifies, and effectively applies a passage of Scripture."[58] He built his advocacy for such preaching on the observation "that expounding the Scripture seems to be the original idea in preaching" throughout the Old and New Testaments.[59] Ray communicates his perspective on the issue in the following passage:

> When I am to make a sermon I have found it an easy job quickly performed to deduce a topic from a text and make a rhetorical outline of that topic and dress it up in platitudinous superficialities and palm it off as a message from the Word of God. But I have found it difficult, laborious, and time-consuming to dig out an adequate interpretation of a passage of Scripture and coordinate the results of that patient digging in an effective, logical outline. Because I have allowed so many little "higglety-pigglety," inconsequential enterprises to break in on my time, I have felt it necessary to follow the line of least resistance and thus have I, and doubtless thus have you, formed the habit of preparing mainly topical sermons. I am an "old dog" now and they tell me that it is hard to teach an antiquated canine a new trick, but I say to you solemnly that if I could call back fifty years, I should

---

predominating characteristic?"

[58] Ibid., 47. Ray's definition of expository preaching reveals the influence of Broadus, whose book, *A Treatise on the Preparation and Delivery of Sermons*, he utilized throughout his career as professor of homiletics at Southwestern Baptist Theological Seminary. Because of this work, Broadus is the homiletician credited with giving the Baptist sermon a distinctive shape through explanation, argumentation, illustration, and application.

[59] Ibid., 48. This is one of five arguments that Ray makes for expository preaching. The remaining four are as follows: expository preaching was the method of Jesus; it requires the preacher to have a higher knowledge of Scripture; it allows for difficult and confrontational texts normally avoided to be dealt with in natural progression; and finally, it greatly reduces the possibility of a preacher misunderstanding and misapplying a passage of Scripture.

make it a life's ambition to be a real expositor of the Word rather than a rhetorical declaimer on topics and mottoes.[60]

Although Ray knew "that genuine expository preaching is almost as rare as the once multitudinous buffalo on our Texas prairies," this in no way undercut his conviction "that expository preaching is the ideal method—that is the method most profitable, both to the preacher and to his people."[61] This conviction concerning expository preaching harks all the way back to the nature of the Bible itself. As did Broadus and Carroll, Ray believed that the very words of Scripture are inspired by God, which means that the words of Scripture as signs signify the very ideas of God.[62]

If this is true, then the most direct, efficient, and accurate method for communicating God's ideas expressed through inspired human language is expository preaching.[63] If God's inspired Word expresses His ideas, then how could communicating anything other than those very ideas be labeled preaching? In short, Ray's philosophy of expository preaching is rooted in none other than the reality of the verbal plenary inspiration of the Bible.

Finally, Ray emphasized that expository preaching manifests its greatest quality by pointing to the person and work of Jesus Christ. Ray gives voice to this deep conviction by recalling a dream wherein his wife, who was then dying of disease, had come back youthful, riding a white horse, and saying:

---

[60]Ibid., 81-82. Secondary sources confirm that Ray was an advocate of "the classical expository sermon with unity and orderly structure" and that "most of his sermons were expository." See David L. Larsen, *The Company of the Preachers*, vol. 2 (Grand Rapids: Kregel, 1998), 557; and Al Fasol, *With a Bible in Their Hands: Baptist Preaching in the South, 1679-1979* (Nashville: Broadman and Holman, 1994), 118.
[61]Ray, *Expository Preaching*, 81 and 53.
[62]See Carroll, *Inspiration of the Bible*, 20.
[63]Ray positively quotes Lewis O. Brastow, Yale homiletics professor, who claims, "The matter of the sermon must be drawn somehow legitimately out of the text, or drawn through it so as to take fiber, color, shape, and direction from it, and thus a correspondence be realized between the text and the substance, sentiment and object of the sermon." In *The Work of the Preacher: A Study of Homiletic Principles and Methods* (Boston: The Pilgrim Press, 1914), 123. Quoted in *Expository Preaching*, 101-02.

> I am sent back to you with the message I gave you once in the happy days of our youth. The message is: Give a wider place in your preaching to expounding this Book and exalting its matchless Hero. He wrote no line in the Book, but every word in it from its 'In the beginning God' to its last 'Even so, come quickly, Lord Jesus' is a witness to His majestic person and His saving power. I am sent to urge that in preaching this Book you will not fail to speak a good word for Jesus. ... Pack your sermon full of Jesus.[64]

Of all the implications resulting from a belief in the full inspiration and authority of the Bible and their bearing on preaching, maintaining a central focus on Jesus is by far the most natural. Jesus Himself witnesses to the truth that Scripture as a whole testifies about Him.[65] Therefore, expository preaching that, by design, seeks to expose the ideas of Scripture must ultimately point to the One about whom all of Scripture testifies. Ultimately, Ray's philosophy of expository preaching crystalizes in reference to its grounding—the inspiration of Scripture and its goal—that people see Jesus and exalt Him as Lord.

Conclusion

The act of Christian preaching implies that God has spoken and that the Old and New Testaments are the very words of God in written form.[66] Because God inspired human authors to inscripturate His Word and commissioned faithful servants to communicate His Word, the essence of preaching is "re-presenting" the words of God.[67] In fact,

---

[64] Ibid., 54.
[65] "You search the Scriptures because you think that in them you have eternal life; it is these that testify about Me" (John 5:39).
[66] See 2 Timothy 3:15-16; 2 Peter 1:20-21; 2 Peter 3:16. See also Peter Adam, *Speaking God's Words: A Practical Theology of Preaching* (Vancouver: Regent College Publishing, 1996), 37.
[67] Steven W. Smith presents preaching as "re-presenting" God's Word in *Recapturing the Voice of God: Shaping Sermons like Scripture* (Nashville: B&H

the very idea behind the word *kerrusso*, which Paul employs to charge young Timothy to "preach the Word," is of a royal ambassador or town crier commissioned by the emperor to repeat his decrees to the public.[68] Thus, according to the New Testament, preaching is an act that centers on the communication of God's Word. The theological relationship between the nature of Scripture and the act of preaching is intimate, and expository preaching is the homiletical methodology that honors this relationship most fully.

No wonder Ray argued that public preaching was the primary way of winning men to Christ and conforming them more fully to Christ. In light of the importance of preaching, a closing thought from Ray is apropos:

> Most of the men in the ministry today are good men, but most of them are not first-rate preachers. The tragedy of it is that most of them do not seem to realize that preparing and delivering sermons is the main business of the preacher. The result is they spend more time and give more nervous energy and hard work to secondary things than they do the major task. They are setting-hens on porcelain eggs. If God has called a man to preach, he can preach if he will try.[69]

Now, with the importance of preaching in mind, the following chapter will articulate the definition and steps of text-driven preaching.

Academic, 2015), 3. See also 2 Timothy 3:17-4:2.
[68]Walter Bauer, *A Greek-English Lexicon of the New Testament and Other Early Christian Literature,* ed. and trans. William F. Arndt, F. Wilber Gingrich, and Frederick W. Danker [BAGD], 3rd ed. (Chicago: University of Chicago Press, 2000), s.v. "*kerrusso.*"
[69]Ray, *Expository Preaching,* 14-15.

CHAPTER 2

THE STEPS OF TEXT-DRIVEN PREACHING

Part I: Interpreting the Text

"Real expository preaching accurately interprets, intelligently amplifies, and effectively applies a passage of Scripture." – Jeff Ray

Defining Text-Driven Preaching

As Haddon Robinson posits, "Expository preaching at its core is more a philosophy than a method."[70] Ultimately, however, expository preaching is not only a philosophy but also a practice. In fact, unless the philosophy of expository preaching leads to the practice of exposition, then expository preaching does not exist at all.

Unfortunately, true expository preaching often never makes it to the pulpit. Many a preacher accepts the philosophical foundations of expository preaching but denies them in practice. Sometimes, preachers unconsciously reject exposition in practice. Yet, many preachers, despite their verbal affirmations of exposition, often consciously decide to substitute for it in the pulpit. No matter the reason, the rejection reveals a preacher's true homiletical convictions. Pulpit practice proves what one

---
[70] Robinson, *Biblical Preaching*, 5.

believes about preaching. Therefore, the nomenclature of "text-driven" preaching is valuable in part because it distinguishes true expository preaching from what is often mislabeled as "expository preaching."

Although no one method exclusively constitutes text-driven preaching, it is true that certain homiletical practices are either consistent or inconsistent with a text-driven philosophy. Therefore, the key to performing text-driven preaching is to identify the practices that are consistent with a biblical philosophy of true expository preaching. Before leaping to identify these practices, though, a bridge is needed. A natural gap exists between philosophy and practice—hence another reason so many preachers claim to do exposition but fail to do so in practice. The gap is definition—a definition of text-driven preaching, to be exact. A definition of text-driven preaching clarifies its identity, establishes parameters, and provides a guide to appropriate methods for execution. A clear definition of text-driven preaching, therefore, is crucial to practicing it appropriately.

David Allen does not claim to have coined the term "text-driven preaching," but he started utilizing it in the late 1980s as a professor of preaching at Criswell College.[71] By text-driven preaching, Allen means preaching that "attempts to stay true to the substance, the structure, and the spirit of the text."[72] Over time, Allen's colleagues in the School of Preaching at Southwestern Seminary further refined the concept. Steven Smith writes, "Text-driven preaching is the interpretation and communication of a biblical text in a sermon that re-presents the substance, structure, and the spirit of the text."[73]

This will be the definition of text-driven preaching utilized in this work. Do not miss how similar it is to Ray's definition! Perhaps a breakdown of the definition would be helpful. Text-driven preaching is preaching that treats (interpretation and communication) a text (natural

---

[71] David Allen, Interview with Author, Fort Worth, September 19, 2014. When asked, "Who first coined the term 'text-driven preaching'?" Allen replied, "Perhaps I did, but I am not necessarily claiming I did."

[72] David Allen, "Text-Driven Preaching: Why and What?" (paper presented at the annual meeting of the Evangelical Homiletics Society, Fort Worth, TX, October 13, 2016), 3.

[73] Smith, *Recapturing the Voice of God*, 17.

thought unit of Scripture) on its own terms (substance, structure, and spirit.)

Expressed another way, text-driven preaching is the process of identifying what the text says and communicating what the text says in the way the text says it. The meaning of a text is more than the subject, theme, or topic (substance) of the text. In this way, written communication is similar to verbal communication. The meaning of what someone says is a composite of context, word choice, and manner of delivery. The same sentence spoken different ways in different contexts means very different things. The same principle applies to Scripture. In order to grasp the full meaning of the text, the preacher must not only interpret the meaning of the actual words, but also the context and manner (structure and spirit) in which the words have been written. This means the preacher must first select a natural thought unit of Scripture. Then, the preacher's interpretation and communication must stay true to the substance, structure, and spirit of that text.

More on selecting a natural thought unit of Scripture for the sermon lies ahead. For starters, it is necessary to recognize that written communication (including Scripture) is nothing like an amoeba! "Formless and void" the Scripture is not! Unfortunately, one of the most overlooked realities of language is the inherent structure it possesses. J. Beekman, J. Callow, and M. Kopesec explain, "Thought can only be shared with others by giving it perceptual shape."[74] Verbal communication exists due to structured sounds such as phonemes, syllables, and phonological words. Furthermore, the word "text" signifies a unit of written communication and figuratively expresses the idea of structured meaning. Werner Stenger defines a text as "a cohesive and structured expression of language that, while at least relatively self-contained, intends a specific effect."[75]

In other words, the form of language (speech sounds in their phonological, lexical, and grammatical structures) gives substance to

---

[74] J. Beekman, J. Callow, and M. Kopesec, *The Semantic Structure of Written Communication* (Dallas, TX: Summer Institute of Linguistics, 1981), 8.
[75] Werner Stenger, *Introduction to New Testament Exegesis* (Grand Rapids: Eerdmans, 1993), 23.

cognitive ideas. Language, however, is more than the sum of these forms. Language also has meaning. The components of form are mentioned above. Meaning, however, is composed of referential, situational, and structural meaning, all arranged in a certain semantic structure. Most fascinating is the fact that "there is a finite set of [semantic] communication relations that exists for all languages."[76] This means that the structural rules facilitating the meaning of language are universal and at work in all human communication.

As a result, selecting a natural thought unit of Scripture means the preacher must select his text along the appropriate structural lines of meaning that allow him to treat that text on the terms the author intended. This is why continuous exposition (i.e., running commentary) that simply treats one verse after another until time no longer permits is not text-driven preaching. This method of preaching ignores the structure of the text and thereby jettisons the semantic meaning of the text.

Selecting a natural thought unit of text paves the way for proper text-driven preaching. Next, the preacher's interpretation and communication must stay true to the substance, structure, and spirit of the text. Allen concisely defines each "term" of the text as follows:

> The "substance" of the text is what the text is about (theme) and what it is saying about it. The "structure" of the text concerns the way in which the author develops the theme via syntax and semantics. A text has not only syntactical structure but also semantic structure, and the latter is what the preacher should be attempting to identify and represent in the sermon. The "spirit" of the text concerns the author-intended "feel" or "emotive tone" of the text, which is influenced by the specific textual genre, such as narrative, expository, hortatory, poetic, etc.[77]

---

[76] Allen, "Text-Driven Preaching: Why and What?" 11.
[77] Ibid., 3.

Interpreting the Text

The text *says* something. This is its substance. What the text says, however, is not the text's full meaning. The text also *is* something. The author took the substance of words and constructed them in a specific way. This is the text's structure. Every text is structured to present the words in the specific way that the author intended. Finally, the text *feels* something. The author chose a certain literary form or genre based on the emotive feel he intended to convey. Stories, letters, poems, etc. are general ways an author can package a text, and each type of packaging best conveys certain tones or moods. Therefore, the meaning of a text is the total combination of the words the author selected, the literary design the author constructed, and the emotive feel the author intended. Further explanation of these "terms" of the text will follow. For now, it is only necessary to recognize that in order for preaching to be text-driven, it must do justice to the full meaning of the text by treating it on all of its own "terms."

Performing Text-Driven Preaching

With the definition of text-driven preaching serving as a homiletical bridge between theory and practice, we are now ready to cross over from "what" to "how." In one sense, it is impossible to provide a single, comprehensive list of steps to construct a text-driven sermon on every biblical text. God inspired the Scriptures in all types of literary genres, and each genre possesses its own literary terms. Furthermore, no two biblical texts are exactly alike, which means no two texts are semantically identical. Therefore, there is no one sermon structure (or set of sermon structures) that works for every text. Yet, do not lose heart! This is the beauty and wonder of text-driven preaching! It harnesses the unique message of every single text by providing principled steps any preacher committed to text-driven preaching can follow.

The Primacy of Prayer

The final and most important reality to realize before presenting the steps of text-driven preaching is the importance of prayer. Preaching is more about faithfulness than success. Of course, every preacher desires to see physical and spiritual signs of success, but ultimately, faithfulness is success. God calls preachers to be faithful. God assigns to Himself the role of producing success (transformed hearts and lives). Both the call to faithfulness and our complete dependence on God for all success should drive us as preachers to our knees in prayer.

Moreover, no man naturally volunteers (or should volunteer) to stand and speak for God. Who would dare handle words of life and death? Who would dare take on the responsibility of shepherding souls toward a fixed and eternal heaven or hell? Who desires a stricter judgment for having been a teacher of God's Word? Such questions should be rhetorical. The weightiness of preaching outweighs every earthly scale! As Paul cries, "Who is adequate for these things?" (2 Corinthians 2:16b). The answer: No one! No matter his talent, gifting, personality, knowledge, or charisma, no one is sufficient to be a preacher. The goal and purpose of preaching—the supernatural change and transformation of the human heart—exceeds the capabilities of every man.

On the one hand, we, as preachers, are woefully insufficient. On the other hand, however, God's Word inspired by the Holy Spirit is sufficient. Furthermore, when God calls a man to preach, He sets him apart and equips him for the work. Preaching, therefore, occurs at the intersection of three realities: (1) the insufficiency of the preacher; (2) the sufficiency of the Word; and (3) the sovereignty of God over all results. Here, the paradox of preaching crystalizes. God calls preachers to labor as if the results depend on them. Simultaneously, God calls preachers to entrust the results entirely to Him.

How should we respond to such a paradox? We pray! We pray! We pray! Prayer bridges the mysterious space between our feeble human labor and the omnipotent movement of God's hand. Prayer is a place where the transcendence and immanence of God meet in our lives. Prayer is a space where we strive but God accomplishes. No set of homiletical steps for constructing a sermon are complete without saturation in prayer. Though I cannot fully explain it, I plead with you to begin your sermon preparation on your knees asking for God's assistance. I encourage you to pause along the way, return to your knees, and again ask for God's help. Prayer is primary in preaching. Be sure to talk to God before, during, and after you plan to speak for God.

Step 1: Select the Text

Wait a minute … will not any text of Scripture do? Yes and no. Yes, every text in the Bible demands to be preached. However, do not haphazardly select the dimensions of your text. The Bible is a book made up of natural units of thought. The Bible has two primary units—the Old Testament and the New Testament. It gets far more granular than that. The Old Testament consists of 39 books and the New Testament, 27 books. These testaments, made up of 66 books, provide the macro structure to the literary thought units of the Bible. However, each book is also internally structured on the micro level.

Think about it like this. If the Bible is a "body" of literature, then it is composed of body parts. A human body is composed of an upper and lower body. The upper and lower body each have their respective parts. Each of these parts consists of smaller parts. Though every part connects to make the whole, every part is unique and must be understood on its own terms. Understanding and treating an arm is very different from treating an eye. In order to select a text properly, one must understand the literary terms of the text. Scripture is literature. Of course, Scripture is much more than literature, but not less. Thus, preachers must not take for granted the basic qualities of literature, otherwise they risk mistreating what they claim to highly revere.

Literature comes in a variety of forms known as genres. "Genre" is the literary form/species/type of the text that determines how the text communicates and therefore how it should be interpreted. You are familiar with the concept already if you understand the difference between fiction, non-fiction, mystery, biography, self-help, travel, history, poetry, reference, etc. Based on the terms of each type of genre, readers naturally refrain from approaching and interpreting biography in the same way they do science fiction or poetry. Neither should preachers approach and interpret all the genres of the Bible in the same way.

Every text of the Bible is equally inspired and true. Yet, each biblical genre presents its own terms of engagement.

There are many different genres in the Bible. What is encouraging for the preacher, however, is that every biblical genre belongs to one of three macro-genres: story, poem, or letter. In fact, "everything in Scripture is a story, a poem, or a letter."[78] Scholars do vary on exactly how many individual genres the Bible contains. Smith claims, "There are arguably nine discernible genres of Scripture: Old Testament Narrative, Law, Psalms, Prophecy, Wisdom Literature, Gospel/Acts, Parables, Epistles, and Revelation (Apocalyptic.)"[79]

The key is to remember that all nine-plus biblical genres can be categorized according to a common structure that fits within one of the following: story, poem, or letter. Smith's *Recapturing the Voice of God* serves as a primer on preaching each biblical genre, and his synopsis of how an understanding of genre influences proper text selection for preaching is insightful. He writes:

1. Story (Narrative): Old Testament Narrative, Law, Gospels/Acts, Parables
2. Poem: Psalms, Prophecy, Wisdom Literature
3. Letter: Epistles, Revelation

> There is a lot to understand about genre. However, one must at least understand narratives (stories) and their scene structure, Epistles (letters) with their paragraph structure, and Hebrew poetry and its strophe structure (a strophe is to poetry what a paragraph is to prose—a contained unit of thought, much like a verse in a song).[80]

Therefore, the natural thought units of the Bible are not only organized by the two testaments and by their 66 books, but also by the genres contained within each book. Selecting a text to preach requires

---

[78]Smith, *Recapturing the Voice of God*, 27.
[79]Ibid.
[80]Ibid.

Interpreting the Text

identifying the genre of the text and then selecting a natural thought unit based on the terms of that genre. Narrative literature directs the preacher to select a complete story with its respective scenes. Epistolary literature (letters) typically asks the preacher to select a natural thought unit in the form of a paragraph. Poetry requires preachers to select a strophe or strophes grouped by stanza (strophes grouped by theme) that form a poem, prophetic oracle, song, proverb, etc.

One of the most common pitfalls of "expository preaching" occurs when preachers cut (select) a text according to dimensions that deform its natural thought structure. Text-driven preaching is treating a text on its own terms, and that begins with extracting a natural thought unit of the Bible. To do otherwise is at best to present the truths of Scripture in a way that is foreign to the way God inspired them.

In summary, select a text for preaching in line with the natural thought dimensions provided by the genres of story, letter, and poem. With this in mind, most preachers will find themselves in one of two scenarios when selecting a text. In scenario one, the preacher selects a text for a one-time occasion. In scenario two, the preacher selects a text in the context of a local church where he preaches weekly.

a. Selecting a Text for Occasional Preaching

Selecting a text for the occasional preaching opportunity tends to be the most difficult for beginning preachers. The Bible offers so much. Where to begin? In this situation, the place to begin is the same as every other preaching situation—on your knees in prayer before the One who called you to speak on His behalf. Prayer must precede preaching. Prayer must permeate the preparation for preaching. Prayer must coincide with preaching (more on this one to come.) Between prayer and preaching, a symbiotic relationship exists. Effectively communicating for God depends upon effectively communicating with God. Therefore, begin the text selection process on your knees. Then, while remaining in a posture of prayer, dive into the Word. Read, explore, and review various texts. Ask God to guide you to the text His people need to hear, and ask God to give you confirmation and peace concerning that text. To find the right text for the one-time preaching opportunity, pray, read the Bible, and ask God for direction.

b. Selecting a Text for Weekly Preaching

Selecting a text week by week for the Sunday sermon is a different situation. The role of prayer in the process remains the same. However, a pastor shepherding his flock has the advantage of intimate awareness of their needs. This knowledge, taken to God in prayer, along with a knowledge of God's Word, is the formula for selecting a text to preach each Sunday. Ideally, the pastor will follow the Lord's guidance to select a book of the Bible to preach through week by week. Selecting various passages of Scripture to assemble a thematic sermon series is also a possibility. Keep in mind, however, that God's people need a steady diet of God's Word. Preaching consecutively through a book of the Bible provides a planned diet that harnesses not only the thematic consistency of the book, but also the inspired way God chose to package the book. The advantages of text-driven preaching through books of the Bible are myriad and will be discussed later. Worth mentioning now, however, is that preaching book by book is one of the primary ways preachers can treat the Bible on its own terms.

Once a preacher commits to preach week by week through a book of the Bible, selecting the text for each individual Sunday requires homiletical cartography, a process referred to here as "charting." Cartographers construct maps of geographical regions in order to reveal the lay of the land, to establish boundaries, and to provide a navigational guide. In the same way, preachers must chart the biblical book they plan to preach in order to understand the homiletical lay of the text, to establish the boundaries of natural thought units, and to produce a preaching calendar as a guide for week-to-week sermon preparation. Charting is one of the key steps in the process of planning your preaching that promotes consistent text-driven preaching.

Start the charting process by studying the book of the Bible you have selected as a whole. Zoom out and research the background, authorship, original audience, date, and context of the book. Identify the book's genre(s), structure, purpose, themes, key literary devices, characters, etc. Then zoom in and get a feel for the text itself. Read the book as a whole multiple times if possible. Note key observations. Take your time and notice the boundaries distinguishing one natural thought unit (story, poetic strophe, or paragraph) from another.

The goal of charting is to produce a "map" of the boundaries of each natural thought unit of text in the book that includes the following for each text: a rough outline, an attempt at the main idea, preliminary observations, and an assigned calendar date to preach the text.[81] An awareness of the main idea of each text you will be preaching ahead of time serves as a powerful tool to harness illustrations via reading and daily life over the weeks leading up to the sermon. Charting the book you will be preaching ahead of time provides an indispensable guide for your week-by-week sermon preparation.

Step 2: Read, Read, and Re-Read the Text

The exegetical process of interpreting the text begins with the basics. The first step is so basic that many overlook it: reading, reading, and re-reading the text. Many preachers disregard this step to their own peril. Yet, it is arguably the most important of all the interpretive steps.

a. Examining the Whole

Grasping the full picture of the text requires repetitively reading it. G. Campbell Morgan, the great British expositor, read the text at least 40-50 times before preaching it. At minimum, one should read the text 20 times. Not all 20 readings must take place in one sitting. Spread the reading over two or more days, if possible. The results of repetitive reading never cease to amaze. The more one reads, the more one sees.

---

[81] Great preaching requires planning. Charting is one way of familiarizing yourself enough with a Bible book so that you can assign upcoming texts to specific dates on the calendar. This enables the preacher to study, research, pray, and plan according to the upcoming texts. This level of planning also enables worship songs and entire worship services to coordinate with the content of the text. For more on planning your preaching, see Stephen Nelson Rummage, *Planning Your Preaching: A Step-by-Step Guide for Developing a One-Year Preaching Calendar* (Grand Rapids: Kregel, 2002).

Pay careful attention to the context as you read and take notes of observations and questions. Zoom back out periodically and read the text in the context of the surrounding paragraphs or storyline. Compile your study notes in one central location—physical notepad, word processor, etc. Personally, I begin my study notes on a particular passage with the heading "reading notes."[82] Under this heading, I record every observation and question I have of the text. Beginning the process of interpreting the text by reading it repeatedly is the equivalent of placing a piece of meat in a slow-cooking crock-pot. The more one reads the text, the more tender it gets. Eventually, the message falls right off the bone.

By reading the text repeatedly, you gain a familiarity with the text that will also aid the translation process. Therefore, after reading the text as a whole 20 or more times in English, translate the text from the Greek or Hebrew to the degree your exegetical skills allow. Whether or not full translation is possible for you, do compare the various English translations at this point. Include your translation and/or English version comparison notes in your study document under the heading "Translation and Notes." Translating the text takes your exegetical understanding from 2D to 3D, from black-and-white to full color.

b. Examining the Parts: Epistolary Literature

With a rough translation complete, zoom in and read the text more closely. Zooming in begins at the sentence level for epistles, where thought units typically consist of one paragraph. Identify the individual sentences of the Greek text. Distinguish independent clauses and dependent clauses. Mark grammatical features (subject, verb, predicate, etc.) and the punctuation of each sentence. Move to the phrases within each sentence, noting what they depend on or modify. Note parts of speech (nouns, pronouns, prepositions, conjunctions, etc.) and identify key words. Major on verbs and verbals (participles and infinitives) by parsing each one. As David Allen emphasizes, "Verbs are the load-

---

[82]After "Reading Notes," the following headings further organize my study notes: Translation and Notes, Text Structure, Illustration and Application Ideas, and Commentary Notes.

bearing walls of language," especially for epistolary literature.[83] Other non-verb key words will be worthy of further study as well. Word studies are well worth the effort when performed accurately to avoid potential exegetical fallacies.[84]

c. Examining the Parts: Narrative Literature

Examining the parts of narrative literature mirrors in many ways the process for epistolary literature (letters). However, instead of zooming in to examine individual sentences, examine the individual scenes in the story. The elements of setting, plot, characters, point of view, and rhetorical devices collectively communicate the meaning of the text.

The setting of a story is twofold. First, there is the physical, historical, and cultural setting of the story. Second, there is the literary setting. This is where and how the story unit falls into the larger macro narrative of the biblical book and Bible as a whole.

The next element of the story is the plot, which is the primary element driving the story's development. Aristotle went so far as to call the plot the "soul" of the story.[85] Practically, this means the plot functions to "highlight ideas, induce suspense, and fulfill expectations."[86] Most stories have a plotline built with a unique combination of the following elements: background, initial situation, conflict, rising tension, climax, resolution, and conclusion. Identify the role of each scene and how each scene relates to the narrative as a whole. The collective parts played by each scene determine the plot, and the nature of the plot determines the specific kind of story you are preaching.

Stories typically develop according to established patterns. Comedy and tragedy are the two most common plot patterns, but at least a dozen

---

[83] Allen, "Text-Driven Preaching: Why and What?" 7.
[84] D.A. Carson's *Exegetical Fallacies,* 2nd ed. (Grand Rapids: Baker Academic, 1996) is a useful guide to help preachers avoid some common exegetical pitfalls.
[85] Aristotle, *Rhetoric and the Poetics,* trans. W. Rhys Roberts and Ingram Bywater (New York: Random House, 1984), 1450a. Also, see Jeffrey D. Arthurs, *Preaching with Variety: How to Re-create the Dynamics of Biblical Genres* (Grand Rapids: Kregel, 2007), 68.
[86] Arthurs, *Preaching with Variety,* 71.

exist.⁸⁷ A comedy is a "U-shaped story that begins in prosperity, descends into tragedy, and rises again to end happily."⁸⁸ A tragedy is "the story of exceptional calamity. It portrays a movement from prosperity to catastrophe."⁸⁹ Discovering the particular pattern of the story clarifies the trajectory and purpose of the text.

The characters constitute the third element to analyze in every story. The characters are the players in the plot. Remember, plot is primary. Therefore, studying the characters of the story means understanding "the function of characters in relationship to the plot."⁹⁰ Distinguish the major character(s) from minor ones. Pay particular attention to any character descriptions offered by the narrator. Observe the actions and speech of each character. Finally, do not forget the potential significance of character names to the story.

The fourth element through which to analyze a narrative text is point of view (narration). If possible, identify the narrator or author. Sometimes, this will not be possible, but always remember that the narrator is inspired, which means every detail regarding what he says and how he says it is intentional and crucial to the meaning of the text. The author is doing something with what he is saying, so let him be your guide.⁹¹ Tactics like irony, metaphor, repetition, humor, allusion, foreshadowing, etc. are all windows revealing what the author

---

⁸⁷Steven D. Mathewson adapts Leland Ryken's list of plot motifs and names them as follows: quest (hero), death, rebirth, initiation, journey, tragedy, comedy, crime and punishment, temptation, rescue, suffering, Cinderella (rags-to-riches), and revelation. In *The Art of Preaching Old Testament Narrative* (Grand Rapids: Baker Academic, 2002), 48.
⁸⁸Leland Ryken, *How to Read the Bible as Literature ... and Get More Out of It* (Grand Rapids: Zondervan, 1984), 82.
⁸⁹Ibid., 83.
⁹⁰Mathewson, *Preaching Old Testament Narrative*, 57.
⁹¹This claim is a major premise of Abraham Kuruvilla's *Privilege the Text! A Theological Hermeneutic for Preaching* (Chicago: Moody, 2013). Kuruvilla writes, "In any text, an author is always doing something with what he/she is saying. This concept is particularly critical for biblical interpretation for preaching, an endeavor geared to accomplish life-change. For such purposes, one must view the biblical text as saying something in order to accomplish some purpose. Without comprehending what the author is doing with what he is saying, there can be no valid application" (52).

is doing. The elements of setting, plot, characters, point of view, and strategic rhetorical devices collectively communicate the meaning of a narrative text.

d. Examining the Parts: Poetic Literature

Poetry as a biblical genre is most often associated with the book of Psalms, and rightly so. The Psalter is a collection of songs or musical poems. However, songs and many other forms of poetic literature not only constitute other whole books of the Bible, but also various portions of many books. Prophetic books such as Hosea, Joel, Amos, Obadiah, Micah, Nahum, Habakkuk, and Zephaniah are almost entirely poetic; and Isaiah, Jeremiah, Jonah, and Zechariah contain extensive portions of poetry. Furthermore, songs and other forms of poetic literature contribute to Genesis, Exodus, Deuteronomy, Judges, 1 & 2 Samuel, 1 & 2 Kings, Proverbs, Lamentations, Job, Song of Songs, the Gospels, and many New Testament letters. Therefore, preachers must realize that biblical poetry constitutes a significant portion of the Scriptures.[92]

The diverse nature and frequently embedded position of poetry within other genres presents a challenge to preachers. Poetic forms are vast. How do preachers properly approach them? Step one, identify the specific type of poetry in the text (psalm, prophetic oracle, war song, lament, hymn, creed, wisdom saying, praise song, dialogue, proverb, riddle, admonition, allegory, confession, beatitude, etc.).[93] Discovering the type of poetry under examination reveals the specific purpose that the author intended to accomplish. This exegetical step is the most vital, for it assists in answering the ultimate question, "What did the inspired author intend?"[94]

---

[92] Smith lists the subgenres of "poem" as Psalms, Prophecy, and Wisdom Literature in *Recapturing the Voice of God*, 29. However, poetry is not limited to these subgenres alone. Poetry contributes to the canon from the Pentateuch to the New Testament.
[93] Providing a complete listing of poetic subgenres is beyond the goal here. However, preachers should utilize helpful tools on biblical literature to help them identify which type of genre or sub-genre they are working with.
[94] Robert Plummer, *40 Questions About Interpreting the Bible* (Grand Rapids: Kregel, 2010), 244.

Step two, study the text with an understanding of how Hebrew poetry functions. With a knowledge of the specific type of poetry at hand, you are primed to examine the text more closely. However, a knowledge of how Hebrew poetry communicates is crucial for accurate interpretation. The three primary characteristics that contribute to the form and function of Hebrew poetry are metrical patterns (repeated syllable or stress patterns), parallelism, and metaphorical language.[95] Unlike English poetry, Hebrew poetry rarely rhymes. Yet, "rhythm is one of the major identifying marks of Hebrew poetry."[96] Therefore, preachers, especially those able to work with the Hebrew text, are able to utilize rhythm as a major criterion for identifying a text as poetic.

Parallelism, however, is by far the most comprehensive characteristic of Hebrew poetry.[97] It not only helps identify a text as poetic, but it also provides insight into the structure and meaning of the text. The three most basic forms of parallelism are synonymous parallelism, antithetical parallelism, and synthetic parallelism.[98] First, identify the pattern of the poetic lines and group the strophes (stanzas) that go together. Thought development, stylistic changes, chiasm, and alliteration all work to reveal the breaks between strophes. After identifying the poetic structure, examine the type of parallelism at work in order to understand how each strophe operates.

---

[95] Grant R. Osborne, *The Hermeneutical Spiral: A Comprehensive Introduction to Biblical Interpretation* (Downers Grove: IVP, 2006), 224-31.

[96] Ibid., 225.

[97] According to Dan McCartney and Charles Clayton, "Parallelism occurs where two or more lines of approximately equal length (in number of syllables) and similar grammatical structure deal with the same subject. The second line provides a bit more information or a different depiction than the first line, either by addition, contrast, or specification," in *Let the Reader Understand: A Guide to Interpreting and Applying the Bible*, 2nd ed. (Phillipsburg, NJ: P&R, 2002), 230.

[98] Synonymous parallelism—"The second or subsequent line repeats or reinforces the sense of the first line, as in Isaiah 44:22." Antithetical parallelism—"The second or subsequent line contrasts the thought of the first, often reinforcing the first line by the contrast, as in Hosea 7:14." Synthetic parallelism—"The second or subsequent line adds to the first line in any manner that provides further information, as in Obadiah 21." See Gordon D. Fee and Douglas Stuart, *How to Read the Bible for All Its Worth*, 3rd ed. (Grand Rapids: Zondervan, 2003), 198-99.

The third characteristic of Hebrew poetry is metaphorical language. This type of language summons emotion and enhances memory. Stylistic devices such as alliteration, acrostics, chiasm, hyperbole, paronomasia (play on words), and vivid imagery often play a strategic role. Such lyrical rhetoric and imagery pull the reader into the text and provide preachers with creative tactics to communicate the text. The key is to harness these poetic elements correctly.

First, the lyrical nature of poetic language conveys meaning more by the whole than by individual parts. Songs express their message by the complementary relationship of chorus and verse rather than by isolated words. Therefore, preachers must realize that "word studies are not as determinative in the Psalms as they are in the New Testament Epistles."[99]

Second, the figurative language or metaphors that frequent biblical poetry demand careful treatment. Often the author does not intend the image or metaphor to be interpreted literally. Therefore, preachers must be sure "to look for the intent of the metaphor" and then "translate it into the reality it is pointing to."[100] Moreover, the images serve the purpose of practical illustration more often than doctrinal expression. In other words, typical biblical poetry is not primarily intended to codify propositional doctrine (New Testament hymns/creeds being an exception), though it certainly possesses and reflects it. Thus, preachers must avoid the pitfall of putting more theological weight on a metaphor than the author intended. Avoid this mistake by identifying how the author situates the metaphor within the structure and context of the poem.

To summarize the process of examining biblical poetry, begin by identifying the specific type of biblical poetry at hand. Second, read the poetic text in light of how Hebrew poetry functions (meter, parallelism, and metaphor.) Finally, keep the following general guidelines in mind. Note the historical background of the poem/poetic text if possible. Study the parts of the poem in light of the whole. This is especially

---

[99] Osborne, *The Hermeneutical Spiral*, 225.
[100] Fee and Stuart, *How to Read the Bible,* 208.

crucial for books like Job and Ecclesiastes. Even the book of Proverbs must be seen as a whole in order to understand accurately the intent of individual sayings. Overall, the genre of biblical poetry presents some of the most diverse texts for the preacher to tackle. An informed approach, however, positions the preacher to harness its unique characteristics for the sake of his hearers.

By the end of step two, the majority of the exegetical heavy lifting is complete. You have identified and interpreted each exegetical piece of the text. Now you must determine precisely how this text fits together in order to see and articulate its structure. This step is perhaps the heart of text-driven preaching. Almost every biblical preacher completes some form of steps one and two. What happens next, however, is the key to text-driven preaching. You now understand what the text says (substance). The next step will prepare you to say what the text says in the way the text says it.

Step 3: Determine the Structure of the Text

When explaining the steps of interpreting a text, Jeff Ray pauses to mention "some personal, intellectual, and temperamental gifts the preacher must have if he is to be a dependable and helpful interpreter of the Scriptures."[101] Ray writes, "To begin with, I should say he must have been from the beginning endowed with some native literary instinct and by one method or another he must have developed that instinct."[102] Ray argued that preachers must have a fundamental understanding of the way language works if they are going to handle the Scriptures properly. Although each preacher has his own degree of native instinct, the good news is that this understanding can be learned. In fact, it must be learned in order to do text-driven preaching.

One of the primary differences between elastic definitions of expository preaching and true text-driven preaching is the ability to grasp the structure of the text and allow it to drive the development of the sermon. Literary instinct, as Ray put it, is certainly helpful for

---

[101] Ray, *Expository Preaching*, 31.
[102] Ibid.

the task. Fortunately, however, good resources exist that succinctly articulate how language works, enabling any preacher to elevate his literary instincts. The appendix included in this volume is a summary and paraphrase of one of these resources, *The Semantic Structure of Written Communication* by Beekman, Callow, and Kopesec. This work is an introduction to how language works. One would do well to read it entirely. However, the distillation of the content in the appendix presents a primer for preachers seeking to divide rightly the Word of truth.

a. Grammatical Structure

Every text possesses two types of structure. First, every text possesses word structure. Word structure or grammatical structure (also known as surface structure) names the specific way the author arranged the words of the text. Remember, this arrangement is inspired and conveys meaning. Determine the grammatical structure of the text by producing a grammatical diagram.

Producing a grammatical outline is most critical when treating epistolary literature. Notice how diagramming begins to unlock the structure of the text in the examples below. Sentence structure, subjects, verbs, direct and indirect objects, conjunctions, modifiers, etc. all rise to the surface in a grammatical diagram. Poetry and narrative literature depend less on grammatical structure to convey meaning than epistolary literature. However, diagram poetic literature as much as practically possible, especially individual psalms and proverbs. When working with narrative literature, diagram (map out) the scenes in the story. Do pay close attention to sentences that convey vital information or produce a crucial turn of events. These sentences in the story are worth diagramming.

b. Semantic Structure

In addition to word or grammatical structure, every text possesses idea structure. The author not only arranged the words of his choice into a certain structure, but he also related the ideas of the text together in a certain way. Think of the text as a family tree. Each person in a family tree relates to every other person in the family tree via a specific type of relationship—son, daughter, husband, wife, in-law, cousin, etc. In the same way, every idea within the text relates to every other idea in the text via a specific relationship.

The relationship(s) between ideas (structure of ideas) within the text is known as semantic structure. Semantic structure is the "master" structure of the text. More often than not, the grammatical structure and the semantic structure of a text will work together to reveal the unity, coherence, and prominence present in every natural thought unit of text. However, in special cases, the semantic structure may override the grammatical structure to reveal what is most prominent. The example below from Philemon presents such a case.

The key to remember is that the author has arranged the ideas in the text via a specific set or type of relationship. These relationships must be discerned in order for the structure of the text to drive the structure of the sermon. For example, Psalm 23 presents the primary idea (head) that "The Lord is my shepherd, I shall not want." Every verse that follows verse 1 answers (that is, provides grounds for) how the Lord is my shepherd and why I shall not want. Second Peter 2:4-10 argues the primary idea found in verse 9 that God knows how to rescue the godly from trials and how to keep the unrighteous under punishment for the day of judgment. Verses 4-8 all provide historical cases (reasons why), including angels, the ancient world, Noah, the cities of Sodom and Gomorrah, and Lot, all to prove the point made in verse 9. First John 2:15-17 communicates one command (do not love the world) with two supporting reasons why one should not love the world. Hebrews 1:1-4 proclaims that, in these last days, God has spoken fully and finally through His Son. Verses 2b-4 support that claim by clarifying the identity of God's Son with seven descriptions.

Semantic structure consists of the arrangement of ideas in the text. No two texts in Scripture arrange ideas in exactly the same way. What a journey of discovery preachers have before them! Of course, this might also seem daunting. The encouraging thing to keep in mind is that the types of relationships that human language possesses are not infinite! In fact, as Beekman, Callow, and Kopesec argue, all human communication depends on a finite set of communication relationships. Once you become familiar with them, discerning them becomes more and more natural. Consult the appendix for more insight.

c. Constructing an Exegetical Outline of the Text

The goal of determining the grammatical and semantic structure of the text is to produce an exegetical outline that will serve as the template for the final sermon outline. The grammatical outline produced at the beginning of step three is helpful, but the grammatical outline is not sufficient to produce an exegetical outline of the text for preaching. The grammatical outline captures the structure of the words or *form* of the text. The semantic analysis provides the structure of the ideas or *meaning* of the text. When the two are properly understood together, an exegetical outline is possible.

Exegetical Outline | Philemon 21-25

For example, notice the simplified grammatical outline of Philemon 21-25 (ESV). This final thought unit of the letter contains four sentences.

(v. 21)
Confident of your obedience
I *write* to you
    knowing that you *will do* even more than I *say*.

(v. 22)
    At the same time
(You) *prepare* a guest room for me
    for I *am hoping* ... I will be graciously *given* to you
        that through your prayers

(v. 23)
Epaphras ... *sends* greetings to you
    my fellow prisoner in Christ Jesus

(v. 24)
(and) Mark, Aristarchus, Demas, and Luke … (greet you)
   my fellow workers

(v. 25)
The grace … (be) with your spirit.
   of the Lord Jesus Christ

If examining the grammatical structure alone, this text would appear to have four structural elements. However, the grammatical structure fails to convey how these structural elements relate to one another. Are they each equivalent to one another, or is there an internal hierarchy that organizes the meaning so that some ideas are more prominent? This is where an understanding of the semantic structure completes the picture.

First, an analysis of the semantic structure of Philemon 21-25 reveals that verses 21-22 operate together. The primary indicator is the adverb ἅμα, meaning "together" or "at the same time." This adverb links the content of verse 22 to verse 21 through simultaneous time. Yet, are the ideas of verse 21 and verse 22 truly parallel or hierarchically equivalent? No, because the content of verse 22 is a diversion from the primary content of the letter referred to in verse 21. Therefore, semantic analysis reveals that although verse 21 and verse 22 function together as an internal unit of verses 21-25, verse 21 carries the primary idea, and verse 22 relates to that primary idea with a peripheral comment.

Verses 23-24 form the second constituent of the paragraph, greetings. Verse 25 stands distinguished as the third and final element by communicating a closing benediction. Therefore, although Philemon 21-25 grammatically possesses four sentences, there are actually three internal semantic units (propositional clusters.) Based on these three semantic units, the following exegetical outline emerges:

    I.   Paul expresses his confidence in Philemon's obedience and requests a guest room (v. 21-22).

II. Paul sends greetings to Philemon from his fellow co-workers (v. 23-24).
III. Paul asks for God's grace to be with Philemon, his family, and the church in his house (v. 25).

Exegetical Outline | Psalm 32

The following example from Psalm 32 does not include a grammatical outline. Diagramming each sentence in the psalm would be a helpful exercise. However, the poetic genre shifts the structural emphasis from sentence structure to strophe structure, especially the holistic structure created by the poem's strophe. Notice how the exegetical outline below captures the chiastic structural movement of Psalm 32.

A (v. 1-2) Blessed is the one who has been forgiven.
   B (v. 3-4) David testifies of his experience of failing to seek forgiveness.
      C (v. 5) David confessed his sin to God and was forgiven.
         (v. 6) *David exhorts all to seek forgiveness while it is available.*
      C^1 (v. 7) David confesses the reality of God's deliverance.
   B^1 (v. 8-9) David testifies that he will teach others based on his experience.
A^1 (v. 10-11) Blessed is the one who trusts in the Lord.

The skeletal structure of Psalm 32 connects via the literary device of chiasm. Chiasm is a specific type of parallelism where two or more elements are followed by a mention of those elements in reverse order. Chiasm reinforces by repetition and spotlights the content at the chiasm's center. In this case, this center content is the instruction David desires to communicate: "Therefore, let everyone who is godly offer prayer to you at a time when you may be found" (ESV). Three grounds precede the instruction, and those same three grounds, though slightly nuanced, follow the instruction. The exegetical outline highlights the text's most prominent content and displays the poem's development as a whole.

Exegetical Outline | Jonah 1

Scene 1 (v. 1-3): INITIAL SITUATION AND CONFLICT
God calls Jonah to arise and go to Nineveh, but Jonah goes down to Joppa to find a ship to flee from presence of the Lord.

Scene 2 (v. 4-6): RISING CONFLICT
Despite the storm God hurls on the sea, Jonah goes down into the ship, but the captain calls Jonah to arise and call out to God.

Scene 3 (v. 7-10): CONFLICT CLIMAX
The sailors discover the storm has come because of Jonah, who is fleeing from the presence of the Lord.

Scene 4 (v. 11-17): INTERVENTION AND FINAL RESOLUTION
The sailors hurl Jonah down into the sea, but God swallows him up with a great fish.

The meaning of narrative literature depends even less upon individual sentence structure and more on the development of scenes as a whole. Therefore, the exegetical outline above traces the scenes according to the part they play in the larger plot. Each scene distinguishes itself from the others by the turning points in the story. Most often, these turning points occur due to new actions (stimuli) taken by the characters or a change in location or timing. Recognizing the parameters of each scene in the narrative is crucial because the author conveys his message along these lines.

d. Warning: The Exegetical Outline is not the Sermon Outline

The exegetical outlines above remain in the raw form (wording/specifics) of the text. This is as it should be for now. At this point, the goal is only to produce an exegetical outline from the grammatical and semantic structure of the text. One of the greatest mistakes expositors often make, however, is stopping the sermon-building process here. They assume their exegetical outline is sufficient for a sermon outline. This assumption is often the culprit behind the accusation that expository preaching is either boring or lacks a clear main idea. A sermon outline fashioned with the names, places, and circumstances of the first century (or earlier) bores a 21st-century listener. Furthermore, an exegetical outline alone cannot organize and clearly convey the main idea of the text. At this point, the preacher has unfinished homiletical business.

Step 4: Identify the Exegetical Main Idea

Delaying the identification of the main idea of the text until now might seem counterintuitive. The main idea, however, is not fully discernible until the preacher comprehends the grammatical and semantic structure of the text. The structure of the text serves to highlight that which is most prominent. The information that possesses the greatest prominence (either natural or marked) is the main idea. Whatever is most prominent will be the information that every other piece of the text supports and subordinately stands in relationship to. Like the hub of a wagon wheel, the main idea is the organizational center. Therefore, the wonderful part about step four is that, once the first three steps are complete, the main idea should leap off the page.

In order to see and seize the exegetical idea of the text, preachers must understand the difference between an idea and a subject. As mentioned above, it is true that at the core of any thought unit of Scripture will be a subject, concept, topic, or theme. However, none of these things equals a complete idea. Ideas are bigger. Ideas are more specific. Ideas are more complete. An idea begins with a subject, concept, topic, or theme; but it must possess something else in order to be an idea—a complement. Remember, every thought unit of Scripture not only speaks to a concept (subject, topic, theme) but also says something very specific about that concept. Therefore, the main idea consists of what the text is talking about (subject) *and* what the text has to say about it (complement).

For example, "discipleship" is a concept, subject, topic, or theme. Discipleship by itself, however, is not a complete idea. It lacks a complement. Yet, notice the following sentence: "Discipleship is costly." Here is both a subject, "discipleship," and a complement, "is costly." This is a complete idea. Here is a hint that will assist in capturing the main idea of the text: Always articulate the main idea of the text in a complete sentence. Forcing yourself to express the main idea as a complete sentence will ensure that you grasp not only what the text is talking about (subject) but also what the text is saying about it (complement).

The importance of the single idea for every sermon is well attested. Ray put it like this: "A sermon is half preached when the preacher gives his audience a fresh, gripping theme [main idea] well stated."[103] Robinson notes, "Students of public speaking and preaching have argued for centuries that effective communication demands a single theme."[104] Perhaps J.H. Jowett articulates it best:

> I have a conviction that no sermon is ready for preaching, not ready for writing out, until we can express its theme in a short, pregnant sentence as clear as crystal. I find the getting of that sentence is the hardest, the most exacting, and the most fruitful labor in my study. To compel oneself to fashion that sentence, to dismiss every word that is vague, ragged, and ambiguous, to think oneself through to form of words which defines the theme with scrupulous exactness—this is surely one of the most vital and essential factors in the making of a sermon: and I do not think any sermon ought to be preached or even written, until that sentence has emerged, clear and lucid as a cloudless moon.[105]

The necessity of the single idea has even led some preachers to subordinate the place of exposition for the sake of single-idea

---

[103] Ray, *Expository Preaching*, 110.
[104] Robinson, *Biblical Preaching*, 17.
[105] J.H. Jowett, *The Preacher: His Life and Work* (New York: George H. Doran, 1912), 133.

communication.[106] Ultimately, this is a reaction against boring and ineffective expository preaching. It is a reaction against rattling off three alliterated points every Sunday with no main idea tying them together. Such preaching does not perceive the semantic structure of the text that would have clarified the main point of the text and allowed it to guide every aspect of the sermon.

In step four, the goal is only to capture the main idea of the text in the way the author originally meant it for the original audience. This form of the main idea is called the exegetical idea—"what the biblical writer was saying to the biblical readers."[107] Philemon 21-25, Psalm 32, and Jonah 1 continue as examples.

Exegetical Main Idea | Philemon 21-25

I. Paul expresses his confidence in Philemon's obedience and requests a guest room (v. 21-22).
II. Paul sends greetings to Philemon from his fellow co-workers (v. 23-24).
III. Paul asks for God's grace to be with Philemon, his family, and the church in his house (v. 25).

At first glance, nothing appears to tie verses 21-25 together under one exegetical idea. Therefore, in a case like this, preachers often proceed to preach three independent ideas that cover the content of the text but

---

[106] Andy Stanley and Lane Jones, *Communicating for a Change* (Sisters, OR: Multnomah, 2006). Stanley and Jones argue that the goal of preaching is "life change," which requires picking one point to communicate. The problem is that they build an entire communication strategy on communicating that one point, which jettisons the exposition of a natural thought unit of Scripture. This strategy downplays the sufficiency of Scripture and elevates trust in a rhetorical method. Stanley and Jones do not appear to realize that communicating one main point in a sermon is not only possible but also necessary without forsaking expository, text-driven preaching.

[107] Haddon Robinson, "Better Big Ideas: Five Qualities of the Strongest Preaching Ideas," in *The Art and Craft of Biblical Preaching: A Comprehensive Resource for Today's Communicators,* eds. Haddon Robinson and Craig Brian Larsen (Grand Rapids: Zondervan, 2005), 355.

fail to package the ideas appropriately for the listener. The difficulty with this text is that looking within the paragraph for an exegetical idea for verses 21-25 appears futile. Remember, however, that semantic structure not only determines the relationship between constituents within a paragraph, but also the relationship between paragraphs, sections, and larger divisions of the discourse. The meaning (or main idea) of a paragraph is not only communicated by its internal parts, but also by its external relationship with surrounding paragraphs. Because the meaning of a paragraph is always more than the sum of its parts, one of the most effective means of discerning the exegetical idea of a paragraph is not only to look inside the paragraph, but also to look outside of it to discern the role it plays in the larger context.

In this case, Philemon 21-25 closes the letter as a whole. Therefore, as a closing, it will relate to the main idea of the letter. That main idea is in Philemon 17, where Paul states his purpose for writing: "So if you consider me your partner, receive him as you would receive me" (ESV). A study of the semantic structure of the letter reveals that Paul surrounds verse 17 with grounds to persuade Philemon to fulfill his request. These grounds include love (v. 8-9), divine overruling (v. 15-16), the partnership between Paul and Philemon (v. 17), an offer to make up financial loss (v. 18-19), a reminder of Philemon's indebtedness to the apostle (v. 19b), and the desire for a friend's help in relieving anxiety (v. 20). Therefore, knowing the semantic operation of the letter as a whole prompts the reader to expect an appropriate conclusion. Immediately, verse 21 fulfills that expectation with a seventh and final ground supporting verse 17—namely, Paul's personal confidence that Philemon will obey his request. What is Philemon 21-25 talking about (subject)? Paul's confidence in Philemon's obedience! What is Philemon 21-25 saying about Paul's confidence in Philemon's obedience (complement)? Paul is confident that Philemon's obedience will equal and exceed receiving Onesimus as a brother in Christ! **Exegetical idea:** *Paul is confident that Philemon will obey and exceed his request to receive Onesimus as a brother in Christ.*

Interpreting the Text

Exegetical Main Idea | Psalm 32

A (v. 1-2) Blessed is the one who has been forgiven.
  B (v. 3-4) David testifies of his experience of failing to seek forgiveness.
    C (v. 5) David confessed his sin to God and was forgiven.
      (v. 6) David exhorts all to seek forgiveness while it is available.
    C^1 (v. 7) David confesses the reality of God's deliverance.
  B^1 (v. 8-9) David testifies that he will teach others based on his experience.
A^1 (v. 10-11) Blessed is the one who trusts in the Lord.

Psalm 32 is a *maskil* of David, a psalm intended for guidance or instruction concerning the subject of forgiveness. Therefore, this psalm will instruct the reader concerning forgiveness, and it does so most explicitly in verse 6: "Therefore, let everyone who is godly offer prayer to you at a time when you may be found; surely in the rush of great waters they shall not reach him" (ESV). In other words, ask God for forgiveness before it is too late, for God is salvation! Everything else in this psalm surrounds verse 6 in chiastic fashion—what David did and his experience (v. 5, 7), David's silence (v. 3-4) offset now by his counsel (v. 8-9), and the proverbial truths regarding the one who is forgiven (v. 1-2, 10-11). What is this psalm about (subject)? Forgiveness. What does this psalm say about forgiveness (complement)? It says to seek forgiveness while it is available.[108] **Exegetical Idea:** *David instructs sinners to pray for forgiveness while it is available.*

Exegetical Main Idea | Jonah 1

Scene 1 (v. 1-3): INITIAL SITUATION AND CONFLICT

---

[108]Psalm 32 certainly says more than this about forgiveness. However, this is the most prominent thing the psalm says about forgiveness. Everything else in the

God calls Jonah to arise and go to Nineveh, but Jonah goes down to Joppa to find a ship to flee from presence of the Lord.

Scene 2 (v. 4-6): RISING CONFLICT
Despite the storm God hurls on the sea, Jonah goes down into the ship, but the captain calls Jonah to arise and call out to God.

Scene 3 (v. 7-10): CONFLICT CLIMAX
The sailors discover the storm has come because of Jonah, who is fleeing from the presence of the Lord.

Scene 4 (v. 11-17): INTERVENTION AND FINAL RESOLUTION
The sailors hurl Jonah down into the sea, but God swallows him up with a great fish.

Of the three primary genres of Scripture, perhaps the most difficult from which to discern the main idea is narrative. Narrative literature expresses a chronological sequence of events driven by the pairing and chaining (multiple pairs linked together) of stimulus (cause) and response (effect). Of course, a simple summary of a narrative text does not capture the main idea. Authors narrate events, which communicate their message indirectly. In order to comprehend the main idea, preachers must learn to see what is most prominent in narrative literature. Beekman, Callow, and Kopesec explain:

> Since the final response in a chain usually represents the Resolution or Outcome to the Story, there is a movement from the information with lesser prominence to that with more prominence or significance. ... The statement of the theme (main idea) for such units would come from the Resolution or Outcome, together with whatever

---

psalm about forgiveness relates subordinately to the idea of seeking it while it is available.

information from the Problem or Occasion that needs to be stated in order that the statement of the Resolution or Outcome makes sense. The final response(s) of an episode are thus the most prominent units within the episode.[109]

Although narrative literature normally does not directly state the main idea the author is communicating, the final elements of the story usually provide the information to complete the story and therefore reveal the author's main message.

Additionally, narrative literature most often presents ideas through events centered on characters and their actions rather than propositional statements. Therefore, it is critical to understand each character and to determine which characters play major or minor roles. Major characters usually play a major role in how the main idea is communicated. The combination of characters interacting in a specific time and place forms a plot. Every plot is unique, but they generally proceed according to the following pattern: initial peaceful situation, conflict, conflict climax, intervention, final resolution. The details of the plot unfold through the characters' actions until the story concludes and the plot is complete. Therefore, discerning the main idea of a narrative text is only possible by viewing the story as a whole.

A study of Jonah 1 reveals several elements the author uses to communicate the main idea. First, words like "arise," "picked up," and "swallow up," offset by the opposite ideas of "flee," "went down," "gone down," and "lain down," creates a contrast, highlighting the downward spiral of Jonah's disobedience. The author zooms in further on Jonah's disobedience by repeating the phrase "away from the presence of the Lord." God has called Jonah to arise and go, but Jonah is going "down," away from the presence of the Lord. The results of Jonah's disobedient flight are not only negative, but are also increasingly disastrous—a great storm, thrown into the sea, and finally found in the belly of a fish. Jonah has gone down as far as he can go, but he cannot escape God's presence. What is this particular part of Jonah about (subject)? It is

---

[109]Beekman, Callow, and Kopesec, *Semantic Structure*, 137.

about disobedience, specifically seeking to get away from God. What does this story say about disobedience (complement)? It says failing to obey God is disastrous, and seeking to run away from His presence is futile. What is the exegetical idea? **Exegetical Idea:** *Jonah disobeys God's command by attempting to run away only to endanger his life and discover that he cannot get away from God.*

The key is to remember that every natural thought unit of Scripture (paragraph, poem, or story) is talking about something (subject) and saying something specific about it (complement). This main idea must be determined in order to perform text-driven preaching. To find it, zoom in and examine how the internal parts of the text relate to one another. Zoom out and examine how the unit as a whole relates to the surrounding units. Ask yourself: What question is this text answering? Why did the author include this paragraph, poem, or story? What is the author's intent? As you zoom in and out and ask these questions, the main idea will come into focus. Step four is complete when the exegetical main idea is expressed in a single sentence.

Excursus: Consulting Commentaries

No doubt, by now, the question of when and how to utilize commentaries has arisen in your mind. The time has now arrived. Commentaries are critical tools for preachers. However, commentaries must be used properly. Improper use can create an unhealthy homiletical dependence. This dependence robs preachers of the fruit and joy of their own study. This dependence may also tempt the preacher to present the work of others as his own. Yet, despite these dangers, commentaries offer fields of homiletical gold. The key is to mine at the proper time and with utmost integrity.

The goal of consulting commentaries is to broaden and deepen your understanding of the text (interpretation) and enhance your ability to preach the text (communication). Therefore, approach commentaries with these two categories in mind: interpretation and communication. Furthermore, commentaries typically fit within one of four categories corresponding to their primary purpose of either interpretation or communication. Commentaries purposed to enhance interpretation are exegetical and expositional commentaries. Commentaries designed to enhance communication are homiletical and devotional commentaries. Each type of commentary proves useful for preachers when consulted accordingly.

Exegetical commentaries are the most technical, as they normally deal with the text in the original language. The exegetical elements of authorship, background, literary setting, grammar, syntax, structure, and other textual items are addressed. Expositional commentaries are less technical than their exegetical counterparts. These commentaries may deal with the original language to some degree but more often focus on the themes and explanation of the text. Think of expositional commentaries as in-depth Bible study notes.

Although homiletical and devotional commentaries may also enhance one's understanding of the text, they are primarily designed to enhance one's ability to communicate the text via explanation, illustration, or application. Homiletical commentaries are similar to sermons in written form. In fact, many commentary sets are the collected sermons of individual or various preachers. Devotional commentaries are usually the most simplistic and most application-oriented of all the commentary types. Though they may never dive into the technical details of the text, they may offer the preacher an explanatory phrase, quote, word picture, illustration, or specific application that is well worth citing and repeating.

As a rule, wait to consult commentaries until after you have completed the first four steps of text-driven preaching. These four steps constitute your own process of interpreting the text, and the premature consultation of commentaries risks short-circuiting it. Remember, the purpose of exegetical and expositional commentaries is to broaden and deepen your understanding of the text, not replace it with another's. Therefore, think of commentaries as a way to deepen and test your interpretation (exegetical/expositional) and provide creative ideas for communication (homiletical/devotional)—the purpose of the final three steps of text-driven preaching. The following graphic represents the proper place of commentaries within the seven-step process:

The 7 Steps of Text-Driven Preaching

Part I: Interpreting the Text
1. Select a Natural Thought Unit of Text
2. Read/Read/Re-Read the Text
3. Determine the Structure of the Text
4. Identify the Exegetical Main Idea of the Text

COMMENTARIES…

Part II: Communicating the Text
5. Convert the Structure and Exegetical Main Idea into a Sermon Outline and Homiletical Main Idea
6. Flesh out the Explanation, Illustration, Argumentation, and Application
7. Write the Introduction and Conclusion

Consulting four to five solid commentaries in the process of preparing a sermon is a good norm. Commentaries may be purchased in sets, and there are many wonderful sets available. However, keep in mind that every author will be more or less skilled in writing on specific books of the Bible. Therefore, seek to acquire the best individual volumes written by the most dependable and qualified authors. A good goal would be to own four to five good commentaries on every book of the Bible. Several great commentary guides exist to help in this process.[110]

---

[110] David L. Allen, *Preaching Tools: An Annotated Survey of Commentaries and Preaching Resources for Every Book of the Bible* (Fort Worth: Seminary Hill Press, 2016); Tremper Longman III, *Old Testament Commentary Survey,* 4th ed. (Grand

CHAPTER 3

THE STEPS OF TEXT-DRIVEN PREACHING

Part II: Communicating the Text

"It is difficult, but not impossible, to be at the same time the potent expositor and the soul-stirring orator." – Jeff Ray

Congratulations, preacher! You have summited the exegetical mountaintop. You charted your text. You poured over the text's substance, structure, and spirit. You have trekked every inch of the text to the top and taken in all the details along the way. The only problem … you are the only one at the top of the mountain, and no matter how loud you preach from the top, no one can hear you at base camp below. Somehow, you must now descend. The meaning and message of the text must be packed and loaded for transportation down the mountain to listeners waiting below. Making it down is not an option. God's people wait in need of God's Word. Proceed with caution. The descent is more arduous than it appears.

Rapids: Baker Academic, 2007); D.A. Carson, *New Testament Commentary Survey*, 6th ed. (Grand Rapids: Baker Academic, 2007).

Step 5: Convert the Structure of the Text into a Sermon Outline, and the Exegetical Main Idea into a Homiletical Main Idea of the Sermon

Part of the fruit of steps one through four includes an exegetical outline of the text and an exegetical idea that captures the main idea of the text. Essentially, the exegetical idea is what the author said (substance), and the exegetical outline (structure) is in part how the author said it. Both elements are necessary for text-driven preaching, which re-presents the substance, structure, and spirit of the text in a sermon. However, re-presenting what the author said the way the author said it requires converting the exegetical main idea and outline into a homiletical main idea and outline. Descending from the exegetical mountaintop starts with this step.

a. Re-Presenting What the Author Said

The goal of preaching the Word is for people to obey the Word. Therefore, it is not enough for preachers simply to repeat what the Bible says. Preachers preach (proclaim, explain, illustrate, argue, apply) in order to present the timeless truth of God's Word for today. Preaching bridges the gap between what the text said to the original audience and its significance for the present audience. Anchored by authorial intent, the meaning or truth of the text never changes. However, the significance and application(s) of the text often does change based on context of the audience along the timeline of God's unfolding plan of salvation. Thus, what the text says must be re-presented in accordance with the author's intention via preaching for people today.

This sounds simple. It is more complex, however, than most think. It is one thing to understand by exegesis what the author said. It is another thing to grasp the significance of what the author said for today's audience and express it in words that connect. Joel Gregory explains:

> For the most conservative and cautious interpreter the distance between the study desk and the pulpit seems

to be a great chasm. Getting the word from Palestine to Pittsburg, from Jerusalem to Jersey, challenges all....[111]

Creating the chasm between the text and the current congregation is the issue scholars call distanciation—"the cultural gap between biblical times and today."[112] Successfully crossing the gap between the then of the text to the now of the audience is one of the most difficult aspects of preaching. Yet, traversing the chasm is both imperative and possible. After all, according to Romans 15:4, "Whatever was written in earlier times was written for our instruction." Moreover, in 2 Timothy 3:16-17, Paul writes, "All Scripture is inspired by God and profitable for teaching, for reproof, for correction, for training in righteousness; so that the man of God may be adequate, equipped for every good work."

The goal of step five is to convert the exegetical main idea and outline into a homiletical main idea and outline. Here, the preacher finds himself on the edge of the precipice. Here, he must leap—and leap well—to feed the sheep faithfully. To leap well, the preacher must bear in mind everything gathered in the exegetical process revealing what the text originally meant to the original hearers. This includes as much knowledge of the time, place, background, and context of the text as possible.

With this information, the preacher interprets what the author intended to accomplish with what he was saying. What was the author's purpose? What was the author doing with what he was saying?[113] Canonically speaking, the author's purpose will always fit within the parameters of revealing who God is, who man is, and the necessary response man must have to God in order to respond in obedience and faith. In other words, the agenda of every text is theological. It speaks to God, man, and man's proper response to God.[114] Thus, preachers

---

[111]Joel Gregory, "Interpretation in Preaching," *Southwestern Journal of Theology* 27, No. 2 (1985): 10.
[112]Osborne, *The Hermeneutical Spiral*, 441.
[113]Kuruvilla, *Privilege the Text*, 48.
[114]Daniel M. Doriani, in *Putting the Truth to Work: The Theory and Practice of Biblical Application* (Phillipsburg, NJ: P&R Publishing, 2001), 17, concludes, "The whole of Scripture ... focuses on a relationship with God and conformity to his character."

must comprehend the "theological thrust"[115] of the text by paying "close attention to the text, not just what is being said, but also how it is being said, and why."[116] Preachers must not attempt to cross the chasm without a clear and comprehensive knowledge of what the text says.

With a knowledge of the text in hand, preachers are prepared to cross the chasm from the text to the congregation via the bridge built by the theology of the text. Kuruvilla's words are again instructive. The theology of the text "functions as the bridge between text and praxis, between the circumstances of the textual inscription and the lives of the reading community."[117] The theology of the text constructs the bridge from the then to the now because it articulates the timeless truth equally applicable to both the original and modern audience. Therefore, in order to convert the exegetical main idea and outline to a homiletical main idea and outline, the preacher must first identify and stand on this theological bridge.

Sometimes the original meaning and application of the truth communicated by the text are directly applicable to the modern audience. "Love your neighbor as yourself" (Mark 12:31) is a prime example. At other times, however, the distance between the text and the modern audience is more obvious. For example, Exodus 23:19 states, "You shall not boil a young goat in the milk of its mother." Texts like this one require the preacher to climb what Robinson calls a "ladder of abstraction."[118] Climbing the ladder means ascending above the time-specific situation of the text to see the truth about God and man informing the timeless message of the text. Though modern congregations are not likely to be tempted with boiling young goats on Monday, they can be influenced by current pagan practices of idolatrous worship. Therefore, the timeless

---

[115] Kuruvilla, *Privilege the Text*, 102.
[116] Doriani, *Putting the Truth to Work*, 102 and 105.
[117] Kuruvilla, *Privilege the Text*, 116-17.
[118] Haddon Robinson, "The Heresy of Application" in *The Art and Craft of Biblical Preaching: A Comprehensive Resource for Today's Communicators*, eds. Haddon Robinson and Craig Brian Larson (Grand Rapids: Zondervan, 2005), 308. When a text does not allow direct application, Robinson instructs, "Abstract up to God" and "find the depravity factor ... what in humanity rebels against that vision of God."

truth about God, man, and man's proper response to God communicated by Exodus 23:19 applies to people today—avoid imitating any and all actions that imitate idolatry!

Having comprehended what the text is saying, having understood the text's theological and timeless truth, the preacher is now ready to take the exegetical main idea and convert it into the homiletical main idea of the sermon. First, use words that will relate to your 21st-century audience. Second, whenever possible, state the homiletical main idea in terms of application. Keep in mind that a homiletical main idea must be a complete idea, so you must express it in the form of a complete sentence. The homiletical main idea must also be memorable, repeatable, and "sticky." Keep it short and simple. Anything longer than 15-18 words is typically too long. According to Ray, "A sermon is half preached when the preacher gives his audience a fresh, gripping theme [homiletical main idea] well stated."[119]

A word of warning is appropriate here. Remember why Robinson claimed sermons often fail? They often fail not because they have too many ideas. They fail because they have too many unrelated ideas. Preacher, your homiletical idea (the main idea of your sermon) is the tip of your sermon spear. If the full weight of the spear (body of the sermon) cannot align behind the tip (main idea), then the spear (sermon) cannot fly straight and will not penetrate the mind and heart of the listener. Furthermore, the homiletical idea will not function properly unless repeated during the course of the sermon at least five to seven times. Audiences rarely remember a statement stated a mere two or three times. To guide the sermon well, the homiletical idea must lodge in the people's mind, requiring it to be often on the preacher's lips. Most beginning preachers fail to recognize the power and significance of a well-crafted, sticky, and oft-stated homiletical idea. The homiletical main idea is the heart of re-presenting what the author said.

---

[119] Ray, *Expository Preaching*, 110.

Philemon 21-25
Exegetical Main Idea:
Paul is confident that Philemon will obey his request by receiving Onesimus as a brother in Christ.

Homiletical Main Idea:
Obedience to the Gospel is not included, but expected.

Notice that the homiletical idea for Philemon 21-25 seems almost totally unrelated to the exegetical idea. Yet, does it faithfully communicate the meaning of the text for the audience today? Yes, because verses 21-25 are Paul's final shot at hitting the target of Philemon doing what he has asked him to do, and the way the text puts it is "obedience." Obedience to Paul? No, in the context of the letter as a whole, it is clear that Philemon's willingness to do what Paul has asked him to do is actually obedience that should result from his "love" and "faith" toward God and all the saints (v. 5). Love and faith are primary proofs that the Gospel has taken root in someone's life. If someone has love and faith, they show fruit of having accepted the Gospel.

Philemon has accepted the Gospel. So what is this letter all about? It is about Philemon applying the Gospel, being obedient to what the Gospel calls him to do in every situation in life—in this case, a very particular situation concerning a runaway slave. Obeying the Gospel is doing what love and faith demand in any and every situation in life. "Obedience to the Gospel is not included" plays off a popular advertising tagline ("Batteries not included") and communicates that once someone accepts the Gospel, it is expected (Paul's confident expectation) that they obey the implications of the Gospel.

Psalm 32
Exegetical Main Idea:
David instructs sinners to pray for forgiveness while it is available.

Homiletical Main Idea:
Find forgiveness from God before it is too late.

The conversion of the exegetical idea to the homiletical idea for Psalm 32 is noticeably straightforward. Such can be the case when the text communicates its main idea in wording directly applicable to a modern audience. Of course, the name David drops. The imperative form as the essence of an instructional psalm remains along with the obvious urgency imposed by an expiration date.

Jonah 1
Exegetical Main Idea:
Jonah disobeys God's command by attempting to run away only to endanger his life and discover he cannot get away from God.

Homiletical Main Idea:
Running from God is ridiculous.

The author never directly says running from God is ridiculous. However, this is exactly what he indirectly but intentionally communicates. Running from God is ridiculous because it is disastrous and actually impossible. Skeptics often label the idea of a great fish swallowing a man as ridiculous. Those with faith actually see that the great irony here is that what one naturally thinks is dangerous and impossible, being swallowed by a fish, is actually serving to highlight what is truly dangerous to attempt and impossible to accomplish: running from God! One might put it like this … it is easier to be swallowed by a fish for three days than to get away from God for one minute!

Reviewing the Examples
Notice that the examples of the homiletical ideas above are full sentences, short, and somewhat catchy. A complete sentence communicates a complete idea. Homiletical ideas should also be short in order to be clear and repeatable. In fact, it is best to repeat your main

idea verbatim in any sermon at least five to seven times. Though hard to believe, stating the main idea two or three times will not be sufficient. Finally, attempting to make the homiletical idea catchy aims at making it stick with the listener. The goal is for this idea to adhere firmly in the mind of your listeners—much like a song sticks in your head. It should be like chewing gum that clings to whatever it touches. "Catchy" does not mean it has to be corny or entirely alliterated, etc. Such rhetorical strategies can be useful as long as they help the idea ring and refrain from the ridiculous.

b. Re-Presenting How the Author Said It

The exegetical outline serves as a preliminary structural template for the sermon outline. Remember, text-driven preaching is "the interpretation and communication of a biblical text in a sermon that re-presents the substance, structure, and the spirit of the text."[120] The only way a sermon can be driven by the structure of the text is if the sermon's structure is derived from the structure of the text. The biblical author utilized a specific (and inspired!) semantic structure to communicate his message. This specific, structural development contributes to the meaning of the text and therefore must be retained to the greatest degree possible.[121] In order to do so, keep in mind the unique and general characteristics of texts.

The Unique and Consistent Nature of Each Text

First, remember that no two natural thought units of Scripture are structured exactly alike. Each one possesses a unique semantic fingerprint. Yet, Beekman, Callow, and Kopesec chart the finite set of semantic relationships that exist. Therefore, although each linguistic unit of Scripture is structurally unique, it is possible to identify each semantic relationship present in each text.

---

[120] Smith, *Recapturing the Voice of God*, 17.
[121] "Does not the outline have a right to be shaped by the text as much as the content of the message? To be truly biblical one must contour the message around the contour of the text," Gregory, "Interpretation for Preaching," 16.

The General Ways Ideas (Texts) Develop

Second, bear in mind the general ways an idea can develop. Ideas develop by moving from the general to the specific, from the specific to the general, or some combination thereof. Deductive development occurs when an idea develops from the general to the specific. This means a deductive sermon will begin with the general main idea and proceed by articulating the details. Inductive development works in reverse. The details come first until they accumulate to reveal the general main idea at the end. New Testament epistles typically operate deductively as they explain ideas, prove propositions, and apply principles.[122] Old Testament narrative, however, moves inductively as the initial details of the story build and culminate in the story's conclusion and overall message.

A combination of inductive and deductive development occurs with "semi-inductive form" and "induction-deduction."[123] Semi-inductive development is common when a subject (incomplete idea) is presented in the introduction and is subsequently completed (complement provided) by each point in the body of the sermon. An example would be a sermon that presents the idea of heaven in the introduction followed by five truths about heaven in the body. Induction-Deduction works by presenting the main idea in the middle of the sermon. The beginning of the sermon inductively provides details that lead up to the main idea. The second half of the sermon deductively handles the idea, proposition, or principle.

The point is to have an understanding of the general ways ideas develop. Preachers must not view deductive, inductive, or a combination thereof as homiletical templates to force upon any text. Rather, preachers must surrender to the unique semantic development of each text while understanding that each text will generally develop its idea deductively, inductively, or by some combination thereof. Remember, the way in which the human authors and divine Author developed the ideas presented in Scripture is a matter of inspiration. Therefore, a hallmark

---

[122]Robinson lists the most common deductive arrangements as "an idea to be explained," "a proposition to be proved," and "a principle to be applied," in *Biblical Preaching*, 78-84.
[123]Ibid., 85-87.

of text-driven preaching is abiding by the fact that the text supplies the form (structure) of the sermon. What every text-driven preacher must do is simply discern the sermon template that God has already inspired.

Converting the Exegetical Outline into a Homiletical Outline

Converting the exegetical outline into a homiletical outline requires the following: a homiletical main idea, an understanding of the unique semantic structure of the text, and a knowledge of the general way the text develops. It is important to deal with the homiletical idea first so that the wording of the homiletical outline flows out of and is consistent with the homiletical idea. Converting the exegetical outline to the homiletical outline proceeds along the same lines as moving from the exegetical to the homiletical idea. Travel the path from text to theology to current congregation. The wording of each portion of the outline should remain in complete sentences and, as much as possible, show consistency with the homiletical idea. Consistent wording should be possible because the homiletical idea should encompass every aspect of the outline.

First, simplify the exegetical outline in order to transform it into a homiletical outline. No matter how complex or detailed the exegetical outline is, the sermon or homiletical outline must be simple. Sub-points are rarely a good idea for homiletical outlines. Listeners do well to identify main points of an outline, much less smaller and more subtle sermon moves. Although exceptions do exist, three to five main outline points, scenes, or moves typically work best. Therefore, the number of divisions in the homiletical outline will not always match the number in the exegetical outline. Effective communication requires a degree of simplicity, meaning it is sometimes necessary to consolidate portions of the exegetical outline when converting it to a homiletical outline.

Second, reword the outline to express each sentence in 21st-century language that, whenever possible, is application-oriented. Lose any theological jargon that is not essential to the meaning of the text or vital for your audience to understand.[124] Eliminate language that

---

[124] Theological heavyweights such as justification, redemption, sanctification, propitiation, glorification, etc. are not everyday terms, but they are biblical terms that communicate the richness of the Gospel. Teach these vital terms to your

is not clear, readily understood, or easily explained. Keep complete sentences, but be concise and to the point. Also, word each point, scene, or move in a parallel grammatical fashion as the examples show below. Mixed sentence structure within the homiletical outline undercuts the prominence and clarity of the sermon's navigational beacons. Each sentence of the outline should be a complete thought that contributes to the development or explanation of the homiletical idea. State these sentences similarly to assist their status as pillars of the sermon.

Philemon 21-25
Homiletical Main Idea:
Obedience to the Gospel is not included, but expected.

Homiletical Outline:

I. Gospel Obedience Needs Encouragement and Accountability (v. 21-22).
II. Gospel Obedience Requires Individual and Collective Effort (v. 23-24).
III. Gospel Obedience Depends on Grace (v. 25).

This homiletical outline is a classic deductive sermon. The sermon could open with the illustration of a product for sale, advertised by a commercial that ends with, "Batteries not included." Of course, batteries are the very thing that make the product work! Next, in comparison with the batteries not included from the seller but expected to be supplied by the buyer, the preacher should explain the offer of the Gospel that does not include, but expects, obedience. This Gospel obedience is the essence of Philemon because Paul is writing to exhort him to do what is right for Onesimus in light of the Gospel. The main homiletical

---

people. Jerry Vines and Jim Shaddix argue that every community shares language that "ties them together" and that, "If the church loses its language, it will lose an important aspect of its community." In *Progress in the Pulpit: How to Grow in your Preaching* (Chicago: Moody, 2017), 78.

idea should then be stated and repeated for emphasis. A transition will bridge the gap between the introduction and body of the sermon. For example, "The message of our text is, 'Obedience to the Gospel is not included, but expected.' Notice how Philemon 21-25 gives us three *truths*[125] regarding the obedience that God expects from us as His followers. The first *truth* from verses 21-22 is…."

Notice that each main point of the outline shares consistent language with the homiletical idea. This reinforces the fact that each point teases out an aspect of the main idea. Notice also that each main point is a complete sentence expressed in parallel fashion (subject, finite verb, predicate). Alliteration is omitted in this particular example, but is another tool that assists with emphasis and retention when used properly. Finally, notice the number of points for this outline rests on the structural makeup of the text.

Psalm 32
Homiletical Main Idea:
Find forgiveness while it can be found.

Homiletical Outline:
    A (v. 1-2) Life is good for the forgiven.
        B (v. 3-4) Life is not good for the unforgiven.
            C (v. 5) God grants forgiveness when we confess our sin.
                (v. 6) *FIND FORGIVENESS WHILE IT CAN BE FOUND.*[126]

---

[125] The word "truths" in this transitional sentence functions as the homiletical key word. "The key word is a plural, abstract noun that names a category to classify the sermon division statements," according to Wayne McDill, *12 Essential Skills for Great Preaching,* 2nd ed. (Nashville: B&H Academic, 2006), 111. This key word adds clarity for the listener as it labels the kind of ideas the outline consists of. In the Philemon 21-25 example, each main point of the sermon outline falls into the category of "truths." In general, the options for key words are almost unlimited. Avoid generic terms, however, such as "things" or "points." These generic terms do little to identify the nature of the ideas in the sermon outline.

[126] Alliteration is a rhetorical device that preachers have consistently relied on. However, it is often overused and sometimes abused. Notice the main idea here does utilize alliteration. Yet, it is subtle and applied to a complete sentence rather

C¹ (v. 7) Those who find forgiveness find salvation.

B¹ (v. 8-9) Those who find forgiveness tell others how to find forgiveness.

A¹ (v. 10-11) Those who find forgiveness find steadfast love and rejoice.

This homiletical outline exemplifies how inductive and deductive development sometimes combine, specifically in an inductive/deductive way. This development was not chosen arbitrarily, but discerned from the semantic structure of the text and retained in order to drive the structure of the sermon. Details of forgiveness begin the psalm and lead to the main idea in verse 6. Then, out of that main idea flow more details that parallel the beginning of the psalm. Earlier, it was stated that most outlines should be kept to no more than five elements. This example serves as one exception due to the semantic structure of the poem. The key is to remain flexible so that the text can drive the sermon. Flexibility guided by simplicity will allow the preacher to remain creative while tethered to the text.

Jonah 1
Homiletical Main Idea:
Running from God is ridiculous.

Homiletical Outline:

Scene 1 (v. 1-3): Jonah runs from God by going down to Joppa.

Scene 2 (v. 4-6): Jonah runs, but God pursues with a storm and an angry sea captain.

Scene 3 (v. 7-10): Jonah runs from God, but he cannot hide from God.

---

than individual words in each point. It does not appear forced. When this is the case, alliteration can help rather than distract.

Scene 4 (v. 11-17): Jonah's run leads to disaster, but God mercifully rescues.

A fully inductive text like Jonah 1 and other narrative units of Scripture operate differently from deductive literature and therefore require a different homiletical approach. First, the outline of a narrative text will most often map the scenes of the story. The goal of outlining the story by scenes is to capture the summary or message of each scene in a single sentence, as exemplified by the outline above. An alternative approach is to word the point or message of each scene in an application-oriented manner. However, this is not always possible, because the main point of the story to be applied typically does not surface until the end. Yet, when subordinate points surface along the way in narrative texts, it is appropriate to word the scenes (outline) according to the application available while the homiletical idea and main application wait until the end.

Finally, keep in mind that the "points" or scene summaries of a narrative sermon outline will function inversely to a deductive sermon. Each division of a deductive sermon will begin by stating the point followed by its detailed development. Inductive sermon divisions, however, begin with the details of the scene and end with the statement of the overall scene summary or point.[127] Step six provides further clarification.

As you complete step five, keep in mind the words of Mark Twain, who said, "The difference between the almost right word and the right word is really a large matter—'tis the difference between the lightning bug and the lightning."[128] The homiletical idea especially, but also the homiletical outline, possesses pinnacle importance regarding word choice. Precision and clarity are crafted. Labor here until your words

---

[127] Mathewson, in *The Art of Preaching Old Testament Narrative*, 124, offers the following tip when outlining narrative sermons: "View main points as endings, not beginnings." For narrative literature, each sermon division begins with details of a scene, dramatically builds, and culminates in the one-sentence statement summarizing the scene.

[128] George Bainton, *The Art of Authorship* (New York: D. Appleton and Company, 1890), 87-88.

both accurately convey the meaning of the text and clearly connect with your audience. The only hard and fast rule when constructing the homiletical idea and outline is to let the text drive the sermon. Avoid the mentality of seeking a template. Rest in the fact that the text provides a template, and relish the joy of discovering it.

The final touch that polishes the precision and clarity of the homiletical outline is to identify the nature of the transitions needed between each portion of the outline. What logic defines the relationship between each point or move in the homiletical outline? This logic determines the type of the transitions needed, which serve as the ligaments between every joint in the sermon. Unless these ligaments are present and in full operation, the sermon cannot move smoothly. Clarity requires transitions that logically link the listener from one portion of the sermon to the next.

Therefore, identify the logic connecting each portion of the homiletical outline. Articulate that logic in transitional statements that link each point/move of the sermon to the next. Think of these transitions as road signs. They remind the listeners of where they are and where they are going.

Step 6: Flesh out the Explanation, Illustration, Argumentation, and Application

Preaching certainly is communication, but it is also much more. Excluding the very voice of God, preaching is the most crucial communication known to man. Heaven and hell hang in the balance. The Sunday morning sermon is not a casual conversation. It should be a full-scale verbal assault on sin, a balm for the soul, and the exaltation of Christ obliterating unbelief and piercing the heart with God's Word. This means preachers must do everything they can to communicate God's Word. What is fascinating, however, are the finite options in the preacher's arsenal.

Completing step five yields the homiletical idea and its development via a homiletical outline. The preacher now has the idea of the text isolated and articulated. Now what? Rhetorically, there are only five things a preacher can do with that idea: state it, explain it, illustrate it, argue it, and apply it.[129] That is it! Each of these actions amplifies the idea from a different angle and is therefore necessary in order to communicate every facet of the idea. Often referred to as the functional elements of preaching (explanation, illustration, argumentation, and application), they add flesh to the bones (outline) of the sermon. The best way to proceed with these functional elements, especially for beginning preachers, is to manuscript them word for word.[130]

a. Explanation: What does the text mean?

Priority number one of step six is articulating exactly what the text means in a clear and compelling way. As homiletics professor and pastor Steven Smith says, "Explanation is your one chance to get the text right!"[131] Smith also writes, "The most help the sermon can be to anyone is when the sermon clearly explains Scripture. Perhaps the greatest compliment a preacher could be paid is, 'Now I understand what the Scripture means.'"[132] Think about the priority of explanation this way—no one can believe and be transformed by truth they do not know. Before the preacher can do anything else with an idea, he must first explain it.

Point to the words of the text and tell the audience what the text means. Deal with any critical words and textual issues. Ask, "What information won't my audience immediately understand?" Ask, "Is this

---

[129] Robinson notes, "When we make any declarative statement, we can do only four things with it: we can restate it, explain it, prove it, or apply it. Nothing else. To recognize this simple fact opens the way to understanding the dynamic of thought," in *Biblical Preaching*, 49.

[130] It is almost impossible to think through every word of the sermon without writing. Writing forces thoughts to connect and crystalize. Writing offers the opportunity to wrestle with word choice. The purpose of writing a manuscript is not memorization, but preparation. The process of writing demands thorough thought and enhances internalization. Both are necessary for effective, extemporaneous communication.

[131] Steven W. Smith, "Building an Expository Sermon" (classroom lecture notes, PRCHG 3313—Introduction to Expository Preaching, Spring 2009, author's personal notes).

[132] Steven W. Smith, *Dying to Preach: Embracing the Cross in the Pulpit* (Grand Rapids: Kregel, 2009), 164-65.

information absolutely necessary or extremely helpful?" Ask, "How can I put the meaning of the text into terms the audience will understand?" Ruthlessly remove everything that is not essential.

You cannot do anything else with an idea until you have properly explained it. Thus, in a way, all of the other functional elements (illustration, argumentation, and application) are servants of explanation. This functional element of preaching more than any other vaults the supernatural truth of God's Word into the minds of the listener. Tell them what the text means!

b. Illustration: What does the text look like?

Good teachers understand that we learn by relating new information to familiar information. This intake by analogy attaches a mental handle to new data enabling the mind to grasp it more efficiently. Illustration is, in a way, a subset of explanation that allows the preacher when explaining an idea to say, "It's like this...." Therefore, illustration moves away from formal description or definition and toward portraying a picture of the truth. The audience hears the truth via explanation. The audience sees the truth via illustration. To illustrate, illustrations are like windows allowing light to penetrate and reveal what is on the inside. The goal of illustrating is enhanced comprehension of the text.

Illustrations may come from almost anywhere and anything in life. The options are endless, including Scripture, science, culture, nature, history, literature, current events, and personal experiences. The very best illustrations are those that overlap both the preacher's and the listeners' experience. Moreover, they will not only appeal to people's minds, but also touch their emotions. Illustration is one of the most powerful tools in the preacher's arsenal. Use it wisely by ensuring the illustration further explains the text without introducing unnecessary distractions. Ultimately, the people need the truth of the text, not an illustration.

c. Argumentation: Why is the text true?

Of the four functional elements of preaching, argumentation might be the most overlooked and neglected element. More often than not, preachers simply assume listeners will either accept what the Bible says as true or reject it as untrue. In some ways, preachers correctly recognize no one has ever been argued into the Kingdom of God. However, does this mean there is no place for argumentation in preaching? Surely not! If so, then apologetics concerning the Christian faith would have no place either.

Preachers should approach argumentation with two types of people in mind. The first person represents the majority of the congregation. This person is a believer but honestly struggles at times with doubt. They are much like the father in Mark 9:24, who cried out to Jesus, "I do believe; help my unbelief!" Like this father, most people in the pew accept the truth and authority of Scripture, but they do need help with their doubts. Therefore, preachers must ask, "What is in this text that my audience will struggle to believe?" Reinforce the items identified with content that will assist in solidifying the listener's faith. Scripture is the ultimate authority. Therefore, the point is not to depend on "better" sources than Scripture. The idea, however, is to utilize other sources such as logic, history, science, other Scripture references, etc. to reinforce the fact that the text is true.

The second type of person in the pew, perhaps in the minority but always present, is the skeptic. This person is an unbeliever who does not believe but very well may want to believe. This is the person Paul had in mind when he wrote in 2 Corinthians 5:11, "Therefore, knowing the fear of the Lord, we persuade men." This is the kind of response Peter had in mind when he wrote in 1 Peter 3:15, "Always being ready to make a defense to everyone who asks you to give an account for the hope that is in you."

Argumentation within the sermon is not always a necessity, and, when present, it need not be long. Argumentation, in fact, should be used more sparingly than any of the other elements. Yet, there are times when argumentation is called for. Preaching in today's culture means speaking to people who are less and less inclined to accept the truth and authority of God's Word. Therefore, give warrant for why people should believe when necessary and do so with gentleness and respect.

d. Application: What does the text say to do?

Ultimately, preaching seeks not only the hearing of the Word, but also the doing of the Word. Application, therefore, is never optional in preaching.[133] According to Jeff Ray, real expository preaching always "effectively applies" the text.[134] Ray understood, as others have argued, "that we do not wholly understand a text unless we can apply it."[135] Application, however, is by far the most difficult of all the functional elements to do well. Robinson warns, "It's when we're applying Scripture that error most likely creeps in."[136]

The journey from the biblical text to the modern world is fraught with hermeneutical dangers that the preacher must be prepared to navigate. Hence Paul's injunction to young Timothy in 2 Timothy 2:15—"Be diligent to present yourself approved to God as a workman who does not need to be ashamed, accurately handling the word of truth." Thus, application that accurately answers the "so what?" and "now what?" of the text results from skilled labor.

The good news is that, by this point, the hardest work required for application is complete. Crossing the chasm from the ancient text to the modern audience via the theological thrust of the text happened in step five. All that remains is the work of exegeting the congregation in order to know exactly how the truth of the text should intersect their lives. Knowing the congregation should be part of the ongoing work of a pastor, supporting the symbiotic relationship between pastor and preacher.

The preacher who proceeds according to the steps outlined above will soon realize the following reality:

> Most texts hold more potential application than one coherent message could develop. The chief task, then, is

---

[133]In the words of John A. Broadus, "If there is no summons, there is no sermon," *On the Preparation and Delivery of Sermons*, rev. by J.B. Weatherspoon (New York: Harper & Row, 1944), 210.
[134]Ray, *Expository Preaching*, 47.
[135]Doriani, *Putting the Truth to Work*, 27.
[136]Robinson, "The Heresy of Application," in *The Art and Craft of Biblical Preaching*, 306.

not finding something to say, but fingering the one *chief* application that drives the central theme of the text and arrays the subpoints around it.[137]

The biblical author wrote the text for a specific purpose—to achieve a desired application. Therefore, sermon application must be driven by the primary purpose of the text revealed by not only what the text says (semantics), but also how the text says it (pragmatics).[138]

Guiding text-driven application will be the homiletical main idea of the text and the genre of the text. The main idea guides the substance of the application, and the genre of the text guides the spirit of the application. Remember, a text-driven sermon is driven by the substance, structure, and spirit of the text. In no other portion of the sermon should the spirit of the text be more obvious than in the application. In order to identify the spirit of the text, preachers must look to its genre.

The "spirit" of the text is the "author-intended emotional design of the text."[139] The specific genre of the text is the first and primary factor influencing the spirit or tone of the text. Psalms, prophecy, epistles, parables, law, narrative, apocalyptic, wisdom literature, etc. all communicate uniquely and therefore "feel" different.[140] However, each genre possesses a degree of tone dexterity. Therefore, preachers must determine the specific mood of their text. Does the text warn, instruct, encourage, inform, plead, etc.? For example, Luke 16 threatens and warns. Psalm 23 encourages and warms. Titus 3:9-11 mandates a procedure to follow. In this way, "the voice of application is embedded in the spirit of the text."[141]

---

[137] Doriani, *Putting the Truth to Work*, 81.
[138] Abraham Kuruvilla explains the function of pragmatics for preaching in *Privilege the Text!* He defines pragmatics as "the analysis of what texts (or speakers/authors) do with what they say" (48). Pragmatics emphasizes "that there is more to understanding what authors are doing than just dissecting out the linguistic, grammatical, and syntactical elements of what the authors are saying" (49).
[139] Smith, *Recapturing the Voice of God*, 21.
[140] Ibid.
[141] Smith, "Building an Expository Sermon," Spring 2009.

With both the homiletical main idea and the spirit of the text in mind, preachers are prepared to articulate the application of the text. This is the time and place to answer the "so what?" and "now what?" of the text. Answer the question, "What message does God want to give these people from this text?"[142] The procedure that produces accurate application mirrors the process articulated above for converting the exegetical main idea and outline to the homiletical main idea and outline. Follow these guidelines:

1. Concentrate on the original message of the text.
2. Recognize any discontinuity between the original audience and the church today.
3. Recognize the overarching continuity between the original audience and the church today.
4. Focus on the goal of the text.[143]

If application seems elusive, look to what the passage reveals about God, man, and man's proper response to God.

Daniel Overdorf takes Greidanus' four steps above and gets even more granular with 10 questions to ask for developing specific application:

1. Biblical Teaching: What did God originally teach through this text?
2. Original Purpose: How did God intend this text to affect its original readers?
3. Comparison of Audiences: How do my listeners compare with the original readers?
4. Listener Need: What listener need does this text address?

---

[142] Adam, *Speaking God's Words*, 133.
[143] Sidney Greidanus, *The Modern Preacher and the Ancient Text: Interpreting and Preaching Biblical Literature* (Grand Rapids: Eerdmans, 1988), 166-75. Areas of discontinuity may include "progressive revelation," "stages in kingdom history," and "culture." Areas of continuity include "one faithful God" and "one covenant people."

5. Sermon Purpose: What should my listeners think, feel, or do differently after having heard a sermon from this text?
6. Sermon Application: If the sermon accomplished its purpose in specific listeners dealing with specific life situations, how might it look?
7. Safeguard: Does this application exalt God?
8. Safeguard: Is this application consistent with the text's teaching and purpose?
9. Safeguard: Will this application motivate and equip listeners to respond to the text?
10. Safeguard: Does this application give expectations or promises only where the text does?[144]

The goal is to develop very specific application while avoiding potential pitfalls. Identifying specific and relevant application is one of the greater challenges in preaching. Second to articulating and repeating a clear homiletical main idea in the sermon, beginning preachers struggle most with *specific* application. Specific application is the fruit of both knowing the text and knowing the audience—both labor-intensive endeavors. This is where rubrics and categories for both the text and people can catalyze specific application.

Doriani suggests thinking through the seven ways the Bible instructs: "through rules, ideals, doctrines, redemptive acts in narratives, exemplary acts in narrative, biblical images, and songs and prayers."[145] Furthermore, he categorizes the questions people ask to help preachers think through specific application:

1. What should I do? That is, what is my *duty*?
2. Who should I be? That is, how can I become the person or obtain the *character* that lets me do what is right?

---

[144]Daniel Overdorf, *Applying the Sermon: How to Balance Biblical Integrity and Cultural Relevance* (Grand Rapids: Kregel, 2009), 102-42.
[145]Doriani, *Putting the Truth to Work*, 82.

3. To what causes should we devote our life energy? That is, what *goals* should we pursue?
4. How can we distinguish truth from error? That is, how can we gain *discernment?*[146]

See the way the text presents its instruction. Identify what question(s) that instruction answers. Then articulate exactly how children, junior high students, high school students, single adults, young married couples, parents, middle-aged adults, senior adults, the congregation as a whole, and any other category of people in the congregation should specifically respond to the text.[147]

Where to place application in the sermon primarily depends on how the sermon is structured. Deductive sermons will normally call for application to be made throughout the sermon—included in each point of the outline. The layout of the elements might look like this:

INTRO
    HOMILETICAL MAIN IDEA
TRANSITION

POINT I
    Explanation
    Illustration
    Argumentation
    Application

POINT II (Add further points as needed for sermon outline)
    Explanation
    Illustration

---

[146]Ibid., 98. Doriani offers these questions not as a template to be forced on every sermon, but rather as a "guide to full-orbed application."
[147]The goal is not to make application to every type of person in every sermon—this is impossible. However, the goal is to apply the text so specifically to as many types of people as time allows so that even the people outside those categories realize (even if only by analogy) how the text applies to their lives as well.

Argumentation
Application

CONCLUSION

Application in inductive sermons, however, typically waits until the story has been preached in its entirety. Only then does the main idea appear and ripen for application. Specific application may surface in each scene of the sermon as the narrative unfolds. However, the main application of a narrative text as a whole hinges on the main idea that must come first. Thus, the layout of a narrative sermon might resemble this pattern:

INTRO

SCENE I
Explanation
Illustration and Argumentation (if needed)
SUMMARY SENTENCE OF SCENE I

SCENE II (Repeat as needed for additional scenes)
Explanation
Illustration and Argumentation (if needed)
SUMMARY SENTENCE OF SCENE II

HOMILETICAL MAIN IDEA

APPLICATION(S)

CONCLUSION

Perhaps the most critical admonition regarding application for Christian preaching is to remember that any and every appropriate application from the text is an implication of the Gospel, which is the Good News concerning the person and work of Jesus Christ. The Bible is God's self-revelation and His story of salvation that culminates in the death, burial, resurrection, and return of Christ (Hebrews 1:1-3). Remember the words of Ray's wife spoken to him in a dream:

> Give a wider place in your preaching to expounding this Book and to exalting its matchless Hero. He wrote no line in the Book, but every word in it from 'In the beginning God' to its last 'Even so, come quickly, Lord Jesus' is a witness to His majestic person and His saving power.[148]

God has finally and fully spoken through His Son, who is the exact representation of the Father, and no one can come to the Father except through the Son (John 14:6). Furthermore, the written Word of God testifies to the living Word, Jesus Christ (John 5:39). Smith articulates the theological "therefore" for preaching when he writes:

> Access to the Father is granted through the Son; access to the Son is granted through his words. ... In the same way that God is completely/perfectly represented in the Son, the Son is completely/perfectly represented in Scripture. ... Think of it in this reverse chronological way:
>
> 1. We re-present the text.
> 2. The text re-presents Christ.
> 3. Christ re-presents the Father.[149]

Every appropriate application from any text in Scripture will always be an implication of "some facet of the person, work, or teaching of Jesus so that people may believe him, trust him, love, and obey him."[150] God has promised every believer that He will finish what He started, namely conforming us completely to the image of Christ, that we might share in His glory as partakers of the divine nature (Philippians 1:6;

---

[148] Ray, *Expository Preaching*, 54.
[149] Smith, *Recapturing the Voice of God*, 12-14.
[150] Sidney Greidanus, *Preaching Christ from the Old Testament: A Contemporary Hermeneutical Method* (Grand Rapids: Eerdmans, 1999), 8.

Romans 8:29-30; 2 Peter 1:4). When communicating application, set the application in the context of believing, knowing, and obeying Jesus Christ as Lord and Savior by the power of the Holy Spirit.

Of course, knowing and obeying Jesus by the Spirit's power is only possible once someone believes in Jesus by faith. Therefore, even if the text for the sermon does not explicitly contain elements of the death, burial, and resurrection of Christ, always be sure to communicate the message of the Gospel, even if only a concise summary for the sake of those who have not yet believed. To one degree or another, every text of Scripture possesses content that naturally platforms the communication of the Gospel. Never take for granted the need to communicate the Gospel in every sermon, no matter your audience. Lost people are almost always listening.

Finally, it is not enough for preachers to apply the text. Specific application that shows listeners what the truth of the text should look like in their lives is outstanding but insufficient. Application must culminate in exhortation. Preaching must persuade. Preachers must plead. Neutrality is not an option between heaven and hell. The truth demands a decision; therefore, so does preaching.

When Paul charges Timothy to "preach the word," he defines preaching as reproving, rebuking, and exhorting. Preaching is more than the proclamation of the truth. It is the presentation of the truth for the purpose of confronting unbelief and disobedience, correcting unbelief and disobedience, and calling for belief and obedience. The return of Christ is imminent. His Kingdom is coming. Jesus will judge the living and the dead. Paul writes, "Therefore, knowing the fear of the Lord, we persuade men" (2 Corinthians 5:11).

Only the Holy Spirit can convince a person of the truth and lead them by faith to believe and obey (1 Thessalonians 1:5). Yet, God has chosen the foolishness of preaching as a tool for the Holy Spirit's work. Therefore, preachers must heed Augustine's admonition:

> It is the duty, therefore, of the eloquent churchman, when he is trying to persuade the people about something that

has to be done, not only to teach, in order to instruct them; not only to delight, in order to hold them; but also to sway, in order to conquer and win them.[151]

Explain the text. Illustrate the text. Argue for the truth of the text when necessary. Always apply the text. Call the congregation to act on the text. Trust the sufficiency of the Scriptures and the power of the Holy Spirit to change hearts and lives.

Step 7: Write the Introduction and Conclusion

The body of the sermon is now complete. All that remains is the beginning (introduction) and the end (conclusion). Putting off the introduction and conclusion until the end might seem counterintuitive, but clarity is worth the wait. How can you properly introduce or conclude something until every detail of that something is clear and complete? The construction of the body of the sermon must precede writing the introduction and conclusion.

As mentioned previously, application poses the most pitfalls for handling the text accurately. Introductions and conclusions pose pitfalls as well, not for interpretation, but for delivery. Introductions and conclusions do not dictate content—the body of the sermon does that. Rather, introductions and conclusions determine the presentation of content and, therefore, determine whether the content connects and remains with the listener.

Think of a sermon like the flight of an airplane. The most difficult aeronautical maneuvers are normally required during two portions of the flight, the beginning and the end. Such is the case for constructing and delivering a sermon.

a. The Beginning | Crafting Effective Introductions

An effective introduction performs its purpose—getting the sermon off the ground and into the air. Getting the sermon into the air and

---

[151] Augustine, *Teaching Christianity*, trans. Edmund Hill, ed. John E. Rotelle (Hyde Park: New City Press, 1996), 217.

up to cruising altitude requires three things: boarding all passengers, fastening those passengers in their seats, and orienting the passengers to the journey toward their final destination. Therefore, an effective introduction will do at least three essential things: (1) Attract the listeners to the sermon; (2) Hook the listeners to the sermon; (3) Orient and guide the listeners to the main idea of the sermon.

1. Attract the listeners to the sermon.

Attracting the listeners to the sermon means activating their interest. Just because someone sits in the pew on Sunday morning does not mean he or she is interested in what you have to say. In fact, you might safely assume half of your audience almost decided not to come, and the other half, though committed to their attendance, came distracted by all the various matters of life. The only way to blaze a trail to the ears of the audience is for the sermon to be the most interesting thing in the room. This means the first two to three sentences of your sermon must be more compelling than Angry Birds, Facebook, Twitter, Snapchat, or anything else on someone's cell phone or tablet or mind in general.

Engaging the audience's interest in order to gain attention is perhaps the most challenging part of the introduction. It requires both keen insight into the life of the listener and creativity. A profound statement, surfacing a felt need, asking a question, humor, a current event, an illustration, challenging the status quo, a short story, etc. stand among the various options a preacher might utilize to interest the audience.

2. Hook the listeners to the sermon.

After attracting the audience in the introduction, it is imperative to hook them with the introduction. Now that the preacher has the audience's attention, he must establish his grip in order to retain it. This is hooking the listeners to the sermon. To change metaphors from flight to fishing, once a fish has taken the lure, the angler "sets the hook" by applying immediate and intense tension to the line so that the hook penetrates and fastens to the fish's mouth. Successfully setting the hook results in the fish having no choice but to go where the angler directs.

Successfully hooking listeners to the sermon requires opening the eyes of the audience to see the value of the sermon. To do so, establish the fact that they need to hear what the text has to say. Convince the audience that they absolutely must listen. Give a glimpse of the difference the truth of the text makes spiritually, physically, practically, temporarily, and eternally. Describe the deprivation of not knowing or heeding the text. Note the gravity of what is at stake both now and forever. Testify to the value of the text in your own life. All of the above and more are routes for setting the hook.

Perhaps you have heard it said that there are preachers you *can* listen to; there are preachers you *can't* listen to; and there are preachers you *must* listen to. A preacher who *must* be listened to not only attracts the listeners' attention in the introduction, but also arrests it so as to hold it for the duration of the sermon. If the hook is not set firmly, the fish is likely to spit it out. Hence the reason why it is almost impossible to recover from a failed introduction. As John Broadus quipped, "Well begun is half done, and ill begun is apt to be wholly ruined."[152]

3. Orient and guide the listeners to the main idea of the sermon.

The third and final purpose an effective introduction must fulfill is to orient and guide the listeners to the main idea of the sermon. This aspect of the introduction is the most critical for the functionality of the sermon. An introduction that does not introduce the main idea of the sermon is bound for disaster. If every part of the sermon hangs on the main idea, as it should, then everything in the introduction should transport the listeners to it. Therefore, before the introduction ends, it must introduce the text and state the main idea of the sermon.[153]

For a deductive sermon, orienting and guiding the listeners to the main idea typically consists of three moves followed by a transition to the body of the sermon.

>Move 1: (General) – Introduces the subject of the text

---

[152]Broadus, *On the Preparation and Delivery of Sermons*, 250.
[153]Jerry Vines and Jim Shaddix, *Power in the Pulpit: How to Prepare and Deliver Expository Sermons*, rev. ed. (Chicago: Moody, 2017), 237.

> Move 2: (Specific) – Further clarifies the subject of the text
> Move 3: (Exact) – States the main idea of the text
>
> Transition: Normally consists of the question the text answers with the main idea, and therefore it serves as the link you need to move from the intro to the body of the sermon.[154]

By the end of these moves, the audience should know exactly what text is being preached and the main idea it communicates. When appropriate, the insertion of a homiletical key word in the transition serves as a guide to the content of the sermon.[155]

Example: 2 Timothy 2:1-7

> Move 1: (General) – The need for faithfulness in ministry...
> Move 2: (Specific) – Faithfulness is needed in light of the great costs of ministry.
> Move 3: (Exact) – In order to be faithful in ministry, we must embrace the cost of ministry.
>
> Transition: How do we embrace the cost of ministry in order to be faithful in ministry?
>
> Homiletical Key Word: *Steps* – 2 Timothy 2:1-7 gives us four *STEPS* we must take in order to embrace the costs of ministry.

The introduction for a sermon on a narrative text operates in a slightly different manner. Much like an introduction for a deductive sermon, it must still attract and hook the listeners' attention. However, it must not give away the full main idea of the text. To do so would rid the

---

[154]Smith, "Building an Expository Sermon," Spring 2009.
[155]Remember that the homiletical key word is a plural, abstract noun that names the category or character of divisions that make up the sermon outline.

congregation of the need to listen to the rest of the story. Instead, partially reveal the main idea by revealing the subject of the story, but not the full idea. Hint at what the story speaks to and how it answers, but do not spoil the ending. Execute introduction move one and perhaps move two. In the place of move three, insert just enough background information on the text to allow the listener to dive into scene one of the story with you. In this way, introductions for narrative sermons are typically shorter by design.

Finally, here are some helpful hints to keep in mind concerning introductions. The introduction helps set the mood for the sermon. Therefore, choose content that is compatible with the genre and purpose of the text. Do not be long. Three to five minutes is plenty. The audience will lose their appetite if you take too long setting the table. Never apologize for anything in the introduction. If you are going to stand up and preach, then preach; do not be sorry. Write the introduction out word for word, even if you do not manuscript the rest of the sermon. Memorize the introduction. During the introduction, maintain eye contact. Establishing your ethos as a speaker is paramount and primarily determined in the first 30 seconds of the sermon. Be creative and avoid being predictable in how you introduce your sermons each week.

b. The End | Crafting Effective Conclusions

Conclusions tend to be the most overlooked portion of sermon construction. Concluding well, however, matches the difficulty of a successful airplane landing. Weather conditions are rarely perfect. Pilot error is always a potential factor. Much is at stake if things go wrong. Last words tend to be remembered most. Therefore, effective conclusions demand as much effort and attention as any portion of the sermon.

Like the introduction, the conclusion must be relatively brief. A conclusion that runs too long may retroactively damage the reception of the sermon. A conclusion works best when communication signals indicate its arrival without an official announcement. Therefore, conclude without telling the audience you are concluding. When well done, the audience will realize exactly what is happening. Be sure not to introduce new information in the conclusion. If an idea does not appear previously in the sermon, it is off-limits for the conclusion. Finally, keep full eye contact with the audience in the course of the conclusion. Dependence on notes at this point is especially detrimental.

Bryan Chapell describes the nature of effective conclusions as follows:

> The last sixty seconds are typically the most dynamic moments in excellent sermons. With these final words, a preacher marshals the thought and emotion of an entire message into an exhortation that makes all that has preceded clear and compelling. A conclusion is a sermon's destination. Ending contents are alive—packed with tension, drama, energy, and emotion. This never means bombast and does not necessitate grandiloquence, since deep feeling and powerful thought are often expressed in the most quiet, sincere terms. Masterful conclusions sometimes thunder, and other times they crackle with an electricity barely audible to the ears, but the best endings always soundly register in the heart.[156]

Chapell boils down the essence of the conclusion to an "exhortation." The conclusion communicates the sermon's ultimate call to action. Fulfilling this purpose requires the conclusion to do four things:

1. Reinforce the main idea.
2. Call for a response.
3. Bring the message to a definite stop.
4. Transition to the invitation.

Reinforcing the main idea includes briefly summarizing, clarifying, and stating the main idea of the sermon. The sermon has said a lot. Now it is time to lean into the one sentence crafted so carefully to be

---

[156]Bryan Chapell, *Christ-Centered Preaching: Redeeming the Expository Sermon* (Grand Rapids: Baker Academic, 2005), 254.

the homiletical main idea. This is the last opportunity to make it stick. Drive it home.

Calling for a response, however, is the most critical portion of the conclusion. Remember, the goal is not for the people to hear the Word only, but also for them to be doers of the Word. Therefore, any and every sermon must culminate in the preacher pleading for the people to put the truth of the text into practice. The "so what" and "now what" of the text must crystalize at this moment. Motivate! Urge! Inspire! Spare no remaining rhetorical energy, effort, or emotion. Aim for the heart, and leave no doubt in the mind regarding what to do in response to the text.

Naturally, the conclusion must also conclude. It must terminate the message in a crisp and clean way. Craft the last sentence or two for maximum impact. Thoughts that are specific, simple, clear, and significant belong here. Every word should be intentional to land the listeners exactly where you intended to take them. Fitting final words echo in the mind and heart of the listener long after the message ends.

Although often considered as separate elements, the sermon's conclusion should naturally transition to an invitation. Unfortunately, many often fail to plan this transition and take the invitation for granted; or worse, they omit it altogether. The context of a worship service, of course, will never facilitate all aspects of obedience a text calls for. However, the worship gathering always provides an atmosphere for responding to the Word with repentance and faith. Therefore, why would preachers not provide listeners an immediate opportunity to do so? Why should preachers plead and urge listeners to heed the Word of God without giving the audience an opportunity to act immediately? R. Alan Streett explains:

> The invitation is that act by which the preacher of the gospel exhorts his hearers and instructs them how to appropriate the content of the *kerygma* in their individual lives. Any sermon that does not include an invitation as well as a proclamation is not New Testament-style preaching. Every sermon should aim to stir the human

will. Truth is something that must be obeyed. It is the gospel invitation that presses home the claims of Christ and calls for an immediate response.[157]

Offering an opportunity to respond constitutes a fundamental element of the Gospel offer.[158] Therefore, exhortation that does not invite a response is contradictory at best. If a preacher trusts the Word to work by the power of the Holy Spirit, should he not look for both immediate and long-term fruit? Giving an invitation creates a time and place for the very purpose of preaching—obedience by faith. Yes, God alone can initiate and enable such a response. Yet, this does not negate the need to ask men and women to respond to what God is enabling by His power and grace. Streett argues:

> Unregenerate man, apart from God's grace, cannot of his own volition repent of sin and turn to Christ in faith. Jesus said, 'No man can come unto me, except the Father which hath sent me draw him' (John 6:44). When the preacher of the gospel calls for men to repent, he calls for them to do the humanly impossible. But he extends the invitation anyway, knowing that it has been preceded by the preaching of the *kerygma*, which is the power of God to save (1 Corinthians 1:18).[159]

---

[157]R. Alan Streett, *The Effective Invitation* (Old Tappan, NJ: Fleming H. Revell, 1984), 37.

[158]"All evangelistic sermons recorded in the book of Acts include both proclamation and invitation" (Ibid.). An encounter with the Gospel or any implication of the Gospel demands a decision. One cannot hear the Gospel and its implications without deciding to accept or reject. Neutrality is not an option. Every time we preach, we preach for a decision—a verdict. Therefore, giving an invitation creates an intentional window of opportunity for listeners to do what you have already asked them to do—decide and act on what they heard! Can every decision the text calls for be acted upon in the invitation? No, of course not, but this does not mean that the intentional window of opportunity to respond should not be extended. The possible decisions/actions that may be made in immediate response to the Gospel are innumerable—the greatest of which is the decision to accept the Gospel and be saved!

[159]Ibid., 45.

Extending an appropriate invitation means naturally moving from the sermon's conclusion to specifying exactly how people should respond during the intentional window of opportunity you are about to offer. Do not re-preach your message in the transition. Do not embark on an extended prayer. Conclude the sermon. Pray briefly. Based on the message of the text, specify exactly what you are asking the listeners to do and what it looks like to do it. Then, be silent. Trust the Holy Spirit. Be ready for those who respond and follow up appropriately.

Final Thoughts on Sermon Construction

Take a deep breath and relax. If you feel that the steps above are tedious or laborious, you are not alone. Genuine text-driven preaching is hard work. In fact, that is the primary reason many do not do it! This book assumes, however, that you have made up your mind not to be lazy. According to Jeff Ray, "The preacher who is unwilling to put in hard work on any detail that will make his preaching more acceptable, more attractive, more effective, has a pitifully low conception of his calling."[160] Would one dare stand to speak for God, knowing he will give an account, without giving it his all?

The work is hard, but perhaps these steps also add an awkward, mechanical feel to the sermon construction process. Wonderful! This means you are doing it right. Learning new methods and skills always feels unnatural at first. New moves take time to become instincts. With each repetition, however, the process will become more fluid. It will feel natural and will ultimately happen without giving conscious thought to each step. Therefore, embrace the work. Embrace the awkwardness. Commit yourself to consciously focusing on each step. Before you know it, these steps will happen naturally.

Finally, remember that the most important thing you can do when preparing a sermon is pray.[161] As encouraged previously, pray before the

---

[160] Ray, *Expository Preaching*, 15.
[161] Charles Spurgeon writes, "I take it that as a minister *he is always praying*. ... He is not always in the act of prayer, but he lives in the spirit of it. ... The fact is, the

process begins. Pray during each stage of preparation. Pray after the sermon is complete, and even pray as you preach! Most preachers in the act of preaching experience secondary trains of thought in their minds as they maintain a primary train of thought producing their speech.[162] Use those secondary trains of thought to pray! Perhaps Augustine best summarizes the importance of prayer for preachers. He writes, "Let him be a pray-er before being a speaker."[163]

---

secret of all ministerial success lies in prevalence at the mercy-seat," in *Lectures to My Students* (Grand Rapids: Zondervan, 1954), 42-49.

[162] Ibid., 193. Spurgeon recalls counting at least eight separate trains of thought in his mind while he preached. Thus, he writes, "It is the Holy Spirit's work to maintain in us a devotional frame of mind whilst we are discoursing. This is a condition to be greatly coveted—to continue praying while you are occupied with preaching."

[163] Augustine, *Teaching Christianity*, 218.

CHAPTER 4

THE ADVANTAGES OF TEXT-DRIVEN PREACHING

"There may have been an expositor who was not a great preacher, but there has never been a great preacher who was not a great expositor."

"I am fully convinced that expository preaching is the ideal method—that it is the method most profitable, both to the preacher and to his people."

– Jeff Ray

Ray realized that his claim that great preachers have always been great expositors might be a little too strong. He even named a few exceptions. Still, Ray argued that the statement is one every preacher should ponder if he truly yearns to be a mighty preacher. Ray's point reinforces what preaching is and what the greatest preaching will always be—an exposition of some portion of God's Word.

The definition of expository preaching Ray articulated allows for a wider range of methods than the one presented here for text-driven preaching. Such is the case historically regarding many expositors and their definition of exposition. This wider methodological range originates from the nature of expository preaching. Exposition is not a singular style or method, "but a theologically driven philosophy of preaching whose purpose is to get as close to the text as possible."[164] A singular philosophy may create multiple methods. Each method, however, is not created equal. Therefore, in the pursuit of faithfulness to Scripture, the various expository methods must constantly be evaluated for their ability to get as close to the text as possible.

In other words, preachers must always be willing to reform their homiletical methods in order to preach the text most faithfully. This commitment warrants the update and revision of Ray's *Expository Preaching* under the subtitle "Preaching that Treats the Text on its own Terms." Ray's conviction concerning the sufficiency of Scripture and his desire to train preachers to exposit the text most faithfully continues. This trajectory highlights the first advantage of text-driven preaching.

1. Text-driven Preaching Glorifies God by Seeking the Utmost Faithfulness to Scripture.

When used to describe preaching, the adjectives "Christian," "biblical," or "expository" are certainly not wrong. However, they are so general that they often give their approval to homiletical methods lacking the ability to communicate the Word of God most faithfully. These adjectives often accept good methods, but not always the best methods. If the preacher's charge is to "preach the Word," is "Christian" preaching good enough? Is "biblical" preaching sufficient? Is "expository" preaching most God-honoring? Perhaps, depending on the definition of such terms. Regardless, should not all preachers hunger to hone their methods to communicate the Word of God most faithfully? Of course! Therefore, the primary advantage of text-driven preaching is its holistic submission to Scripture (substance, structure, and spirit), trusting the sufficiency of Scripture, in order to let the text do the talking.[165]

---

[164]Smith, *Recapturing the Voice of God*, 1.
[165]Alistair Begg, in *Preaching for God's Glory* (Wheaton: Crossway, 2010), quotes J.I. Packer, who suggested that preaching is "letting texts talk" (12).

Christian preaching in the most general sense may only mean that the content of the sermon communicates Christian ideas. Wonderful, but is that the purpose of preaching? Biblical preaching in the most general sense may only mean that every word of the sermon serves to communicate a biblical idea. Great, but is that fulfilling the full purpose of preaching?[166] Expository preaching at minimum may mean *ex*-ing out (excavating/exposing) some *posit* (piece) "of the truth that is in the text and showing it to the people."[167] This sounds admirable, but is this a fair treatment of the text? The fact is, Christian, biblical, and expository preaching can be and often are faithful to the text. The advantage of text-driven preaching, however, is that it offers a more precise definition and method of exposition—one that rivets the preacher even tighter to the authority and sufficiency of God's Word.

"The passage is the voice, the speech of God; the preacher is the mouth and the lips, and the congregation … the ear in which the voice sounds."[168] Thus, text-driven preaching glorifies God by starting with God's Word and giving God's Word full voice to the congregation through the preacher. The advantages to both the preacher and the congregation are great.

2. Text-Driven Preaching Benefits the Preacher.

a. Text-driven preaching protects the preacher.

Attempting to speak for God would be the most audacious act imaginable had not God called and commissioned men to do it. Even still, executing the call carries inherent risks. James 3:1 warns, "Let not many of you become teachers, my brethren, knowing that as such we will incur a stricter judgment." Referring to all people, Jesus said, "But

---

[166] "There is a dramatic difference between the congregation that gathers in anticipation of a monologue on biblical matters from a kindly fellow and the one that has come expecting that when God's Word is truly preached, God's voice is really heard" (Ibid., 33).
[167] Ibid.
[168] Gustaf Wingren, *The Living Word* (London: SCM, 1960), 201.

I tell you that every careless word that people speak, they shall give an accounting for it in the day of judgment" (Matthew 12:36.) If all people will give an account for every word they speak, how much greater the accountability will be for every preacher! Preaching in light of that day should compel us to surrender our words to the text for the sake of being found faithful before God.

Not only will every preacher give an account before God, but also every preacher faces the lesser but present judgment of people. Listeners may accept what the preacher has to say as true, but they may also reject, question, or criticize the preacher's words or right to speak those words. Here, text-driven preaching also protects the preacher. Text-driven preaching platforms the preacher not on his own authority, but on God's authority. Text-driven preaching eliminates the preacher's words and forces people to wrestle with God's words. When a preacher is able to say "Thus saith the Lord" with all integrity, the possibility of being rejected for his own ideas or opinions disappears.

b. Text-driven preaching feeds the preacher.

Before ascending to be with the Father, Jesus exhorted Peter to feed His sheep—the primary duty of a shepherd. Feeding the people of God means providing them with the spiritual food they need to survive, for "man does not live by bread alone, but man lives by everything that proceeds out of the mouth of the Lord" (Deuteronomy 8:3.) A shepherd, however, cannot give what he does not have. Therefore, in order for a preacher to feed his people the Word of God, he must first feed himself from the Word. Text-driven preaching requires patiently studying the Word, laboriously digging into the Word, and earnestly praying over the Word.[169] Text-driven preaching is impossible for the preacher not immersed in the Word of God. This immersion in the text feeds the preacher first and prepares his soul to feed the people.

---

[169] Ray, *Expository Preaching*, 47.

c. Text-driven preaching grows the preacher.

One of the beauties of text-driven preaching is that it forces the preacher to grow in knowledge of the whole Bible, especially when embracing the strategy of book-by-book exposition. Jeff Ray clarifies the scenario:

> The man who preaches only topical sermons may get along with only a superficial knowledge of his Bible provided he keeps up with the newspapers and the magazines and buys a book of sermons occasionally, but if he is to be an expositor of the Word, he must be familiar with its content.[170]

d. Text-driven preaching reduces the possibility of mishandling the Word.

Paul wrote to Timothy, "Be diligent to present yourself approved to God as a workman who does not need to be ashamed, accurately handling the word of truth" (2 Timothy 2:15). The difference between rightly handling the Word and wrongly handling the Word is the difference between eternal life and death. Romans 10:17 states, "So faith comes from hearing, and hearing by the word of Christ." Salvation, therefore, is only possible as a result of hearing the Word of God clearly and accurately.

The high stakes of handling the Word rightly anchored Ray against the tide of topical preaching so prevalent in his day. Ray wrote plainly on the matter:

> The topical preacher has his theme, and he needs a Scripture as a spring-board for the discussion of it. He is under constant temptation to misinterpret some passage of Scripture, notably some short sentence or fragment of a sentence, in order to make it fit his theme. It results in

---
[170]Ibid., 49.

what is usually called an accommodated text. The truth is that while it accommodates the preacher, it usually butchers the text.[171]

When preachers butcher the text, what do they simultaneously do to people's souls? Ray witnessed it frequently:

> Sometimes I go to church and the preacher does that very thing … he takes a Scriptural phrase, separates it from its connection (context), and by a roundabout process of rhetorical suggestion, deduces a theme and delivers a disquisition on the social order or some similar semi-religious topic. … I am far from maintaining that expository preaching guarantees correct interpretation and I certainly do not hold that topical preaching always or even usually results in false interpretation, but if we had studied the question thoroughly, I am quite sure we shall agree that the former more than the latter is apt to result in a sane, well-balanced use of the Word of God.[172]

Text-driven preaching reduces the possibility of mishandling the Word because it attempts to take every possible cue for the sermon from the text. The text communicates its meaning via its substance, structure, and spirit. Any homiletical method that fails to do justice to any of these elements inherently fails to handle the text as rightly as possible.

e. Text-driven preaching supplies the preacher.

Few professions shrink a week more than a preacher's. Every seven days, ready or not, Sunday comes. Unfortunately, many preachers needlessly suffer from Saturday night fever—the ailment afflicting those who grope for a sermon text or topic week by week. Their Bibles call out from beginning to end that their every word "is inspired by God

---

[171] Ray, *Expository Preaching*, 52.
[172] Ibid., 49-53.

and profitable for teaching, for reproof, for correction, for training in righteousness; so that the man of God may be adequate, equipped for every good work" (2 Timothy 3:16-17). Yet, the fever so often deafens the preacher to the Bible's cry.

Text-driven preaching remedies this illness by treating the Bible on its own terms. Ironically, Bible-believing preachers agree that a sermon should treat a natural thought unit of text in its natural context. Yet, so few follow that train of logic beyond the context of individual passages and realize that the larger context of those passages is one of the Bible's 66 books. What homiletical method treats a text on its own terms more than preaching the consecutive, natural thought units of a text through one book of the Bible at a time? God gave the Bible as one book with two testaments collectively containing 66 books. Planning to preach book by book through the Bible one passage at a time eradicates the feverish search for a text that afflicts so many.

Just because book-by-book, text-driven preaching constitutes a preacher's normal mode of operation does not mean, however, that the method should never vary. On the contrary, preachers must periodically stop and allocate a sermon to deal with a pressing issue, a crisis, a congregational need, a specific leading of the Holy Spirit, etc. Furthermore, pastors do well to rotate in doctrinal and topical series from time to time. The key, however, is to keep each sermon text-driven. Doctrinal, topical, and even biographical preaching can all be done in a text-driven manner. Remain open and flexible to the guidance of the Holy Spirit and the needs of the congregation. Never fail to treat a text on its own terms. Pray and plan. Pivot from the plan when led by the Holy Spirit. If you will pray, plan, and be ready to pivot the Scripture, Sunday's sermon will cease to be a mystery.

3. Text-Driven Preaching Benefits the People.

a. Text-driven preaching grows the people's hunger for the Word.

Hunger for the Word of God does not come standard with the human heart. All people are born as children of wrath with their backs toward God (Ephesians 2:3). But praise be to God, those who trust Christ by faith are born again by the living and abiding Word of God (1 Peter 1:23). Hearing and receiving the words of life activates a spiritual hunger in the children of God. Having tasted that the Lord is good, newborn Christians crave the pure spiritual milk of the Word of God that is able to grow them up into salvation. Those who grow to maturity enjoy the solid food of the Word while never losing their taste for the simplicity of milk.

In short, those who are born again by hearing the Word will naturally hunger for the Word. Furthermore, the believer's spiritual appetite functions inversely to their physical appetite. The more physical food one consumes, the less hungry one becomes, and vice versa. One's spiritual appetite, however, works in reverse. The more of the Word one consumes, the more hungry one becomes. Unfortunately, the less of the Word one consumes, the less hungry for it one becomes. Thus, pastors and preachers play a pivotal role in the development of a congregation's hunger for the Word of God.

Text-driven preaching grows people's hunger for the Word because it faithfully re-presents the Word. The hearts of the disciples on the road to Emmaus burned as the Living Word, Jesus Christ, opened up the Scriptures and explained to them the things concerning Himself. This is the effect of God's Word hitting the hearts of His people. The sheep know their Shepherd's voice (John 10:3-4). The more they hear it, the more they long for it. The more people long for His Word, the more they long to see His face. This is the effect of text-driven preaching.

b. Text-driven preaching presents the whole council of God to the people.

Vines and Shaddix partially blame the increasing biblical illiteracy in the church to preaching that is "hop, skip, and jump" from one text to another Sunday by Sunday.[173] This homiletical approach typically follows no systematic plan to present the whole council of God to the people. Therefore, preachers neglect portions of Scripture. Spiritual malnourishment ensues. Begg describes the consequences:

> When the Bible is not being systematically expounded, congregations often learn a little about a lot but usually do not understand how everything fits together. They are like workers in a car assembly plant who know how to add their particular component but remain largely clueless as to how it fits in with the rest of the process. The most dangerous people in our churches are those who are susceptible to all kinds of passing fads and fancies; they often prove to be a trial to themselves as well as to others.[174]

Text-driven preaching performed book by book or in some similar systematic plan, however, enables the proclamation of the whole council of God. Ray argued for the practical advantages as follows:

> "It gives occasion for remarking on many passages of the Bible which otherwise might never enter into the sermon and for giving important practical hints and admonitions which might seem to some hearers offensively personal if introduced into a topical sermon but which are here naturally suggested by the passage at hand." That is to say if, in a topical sermon, the preacher gives an admonition or administers a rebuke, the subjects of it will become offended, saying that he went out of his way to criticize

---

[173]Vines and Shaddix, *Power in the Pulpit*, 50.
[174]Begg, *Preaching for God's Glory*, 31.

them. But if he finds the same thing in the course of the exposition of Scripture, they cannot be offended on the ground that he lugged it in. They will see that there it is in the Scripture, and the preacher could not consistently go around it, and they will gladly acquit him of being offensively personal. The probabilities are they will be helped by that type of admonition or rebuke, but they will be hurt by the other method. ... In the one case they will steel themselves against it as being mere human judgment; in the other they will yield themselves to it as being the wisdom of God.[175]

c. Text-driven preaching teaches people how to read the Word.

Role models often forget about the impact of their influence. Preachers, unfortunately, sometimes do too. For better or for worse, the pew imitates the pulpit. According to Ray, "A strong, virile church was never gathered around a weak pulpit."[176] What is done in the pulpit, especially how the preacher handles the Bible, follows people home. Clever and relevant eisegesis, exegetical omissions, textual abandonment, or any other homiletical acrobatic that dodges the full and unhindered meaning and significance of the text not only deprives the congregation of the truth, but also breeds imitation of these deadly practices at home. Therefore, at minimum, "it is important that the listener does not leave mystified by the way in which the preacher dealt with the text."[177]

In short, preaching teaches people how to read their Bibles.[178] Text-driven preaching teaches people to read their Bibles rightly by modeling sound hermeneutics. It exemplifies how to discern the text's meaning and bridge to its contemporary significance. Therefore, text-driven preaching

---

[175] Ray, *Expository Preaching*, 50-52. Ray begins this portion by quoting from James W. Alexander's *Thoughts on Preaching* (New York: Charles Scribner, 1864).
[176] Ibid., 14.
[177] Begg, *Preaching for God's Glory*, 37.
[178] Paige Patterson concludes, "Good preaching consists in helping people to read the Bible" ("Ancient Rhetoric: A Model for Text-Driven Preachers," in *Text-Driven Preaching*, 26).

best teaches people how to read their Bibles and feed themselves from the Word of God. In this way, text-driven preaching not only provides fish; it teaches people how to fish.

d. Text-driven preaching meets people's greatest needs.

Is every part of the Bible relevant for today? One's answer carries sweeping ramifications. God created everything out of nothing by speaking. He then gathered a portion of the dust created by His voice and fashioned the form of a man. With the same breath used to create all things, God exhaled into that human form of dust, transforming dirt into life. God is the maker of man. "And He made from one man every nation of mankind to live on all the face of the earth, having determined their appointed times and the boundaries of their habitation, that they would seek God, if perhaps they might grope for Him and find Him, though He is not far from each one of us; for in Him we live and move and exist" (Acts 17:26-28a).

If God made man; if God made man's earthly habitation; if God determined mankind's times and places; if man lives, moves, and exists in and through the presence and power of God, then how could God not be aware of mankind's every need? How could Scripture, as God's self-revelation to man, not speak to and meet every human need? Men, cursed by sin and shy of omniscience, feel some of their needs. God, all-knowing and perfect in every way, knows all of man's needs.

This reality should establish a homiletical default—starting with what God has said rather than what men feel. Felt needs are often genuine needs. Yet, they are not always the deepest needs. Text-driven preaching trusts that God knows man's deepest needs and, therefore, allows Scripture, rather than man's needs, to set the homiletical agenda. Simultaneously, text-driven preaching appreciates felt needs and speaks to them from the text. Priority, however, goes to the needs known by God and spoken to in Scripture. Doriani describes the proper balance:

> Good pastors answer the questions people have and address their felt needs, but also inform people when they

should ask different questions and feel different needs. They speak to their people, both as insiders immersed in the community and as outsiders who see things the church cannot.[179]

Is it always wrong to start with a human need and then search the Scriptures for the answer in order to construct a sermon? No, definitely not. A constant practice of this, however, might reveal a preacher's true convictions regarding the relevance of Scripture. Oftentimes preachers claim to believe in the truth, relevance, and sufficiency of Scripture. The only problem … laziness! They take the homiletical path of least resistance. They skip the hard work of exegesis. They do not ascend the mountain to understand the text, nor descend to deliver its meaning. Instead, they point to a text. They drive by it quickly so as not to raise too many questions they do not plan to answer. They then leave the text in the rear-view mirror to perform the "relevant" but far less exacting task of providing cultural Christian commentary on life as man thinks he knows it.

Remember, preacher, the Word does the work. If you subordinate, slight, or gag the Word in any way, do not expect the Holy Spirit to change lives through your personal opinions for living. As a general rule, start the sermon with what God has said, not with what man wants to hear. "By starting with God's Word instead of a popular idea or a perceived need, the preacher will expose the nature and truth of the Triune God to people—which is their greatest need."[180]

"The heart is more deceitful than all else and is desperately sick; who can understand it?" (Jeremiah 17:9). Take the steel of God's Word. Discern the flint of people's felt and unfelt needs from the Word. Strike the flint with the steel. The sparks will light a fire cauterizing the heart. The burn and balm of the Word by the power of the Holy Spirit will not return void.

---

[179] Doriani, *Putting the Truth to Work*, 38.
[180] Tony Merida, *Faithful Preaching: Declaring Scripture with Responsibility, Passion, and Authenticity* (Nashville: B&H Academic, 2009), 12.

The Advantages Of Text-driven Preaching

e. Text-driven preaching nurtures spiritual maturity.

Disobeying the voice of the Lord led to Israel's downfall. They spurned God's Word. They refused to hear. They hardened their hearts. They broke the covenant, and thus, God brought disaster. Yet, God did not give up on His people. God did just the opposite. He made a new covenant. He promised to take His Word, His Law, and write it for His people not on tablets of stone, but upon their hearts (Jeremiah 31:31-34).

How did God write upon the human heart? God became a man in Jesus Christ. Through the Incarnation, God spoke through His Son—the Living Word. When the Living Word ascended back to the Father, the Holy Spirit descended to indwell believers as a helper and guarantee of our eternal inheritance. The Holy Spirit inspired the writing of the New Testament to testify to the Son and the salvation He offers. The moment one calls on Jesus Christ through faith, He comes to dwell in the heart (Ephesians 3:17). Jesus, as the Living Word, is everything God wanted to say to man (Hebrews 1:1-4). God inscribes His Son in and on our hearts when, by faith, we call on Him as Savior and Lord.

Salvation in Christ is both a now and not yet reality. Christ's righteousness clothes us and justifies us before the Father the moment we believe. From that moment on, salvation stands secure while marching forward via sanctification in the life of the believer. Union with Christ by faith turns to a daily process of transformation into the image of Christ. God promised that He would complete the salvation He began in every believer on the day of Jesus Christ. The fulfillment of this promise is none other than the hope of glory, which is "Christ in you" (Colossians 1:27). The final stage of salvation, glorification, awaits every believer the moment they behold Jesus face to face (1 John 3:2).

The will of God, therefore, for every believer is daily growth in Christlikeness. The goal is daily transformation by the daily renewing of our minds (Romans 12:2). The goal is for the God of peace to sanctify us entirely (1 Thessalonians 5:23). The goal is love from a pure heart and a good conscience and a sincere faith (1 Timothy 1:5). The goal is a knowledge of the truth that leads to godliness (Titus 1:1). The goal is to set our eyes on Jesus, to lay aside every weight and sin, and run with endurance the race set before us (Hebrews 12:1-2). The goal is Christ formed in each one of us so that we love Him, look like Him, obey Him, worship Him, share Him, and teach others all that He commanded (Galatians 4:19; Romans 8:28-30; Matthew 28:19-20). Thus, the goal of the Christian life is Christ, and Christ is only available because God sent Jesus Christ as the Living Word and inspired the written Word that testifies to Him (Luke 1:1-4; John 17:17; 20:30-31; Romans 15:4; 1 Corinthians 10:11; Titus 1:1-3).

To put it another way, life only exists because God has spoken. God not only spoke, He wrote (through human authors). And from now until Christ returns, the Word that has been written must be preached (2 Timothy 4:2; 1 Peter 4:10-11). The dead come to life when they hear the Word preached and believe (Romans 10:17). Subsequently, it is the work of the Word of God to teach, rebuke, correct, and train God's people in Christlikeness and to be equipped for every good work (2 Timothy 3:16-17; 4:2). Overall, the sanctification of every believer depends on consistent exposure to the Word of God conforming the heart more and more into the image of Christ.

What happens when God's people are not consistently exposed to the Word of God? Spiritual malnourishment! The author of Hebrews provides a sharp warning:

> Concerning him we have much to say, and it is hard to explain, since you have become dull of hearing. For though by this time you ought to be teachers, you have need again for someone to teach you the elementary principles of the oracles of God, and you have come to need milk and not solid food. For everyone who partakes only of milk is not accustomed to the word of righteousness, for he is an infant. But solid food is for the mature, who because of practice have their senses trained to discern good and evil.[181]

---

[181] Hebrews 5:11-14.

The Advantages Of Text-driven Preaching

Furthermore, Ephesians 4:14 warns that believers who lack grounding in God's Word suffer stunted growth and can be "tossed here and there by waves and carried about by every wind of doctrine, by the trickery of men, by craftiness in deceitful scheming."

Walter Kaiser notes that such is the case for many in the church today. He writes:

> It is no secret that Christ's Church is not in good health in many places of the world. She has been languishing because she has been fed, as the current line has it, "junk food"; all kinds of artificial preservatives and all sorts of unnatural substitutes have been served up to her. As a result, theological and biblical malnutrition has afflicted the very generation that has taken such giant steps to make sure its physical health is not damaged by using foods or products that are harmful to their bodies. Simultaneously a worldwide spiritual famine resulting from the absence of any genuine publication of the Word of God (Amos 8:11) continues to run wild and almost unabated in most quarters of the Church.[182]

According to James Stewart, "The disease of modern preaching is its search for popularity."[183] Picking popularity over faithfulness jettisons the text. Preachers let go of what people need most for the sake of their own personal gain. Instead of feeding God's sheep, selfish shepherds feed on God's sheep. Text-driven preaching, on the other hand, demands the preacher let go of his reputation and surrender to the text. Then, text-driven preaching feeds the soul of the preacher. Next, text-driven preaching provides God's food for His people through the preacher. As both preacher and people grow in and through God's Word, the saints are equipped for the work of the ministry, the body of Christ

---

[182]Walter C. Kaiser, *Toward an Exegetical Theology: Biblical Exegesis for Preaching and Teaching* (Grand Rapids: Baker Academic, 1981), 7-8.
[183]As quoted by Begg in *Preaching for God's Glory*, 29.

builds up, unity of faith and knowledge of the Son of God increase, and mature manhood in the measure of the fullness of Christ draws closer and closer (Ephesians 4:11-13).

CHAPTER 5

THE PUBLIC READING OF SCRIPTURE AS A METHOD OF EXPOSITION

"If, by the way he reads it, the preacher can cause the people to understand the Word of God, how important that he learn to read it well!" – Jeff Ray

Alongside expository preaching, Jeff Ray emphasized the importance of the public reading of Scripture. Colleagues of Ray remember this homiletical trademark and attribute it to both Ray's training in elocution and oratory and Ray's dissatisfaction with the status of public Scripture reading. Concerning the latter, T.B. Maston recalls Ray's comments:

> Often I am mortified and seldom edified by the way the preacher reads his scripture lesson. ... God will hold you and me accountable for the way we hamper, not to say butcher his holy Word by our sloven, unprepared public reading of it.[184]

The intense focus and heightened status Ray gave to the public reading of Scripture surfaced when he wrote, "I am making no extreme statement

---

[184] T.B. Maston, "Jeff D. Ray and Southwestern Seminary," *Southwestern Journal of Theology* 10 (Fall 1967): 75.

when I say that a correct and impressive reading of the scripture to the people is among the preacher's most useful and highest achievements."[185] It comes as no surprise, therefore, that Ray dedicated himself to reading the Scriptures in public with excellence and training his students to do so as well. Those who heard Ray read the Scriptures in public often informed him of the impact. One pastor reported:

> You made me see the beauty of it. Also your method of reading caused me to visualize incidents, persons, and places of what you read. It has been my desire for the past few years to give a bigger place to the public reading of God's Word in the worship services in my pastorates.[186]

Another pastor communicated the influence of Ray's emphasis this way:

> P.S. Just today a good woman told me that her husband said that he enjoyed the Scripture reading so much. He said that I read it better than any man he had heard. You know where I received that training. (Please pardon this immodesty but it was another laurel in your crown.)[187]

Despite Ray's emphasis regarding the excellence public Scripture reading demands, pastors and churches often continue to omit, neglect, or underestimate it. Jeffrey Arthurs writes:

> Scripture reading is often the low point of an already lethargic service. Surveys of church members rank the public reading of Scripture as one of the dullest portions of the gathering. ... In many churches, public reading of the

---

[185]Ray, "Preachers," Ray Collection, Box 5, Folder 216.
[186]W.A. Corkern to Jeff D. Ray, 11 December 1939, Ray Collection, Box 6, Folder 346.
[187]C.S. Cadwallader to Jeff D. Ray, 16 November 1931, Ray Collection, Box 6, Folder 308.

Bible is little more than homiletical throat-clearing before the sermon. ... Many churches that pride themselves on being "Bible churches" feature very little of God's Holy Word. Not only do we relegate Scripture reading to the fringe of "what really matters" in our services, but even when we do read, we often read poorly.[188]

Ray's words on the public reading of Scripture written in *Expository Preaching* in 1940, therefore, remain as relevant, compelling, and necessary for today as they were almost 80 years ago. The remaining portion of this chapter records Ray's exact words on the topic. Ray had a way with words. Hear his voice on reading Scripture with your best voice.

Pulpit Scripture Reading as a Method of Exposition[189]

The Bible puts special emphasis not only upon the matter of reading the Scriptures but upon the manner in which they are read publicly.

In the eighth chapter of Nehemiah, we are told: "Ezra the scribe stood upon a pulpit of wood, which they had made for the purpose. ... And Ezra opened the book in the sight of all the people; and when he opened it, all the people stood up. ... So they read in the book in the law of God distinctly, and gave the sense, and caused them to understand the reading."[190] Doubtless they stopped occasionally to give some verbal interpretation, but the weight of the passage seems to carry the idea that they caused the people to understand the law by the way they read it. This is particularly true when Hebrew scholars without any thought of the point I have in mind tell us that the last line should be translated not "Caused them to understand the reading,"

---

[188]Jeffrey D. Arthurs, *Devote Yourself to the Public Reading of Scripture: The Transforming Power of the Well-Spoken Word* (Grand Rapids: Kregel, 2012), 11 and 14.
[189]This subheading titles chapter eight of Ray's *Expository Preaching*, 113. The words that follow it here present Ray's chapter in its entirety.
[190]Ray uses the KJV throughout this chapter.

but "Caused them to understand *in* the reading," which reinforces my thought that the scribes caused the people to understand the law by their interpretative reading of it.

But in the New Testament, there is still further confirmation of the fact that the Holy Spirit insists upon careful preparation for public Bible reading, that in the reading one may correctly interpret the varying shades of truth the passage contains. Paul, moved by the Holy Spirit, requires Timothy to do that very thing.

In 1 Timothy 4:13, we find him saying to that young pastor, "Till I come, give attendance to reading, to exhortation, to doctrine." So it reads in King James. Moffatt translates it, "Attend to your Scripture-reading, your preaching, and your teaching till I come." Way translates it, "Until I come give constant attention to the public reading of the Scriptures, to personal appeals, to exposition."

In my own mind, there is not a shadow of doubt that Way's translation is the correct one. Timothy had three cardinal, coordinate duties when he stood before a congregation in a public service: (1) Read the Scriptures to them; (2) Teach them; (3) Exhort them. Paul urges him to give constant and impartial attention to all three. Paul had sufficient education and experience and observation to know that if the preacher knows how to read the Bible to his audience intelligently and interpretatively, he can set out and enforce the Scriptural truth with as much clarity as in his teaching and with as much winsome persuasion as in his exhortation. He, therefore, made these three public pulpit functions coordinate—read, teach, exhort.

When the average 20th-century preacher reads this Pauline injunction and, by a process of analogy, applies it to himself, the first thing in his mind is a comfortable pastor's study with many shelves full of books and himself sitting in an easy chair reading one of them. He thinks of Paul telling Timothy to shut himself up in some quiet place where he would not be disturbed and read a book. But that could not have been the case. The probabilities are that Timothy did not have any book. In that day, when books were made by the process of copying by hand, a book was an expensive luxury, which probably Timothy could not afford. To interpret the passage to mean that Paul exhorted Timothy to give his attention to reading books is on par with supposing he meant, "Study books," when in 2 Timothy 2:15, King James Version makes him say, "Study to show thyself approved," etc. Most of the preachers have learned that this word should not be translated "study," but "give diligence." Let us hope that these same preachers or their successors in office will learn somewhere down the dim vista that the *anaginosko* in 2 Timothy 4:13 should be translated "reading aloud," just as they have had to learn that the *spoundason* in 2 Timothy 2:15 meant "give diligence" instead of "study."

Now, let us examine some of the evidence that when Paul used the word *anaginosko*, he meant "reading aloud."

1. Thayer gives as one of the meanings of the Greek word, "reading aloud."

2. In this verse, Paul is setting out three important functions of the preacher. Two of them—teaching and exhorting—are necessarily public functions. Does it not seem natural that the other duty—reading (corresponding and coordinate) would also be a public function?

3. The word *anaginosko* is used 33 times in the New Testament. In all these cases, the context would permit "reading aloud"—in 12 of them, the context not only permits but requires that the word must mean "reading aloud." At the risk of being tedious, these 12 uses of the word are cited *seriatim*:

> Luke 4:16: "He went into the synagogue ... and *stood up* for to *read*."

> Acts 8:28-32: "Philip ... *heard him read* the prophet Esaias." (The word is used three times in this passage.)

> Acts 13:27: "The prophets which are *read* every Sabbath" (unquestionably read in public).

Acts 15:21: "Being *read* in the synagogues every Sabbath day."

2 Corinthians 3:15: "But even unto this day, when Moses is *read* (doubtless in the synagogue) the veil is upon their heart."

Colossians 4:16: "And when this epistle is *read* among you, cause that it be *read* also in the church of the Laodiceans; and that ye likewise *read* the epistle from Laodicea."

1 Thessalonians 5:27: "I charge you by the Lord that this epistle be *read* unto all the holy brethren."

Revelation 1:3: "Blessed is he that *readeth*, and they that hear."

4. In further proof that the word means "reading aloud," let us examine some outstanding commentaries:

Expositor's Greek Testament gives us: "Reading aloud of Scriptures."

Meyer's Commentary on New Testament says the word is "used of the reading of the law and the prophets in the synagogue."

Alford Greek Testament has it: "Attend to the public reading."

The Westminster New Testament says of the verse: "Public reading of the Old Testament and probably by this time of Apostolic letters and evangelical memoirs."

International Critical Commentary: "The public reading as in the Jewish Synagogue."

A.T. Robertson, in *Word Pictures in the New Testament*, says: "Probably in particular the public reading of the Scriptures though surely private reading would not be excluded."

The Pulpit Commentary: "The public reading of the Scriptures."

Of course, my opportunities for research are too limited to justify my speaking *ex-cathedra* on the subject, but I venture to express the opinion that one will hardly find a commentary of recognized authority differing from the opinions in the citations I have presented.

5. A further proof is in the fact that in the third and fourth centuries, we find that the church officers whose duty it was to read the Scriptures in public church meetings got their title from this very word, being called *anagnostes*.

If I am correct in my definition of exposition—that it is the interpretation, amplification, and practical application of a passage of Scripture—then an intelligent, interpretative reading of the passage is one of the methods through which that end is attained. Reading would not help in the middle term of the definition (amplification), but in the other two (interpretation and practical application), correct reading may be made to render invaluable service. This statement will be easily admitted if one keeps in his mind that exposition is setting out before an audience that which exegesis has drawn out in the library or study.

Illustrating how a Scripture may be misinterpreted by an incorrect reading, take 1 Kings 13:13, where an old prophet said to his sons, "Saddle me the ass. So they saddled him the ass." I have heard it read with emphasis on and a slight pause after the two pronouns in a way not very complimentary to the venerable prophet.

Or take another illustration. Luke 2:16 reads: "And they came with haste, and found Mary, and Joseph, and the babe lying in a manger." I recently heard it so read as to convey the idea that there were two grown people and a baby lying in a horse trough. Of course, the sense cannot be set out in the reading without a pause and downward inflection after the word "Joseph."

For another illustration, take 1 Kings 18:27, which reads: "And it came to pass at noon, that Elijah mocked them, and said, Cry aloud: for he is a god; either he is talking, or he is pursuing, or he is in a journey, or peradventure he sleepeth, and must be awaked." Usually, when I have heard a preacher read the passage, his manner of reading made Elijah in entire agreement with the Baalites. He told me in words that "Elijah mocked them," but with his voice, he told me an exactly opposite story. His words were the words of Elijah, but his voice was the voice of a Baalite.

Or take Paul in Romans 12:18: "If it be possible, as much as lieth in you, live peaceably with all men." Except when I did it myself or had one of my students do it in the classroom, I have never heard it read so as to bring out clearly the spirit of the Gospel. All other preachers I have heard have put their emphasis on the preposition "in," which implies that there is a certain amount of fussing that a man has to do because of his very nature. The correct reading, of course, would put the emphasis on the pronoun *you*, which implies that if there is any row raised, somebody else must raise it.

Or take the first verse of that same chapter, "I beseech you therefore, brethren, by the mercies of God, that ye present your bodies a living sacrifice, holy, acceptable unto God, which is your reasonable service." Most of the preachers run the words "holy" and "acceptable" together so closely as to leave the impression on the hearer that the word is "wholly" instead of "holy." In fact, it has not been long since I heard a distinguished brother not only read it like that but stop to comment on it, saying that our lives should be so sacrificial that they will be entirely, completely acceptable unto God. A few years ago, I was reading the verse to a congregation when an intelligent deacon interrupted me, saying I had read it as if the word were "holy." Nothing short of showing it to him in the Bible could convince him that it was not "wholly." May I say parenthetically that this false reading of this particular verse comes about in part at least from the fact that many preachers have become so disgusted with "holy-rollerism" and "sinless-perfectionism" that they have a tendency to soft-pedal the real New Testament doctrine of holy living.

Or take the seventeenth verse of this chapter: "Provide things honest in the sight of all men." How few preachers read it so as to set out the fact that while Paul was strong on good character (provide things honest), he was probably in this verse emphasizing the value of a good reputation (in the sight of all men).

My students often ask my opinion of the habit some preachers have of interlarding the Scriptural lesson as they read with running comments of their own by way of emphasis or explanation. My answer is that there may be a rare exception, but as a rule, it is a bad habit—a habit utterly mutilating the Word of God. They say Spurgeon could do that without breaking the continuity of the reading—but most of us are not Spurgeons. In most cases, a good reader could so read the passage as to set out the emphasis or explanation he seeks to make by his running, extemporaneous comment. But if he cannot do that, then better let it pass altogether, or after he has finished the reading go back to the verse or verses he thinks need exemplification and make his illuminating comment.

For many years, it has been my privilege to listen to preachers read the Bible not only in my classroom but in hundreds of pulpits throughout the land. This experience has forced upon me the conclusion that very few of our preachers give any specific attention to the matter of interpretative, winsome, forceful reading of the Word of God from the pulpit. I have heard a few—I am sorry to say only a very few—really effective Bible readers. Most of our preachers read with sufficient mechanical correctness to give one the story, but they do not read with sufficient emotional response to cause one to see and be thrilled with the picture. Their reading sets out the facts but fails to set out the truth contained in or inferred from or suggested by the facts. Most preachers read white and black but almost entirely without color. I sometimes say to my classes, "Most of you could take a piece of white chalk and draw on the blackboard a picture of Dr. B.H. Carroll, which anybody who ever saw him would recognize, but it arouses no emotion. But the artist takes his colors and so mixes and applies them as to produce the matchless portrait that thrills everybody who enters the Southwestern Seminary reception room." The same is true about reading. Nearly anybody with very little training or thoughtful preparation can so read a Scripture as to set out the dry facts, but it takes not only an artist but a diligent student of the noble art to read it with such skillful, soulful use of pause and inflection and touch and tone color as to thrill the hearer with the living, pulsating truth. From my boyhood, I have given more or less diligent attention to the business of the public reading of the Bible. So far from feeling that time given to this matter has been wasted, I do not hesitate to say that if I had life to go over again, I should give far more time and study to the matter of trying to make myself an effective reader of the Word of God. I readily agree that there are "gifts differing" in this matter of histrionic ability, but I do not believe God ever called any man to preach who could not make a good, even if not brilliant, Bible reader if he would work at it hard enough and long enough.

Some time ago, a gifted but somewhat erratic journalist was writing about one of our most distinguished ministers. He claimed for him, quite correctly, that he was preeminently charming as a Bible reader. He accounted for his skill by the fact that he had never studied the subject. So far as I know, the journalist was right if he meant that the preacher had never formally matriculated in a school of elocution, but I happen to know that, from his youth up, this preacher has been a diligent student of public speaking and particularly of the public reading of the Bible. Constantly studying it, he has sought help from every source within his reach. Just as well say a man can be a good mathematician without studying mathematics as to say he can be a good reader without studying reading. There is no royal road to good reading; it comes only at yon end of hard work.

If, by the way he reads it, the preacher can cause the people to understand the Word of God, how important that he learn to read it well! If the preacher can interpret and practically apply the Word of God by the way he reads it, what answer will he make at the judgment bar if, by sheer indifference and wanton neglect of his talent, he fails to become an effective reader?

PART II:
A HISTORY OF
TEXT-DRIVEN PREACHING

CHAPTER 6

JEFF RAY AND THE HISTORY OF PREACHING

Though often forgotten, Jeff Ray made a lasting contribution to the legacy of expository preaching among Southern Baptists as a teacher of preachers for 37 years at Southwestern Baptist Theological Seminary. Admittedly, no method can measure the exact extent of a historical figure's influence. Ray's role in the history of preaching, however, can be described.[191] Therefore, this chapter will place Ray in his historical context and show where he fits in the history of preaching. Special attention will be given to the lineage of expository preaching, Southern Baptist preaching, and Ray's role in particular. Unfortunately, a gap existed within Southern Baptist preaching regarding exposition. Ray contributed to filling that gap by issuing a peculiar call for expository preaching that contributed to a subsequent paradigm shift within Southern Baptist preaching at large.

The State of Expository Preaching during Ray's Lifetime

As mentioned previously, Ray argued that one was as unlikely to encounter a buffalo on the Texas prairie as he was to hear an expository

---

[191] In similar fashion, Thomas R. McKibbens Jr. argues, "There is no accurate way to measure the influence of modern Southern Baptist preaching. One can only describe the role of preaching, not measure it," in "The Role of Preaching in Southern Baptist History," *Baptist History and Heritage* 15 (January 1980): 64.

sermon.[192] Hughes Oliphant Old concurs and summarizes well the homiletical landscape of Ray's day. He writes:

> Not much expository preaching had been heard during the first half of the twentieth century, and even less in the nineteenth century. The few who did expository preaching usually did it like Charles Haddon Spurgeon, one isolated verse at a time.[193]

Examining the underlying reasons behind the paucity of exposition practiced in the late 19th and early 20th centuries is beyond the scope of this book. It is worth mentioning, however, a few of the factors that produced such circumstances in order to recognize the extreme peculiarity of Ray's call for expository preaching.

First, according to O.C. Edwards Jr., the three preachers most highly regarded in America during the middle to the end of the 19th century were Horace Bushnell, Henry Ward Beecher, and Phillips Brooks.[194] Each of these men eschewed the authority of Scripture and expository preaching. Bushnell specifically "has been called the father of liberalism," with Beecher and Brooks as his disciples, who together brought the American pulpit dangerously close to "selling its birthright."[195] Their preaching emphasized almost everything else besides the Word of God.

The ripening of theological liberalism in America soon gave birth to the Social Gospel movement that emerged and matured within Ray's lifetime.[196] Popularized by Walter Rauschenbusch, a Baptist professor at Rochester Theological Seminary, the Social Gospel as a movement

---

[192]Ray, *Expository Preaching*, 81.
[193]Hughes Oliphant Old, *Our Own Time*, vol. 7 of *The Reading and Preaching of the Scriptures in the Worship of the Christian Church* (Grand Rapids: Eerdmans, 2010), xvii.
[194]O.C. Edwards Jr., *A History of Preaching* (Nashville: Abingdon Press, 2004), 631-32.
[195]Larsen, *The Company of the Preachers*, 529-35.
[196]See Fasol, *With a Bible in Their Hands*, 94. Fasol describes some of the aims of liberalism as applying "scientific methodology to Scripture" in order to disregard the "miracles and the supernatural in general" so that "any notion of divine inspiration of Scripture was rejected" (93).

expressed more interest in the improvement of society than in the salvation of men's souls. As a result, homileticians generally elevated the importance of meeting felt human needs from the pulpit over the priority of expositing a text of Scripture.

After embracing the Social Gospel, American mainstream Protestantism eventually crested between 1930 and 1955 with the preaching of Harry Emerson Fosdick.[197] As pastor of Riverside Church in New York, Fosdick embraced the methodology of educational psychology and championed therapeutic "pastoral counseling through preaching."[198] He was convinced that the preacher must begin with people's perceived problems. Caricaturing expository preaching, Fosdick claimed, "Only the preacher proceeds still upon the idea that folk come to church desperately anxious to discover what happened to the Jebusites."[199] Fosdick enshrined the practice of pastoral counseling from the pulpit and labeled the Bible irrelevant.

Unfortunately, the pulpits of mainstream American Protestantism were not the only ones tuned to the therapeutic and psychological emphases of the day. Charles Dargan reports that Baptists were also turning their attention to psychology and its relationship to preaching beginning with the publication of Spencer Kennard's *Psychic Power in Preaching* in 1901.[200] Additionally, Ray's contemporary counterpart, Charles S. Gardner, professor of homiletics at Southern Seminary, published *Psychology and Preaching* in 1918.[201] Gardner composed this volume as a result of his effort "to teach homiletical psychology to young ministers" and to make up for the lack of effort "to apply modern

---

[197] See Edwards, *A History of Preaching*, 665.
[198] Ibid.
[199] Ibid., 668. Edwards argues, "This pattern of stating in the introduction a main idea about a problem facing members of the congregation, making points about it in the body of the sermon, and appealing to them to live by that message in the conclusion is Fosdick's main contribution to the effort to do pastoral counseling from the pulpit" (669).
[200] Edwin Charles Dargan, *The Art of Preaching in the Light of Its History* (New York: George H. Doran, 1922), 227. See J. Spencer Kennard, *Psychic Power in Preaching* (Philadelphia: G.W. Jacobs, 1901).
[201] Charles S. Gardner, *Psychology and Preaching* (New York: The Macmillan Company, 1918).

psychology to preaching."[202] He expresses his view on the importance of psychology to preaching through the following words:

> But having acquired true ideas of social progress and relations, let him devote himself to developing right emotional dispositions in connection with them, being assured that there is no other work in the whole great process of social advancement so much needed. For apart from proper emotional dispositions, the clearest and most comprehensive ideas and principles are without power to control the actions of men.[203]

Whether or not one concurs with Gardner's claim on the value of applying psychological principles to preaching, it is almost impossible to miss the difference in the language chosen and the emphases made between Gardner and Ray. Part of the language distinction is due to the fact that Gardner's volume differs in subject matter from Ray's *Expository Preaching*. However, both men wrote for their homiletical pupils. Therefore, the very difference in what they deemed of highest priority to publish even at the subject level speaks volumes on what they valued. When Gardner wrote on preaching, he emphasized psychology. When Ray wrote on preaching, he emphasized exposition.

A component of Ray's argument for expository preaching revolves around his claim that "expounding the Scripture seems to be the original idea in preaching."[204] In fact, Ray begins with the method of the prophets in the Old Testament and points to the manner in which Ezra and the Levites read and explained the law of God to the Israelite people in Nehemiah 8. Ray then highlights how Jesus unfolded the Old Testament Scriptures in his preaching and explained their relation to Himself on the road to Emmaus as recorded in Luke 24. Finally, Ray includes the expository methods of Peter at Pentecost, Philip at Gaza, Stephen before his stoning, and Paul through his epistles to the churches. Although Ray

---
[202]Ibid., preface.
[203]Ibid., 114.
[204]Ray, *Expository Preaching*, 48.

recognized how rare expository preaching had become in his time, he realized that the fundamental element of legitimate Christian preaching had always been and should always be the proclamation and explanation of the revealed Word of God.

Unfortunately, the dearth of expository preaching practiced in the 20th century is also indicative of its rarity throughout the two millennia of Christian history. James F. Stitzinger speaks to this reality and the value of recognizing men like Ray who sounded a call for expository preaching. He writes:

> The history of expository preaching begins with an understanding of the revelatory and explanatory preaching recorded in Scripture. Legitimate preaching in the Church Age continues the expository preaching begun in the Bible. History unveils a limited but rich ongoing legacy of biblical expositors up to the present day. These men who poured their lives into expounding God's Word command careful attention from today's expositors.[205]

With a knowledge of Ray's convictions concerning expository preaching in the context of the 20th century, it is now necessary to pan out and view Ray in the broader history of Christian preaching and expository preaching in particular. This panorama will produce the historical context needed to expose Ray's ultimate contributions to the legacy of expository preaching.

Expository Preaching and the Major Movements in the History of Preaching

In order to avoid what could be a jejune historical exercise, one must remember "that the history of recorded preaching is but a small part

---

[205]James F. Stitzinger, "The History of Expository Preaching," *TMSJ* 3.1 (Spring 1992): 5.

of the history of preaching."[206] Furthermore, "no work in the English language is devoted specifically to the history of expository preaching."[207] However, through *A History of Preaching*, Dargan clarifies the origin and essence of Christian preaching as exposition. He writes:

> In the very beginning, and ever as time goes on, these two elements of proclamation and instruction are variously combined in the Christian sermon, which as a part of the congregational worship is occupied with the explanation and enforcement of the mind and will of God as revealed in Holy Scripture. From this origin the history of preaching proceeds through the centuries.[208]

The Birth and Early Years of Christian Preaching (A.D. 70-450)

As Broadus claims, "The prophets were preachers," and therefore, Christian preaching finds its roots in the operation of Hebrew prophecy.[209] John the Baptist embodies the transitional period between Hebrew prophecy and Christian preaching as he prepared the way for Jesus Christ, the "preacher par excellence"[210] and "main foundation of Christian preaching for all time."[211] The hypostatic union of Christ's divine and human natures in conjunction with the fact that He manifested the very message He preached made His preaching unique to a large degree. Yet, Larsen suggests that despite the unrepeatable elements of Jesus' preaching, "the pattern seems to be that Jesus the preacher takes a text of Scripture, reads it, explains it, and applies it."[212]

---

[206]John Broadus, *The History of Preaching* (New York: A.C. Armstrong and Son, 1907), 187.
[207]Stitzinger, "The History of Expository Preaching," 5.
[208]Edwin Charles Dargan, *A History of Preaching*, vol. I (Grand Rapids: Baker, 1954), 553.
[209]Broadus, *History of Preaching*, 12.
[210]Larsen, *The Company of the Preachers*, 40.
[211]Dargan, *A History of Preaching*, 22.
[212]Larsen, *The Company of the Preachers*, 42.

This pattern is the essence of all legitimate Christian preaching, referred to here as expository preaching.

Like the preaching of Jesus, apostolic preaching also possessed certain unique elements. The Holy Spirit undeniably accompanied the apostles and manifested Himself through their preaching with signs and wonders that did not continue with the same frequency into the post-apostolic age. The content of the apostles' preaching, however, "was fundamentally the same as that of the Lord, with only the important difference made by the great facts of his crucifixion, resurrection and ascension, and the great promise of his second coming."[213] The apostles preached this Gospel message both from the Scriptures they already had along with the Gospel tradition that was in the process of becoming Scripture, producing the biblical canon.

Dargan summarizes the time immediately succeeding the apostles well and provides greater insight into how exposition became the mainstay of Christian preaching within the assembly of a local church. He writes:

> The accounts and remains of preaching in the times immediately following the Apostles are very meagre. ... As those who could bear oral witness to the main facts of the gospel history passed away, and the authoritative teachers appointed directly by the Master himself died off, the exposition of the written Word became more and more the essence of preaching as a part of Christian worship.[214]

The transition preaching made to being almost exclusively the exposition of the written Word of God naturally accompanied the end of the New Testament era and the closing of the biblical canon. Therefore, although "the preaching in the Bible" is somewhat unique, it "mandates only one biblical response for the post-biblical age: continue to explain and exposit the message now fully revealed (Hebrews 1:1-13).

---

[213] Dargan, *A History of Preaching*, 24.
[214] Ibid., 553.

All preaching must be expository preaching if it is to conform to the pattern of Scripture."²¹⁵

Unfortunately, the early years of the Christian church known as the Patristic Age (70-430 A.D.) as a whole did not produce a high or consistent level of true exposition. Structurally, preaching during this time most often took the form of an informal homily.²¹⁶ Larsen characterizes the early portion of the patristic period as a time when "Scripture was highly regarded" and preaching was "text-dependent."²¹⁷

As time passed in the patristic period, the general structure of sermons progressed toward a more expository character. Origen is the man above all others credited for this development. Dargan argues, "Before his time Scripture was used in the homilies, but rather by way of quotation and application than as furnishing a text for exposition. But in his hands continuous exposition with hortatory application became the rule."²¹⁸ Allegorical interpretation plagued Origen's expositions of Scripture, yet "he was the first to speak of taking a text and explaining it."²¹⁹ His seminal influence forever united exegesis and preaching so that, from his day, the two have remained intertwined.

In addition to Origen, the influence of Greek oratory wielded its sway on the practice of preaching during this period. Dargan's comments on the official origin of the relationship between preaching and rhetorical theory provide further insight. He writes:

---

[215] Stitzinger, "The History of Expository Preaching," 11.
[216] James Philip, "Preaching in History," *Evangelical Review of Theology* 8, no. 2 (October 1984): 298. Philip documents that "homily" originates from the Latin word, "*homilia*, meaning 'a conversation.' ... This was essentially a simple, unpretentious address, spoken extempore, although not without preparation, with little in the way of structure, and certainly far removed from the grossly ramified structures of later medieval scholasticism."
[217] Larsen, *The Company of the Preachers*, 64. He also quotes William D. Howden, who claims, "'Early Christian preaching was biblical preaching,' in which Scripture was cited as authority and Scripture was applied, usually explicitly" (65).
[218] Dargan, *A History of Preaching*, 41.
[219] Larsen, *The Company of the Preachers*, 73. Broadus credits Origen for his influence on expository preaching, but also makes it clear that Origen's allegorical interpretation of Scripture injured preaching until the time of the Reformation (*History of Preaching*, 55).

> The historic development of a theory or art of preaching arose and proceeded from a combined Biblical and classical (Graeco-Roman) initiative. The Bible furnished the motive, content and inspiration of Christian preaching, while the classic (Graeco-Roman) oratory (practice) and rhetoric (theory) supplied forms and rules for public discourse.[220]

Constantine's Edict of Milan in A.D. 313 further enhanced the formal relationship between rhetoric and Christian preaching. The timing of the official toleration of Christianity coincided with the time when "a great system of education in which the theory of speaking was central, and perhaps the leading element, had come to be thoroughly wrought out and established."[221] Therefore, in order to understand the history of sermon development and the history of expository preaching, one must recognize the role of the homily, the subsequent movement toward a more structured sermon approach dependent on a text for development, and the influence of Graeco-Roman rhetorical theory on the formation and delivery of sermons.

The influence of these elements merged during the Patristic Age, especially through the two leading preachers, Augustine and John of Antioch, known as Chrysostom, who brought this era to a close. Chrysostom (A.D. 343-407) rejected the interpretive methods of the Alexandrian allegorists and practiced Bible exposition via "verse-by-verse and word-by-word expositions on many books of the Bible."[222] The name "Chrysostom" literally means "golden-mouthed," and Broadus claims that, as a preacher, "he has never had a superior, and it may

---

[220]Dargan, *The Art of Preaching in the Light of Its History*, 17.
[221]Ibid., 41. Dargan further claims that "the Greek theory of oratory received its most scientific and enduring expression in Aristotle's work on Rhetoric" and that "there has been little of real value or original thought added to the ancient treatises" (28).
[222]Stitzinger, "The History of Expository Preaching," 14. As a part of the Antiochene school of interpretation, Chrysostom emphasized a more simple, literal, grammatical, and historical interpretation of Scripture.

be gravely doubted whether he has had an equal, in the history of preaching."[223] He "is undoubtedly the prince of expository preachers."[224]

In the West, Augustine (A.D. 354-430) served as the Bishop of Hippo and exerted an influence of monumental proportions on preaching. Unfortunately, he often fell into the allegorical habit of his day. Yet, he committed himself to preaching the biblical text. Dargan reports that "very many of his sermons are expository lectures on books of the Bible," and that taken "all in all Augustine was the greatest Latin preacher."[225]

One of the primary reasons for Dargan's claim is that Augustine produced the first textbook on homiletics, *On Christian Doctrine*.[226] Within this work, Christian preaching and classical oratory officially integrated for the first time. According to Larsen, "In essence, Augustine baptized Aristotle's rhetorical approach through Cicero into the Christian church," which synthesized "biblical truth and classical rhetoric" and produced a "defining hour for preaching."[227] Along with Origen, Chrysostom serves as a fountainhead of performing exposition in the pulpit, and Augustine personifies the intimate and ongoing relationship between Christian preaching and classical rhetoric. All biblical expositors, including Jeff Ray, stand on the shoulders of these three men.

The Medieval Period and Christian Preaching (A.D. 450-1450)

The years roughly spanning from A.D. 450-1450 represent the lowest ebb in the history of Christian preaching. The decline occurred swiftly following Chrysostom and Augustine. Philip summarizes the circumstances as follows:

> Following them there came, however, an ebb-tide, that led inexorably to the decline of the Middle Ages. With

---

[223] Broadus, *History of Preaching*, 77.
[224] Ibid., 79.
[225] Dargan, *A History of Preaching*, 104.
[226] Augustine wrote Books 1-3 in 397 and the final portion, Book 4, which addresses the methods of preaching, 30 years later. See Augustine, *Teaching Christianity*.
[227] Larsen, *The Company of the Preachers*, 87-92.

> Chrysostom, the Greek church spent itself, and after him there was no really great preacher. After Augustine also there was a marked decline for two centuries and a dark period of five or more in the West; and even when western preaching within the Latin church revived, it was a very different kind of preaching, far removed from its expository, homiletic roots, that persisted until the Reformation.[228]

Multiple factors attacked true expository preaching during this era, such as sacerdotalism, the growth of the liturgy, Aristotelian logic, the priority of the Mass and practice of penance over preaching, allegorical interpretive methods, and scholastic theology. Overall, "everything has gone into decline, and preaching could not be exempt."[229] However, categorizing these years as completely dark would be homiletically inaccurate.

The influence of scholasticism emanating from the university schools for clerics was detrimental in many ways to the trajectory of expository preaching.[230] A few lights, however, did shine during this era. The brightest of those lights, perhaps, were the preaching Friars of the 12th and 13th centuries established by Francis of Assisi (1182-1226) and Dominic (1170-1221). Smyth claims that "the history of the pulpit as we know it begins with the Preaching Friars. They met and stimulated a growing popular demand for sermons. They revolutionised [sic] the technique. They magnified the office."[231]

---

[228] Philip, "Preaching in History," 298-99.
[229] Dargan, *A History of Preaching*, 108.
[230] See Philip, "Preaching in History," 300. He argues, "The influence of the scholastic theology of the universities ... took over, and the combination of theology and philosophy, and the application of Aristotelian logic to the interpretation of Scripture, with its speculation, analysis and ratiocination imposed an intolerable incubus upon preaching which virtually destroyed it as an effective means for communicating the gospel. It is not surprising, therefore, that hardly any counterparts to the comprehensive patristic expositions of complete books of the Bible are to be found in mediaeval ecclesiastical literature" (300).
[231] Charles Smyth, *The Art of Preaching: A Practical Survey of Preaching in the Church of England 747-1939* (London: SPCK, 1953), 13.

The roots of the revival of preaching among the friars rested in the renewal of biblical scholarship that occurred in the 12th century. Until this time, the better preaching of the era had generally modeled the patristic method of exposition, which consisted of a running commentary on Scripture. With the new outburst of preaching, however, more attention was given to the nature of sermon form. As a result, "thematic preaching made its appearance" in the 13th century and "produced hundreds of manuals on theoretical preaching."[232]

Alan of Lille stood as the central figure in this process as preaching emerged from the shadows to become "a popular art throughout western Europe" by the end of the 15th century.[233] His preaching manual *The Art of Preaching* provided what some have called "the first formal definition (of preaching) in the 1200-year history of the church," and emphasized the need for sermons to possess a more formal structure "based on a single verse of scripture rather than on an extended passage as a patristic homily would have been."[234] Therefore, by the end of the Middle Ages, a new sermon form characterized by formal structure based on a single text or "theme" emerged. Concerning the history of expository preaching, it is vital to perceive that "an important and easily overlooked aspect of this new form is that it represents the beginning of the assumption that sermons ought to have a pattern instead of taking their shape from the biblical passage expounded."[235]

---

[232]Larsen, *The Company of the Preachers*, 125. According to George A. Kennedy, "what is meant by 'thematic' preaching is systematic, logical preaching, as opposed to the informality and lack of structure of the homily," in *Classical Rhetoric and Its Christian and Secular Tradition from Ancient to Modern Times*, 2nd ed. (Chapel Hill: The University of North Carolina Press, 1999), 223.

[233]Ibid., 222.

[234]Edwards, *A History of Preaching*, 181. Alan of Lille defined preaching as "an open and public instruction in faith and behavior, whose purpose is the forming of [persons]; it derives from the path of reason and from the fountainhead of the 'authorities'" (178). As a result of this transition catalyzed by Alan of Lille, Edwards comments, "The patristic homily was expository preaching while sermons of the High Middle Ages tended to be textual" (180).

[235]Ibid., 221.

The Reformation and Christian Preaching (A.D. 1450-1648)

While it is true that the Medieval Period neglected preaching to a great degree, Broadus claims that "so far as the form of modern preaching differs from that of the early Christian centuries, the difference has had its origin in the Middle Ages" with its emphasis on theme and structure.[236] The problem, however, is that this emphasis led to an extreme that buried "divine truth … beneath the minutiae of logical divisions and distinctions."[237] Smyth sharply critiques this extreme as follows:

> Such preaching may be extremely clever and ingenious, but its connection with the Word of God, though undeniable, is purely superficial and purely formal. There is here no wrestling with the Word, no preaching as of a dying man to dying men. The text of Scripture is supposed to be the preacher's theme: it is in fact merely the peg on which he hangs an academic exercise. … Therefore, Wycliffe demanded a return to the older method of expounding a portion or a chapter of the Bible, instead of extracting a text and constructing a sermon round it.[238]

Individuals like John Wycliffe, William Tyndale, John Huss, Girolamo Savonarola, Erasmus, and John Colet to one degree or another emphasized the centrality of Scripture, which laid the foundation for the Reformation Period (1500-1648.) As a result, the Reformation witnessed "the greatest recovery of the power of biblical preaching in the history of Christianity."[239]

The three primary preachers of the 16th century Protestant Reformation include Martin Luther, John Calvin, and Ulrich Zwingli. These "Reformers subscribed to a view of scriptural authority which made biblical preaching a necessity" and believed that preaching was

---

[236]Broadus, *History of Preaching*, 94.
[237]Smyth, *The Art of Preaching*, 54.
[238]Ibid., 53.
[239]Larsen, *The Company of the Preachers*, 129.

"not chiefly rhetorical or communicational but theological."[240] The homiletical implications of their convictions proved revolutionary. Preaching dethroned the Mass, and the pulpit assumed the highest status in Reformed churches. As the Reformers submitted to Scripture as the highest authority, they preached in order to open and lay bare its contents.

In general, the Reformers looked back to the fourth and fifth centuries and took their homiletical cues from Chrysostom and Augustine, who practiced the exegetical homily. Each Reformer, however, possessed his own unique homiletical technique, and Philip describes a valuable distinction among them germane to the history of expository preaching. He writes:

> But while it may be true that it was Luther who first rediscovered both the form and the substance of this preaching, it was supremely in the Reformed, as distinct from the Lutheran, tradition that the continuous exposition of Scripture, brought into its own by Origen and into its fullest flowering by Chrysostom and Augustine, found its fullest expression and reached its greatest heights. ... Calvin and Zwingli in particular, with Bullinger following them, preached continuously through books of the Bible, often in the greatest detail.[241]

In fact, when Zwingli announced to his congregation in Zurich his intention to preach through whole books of the Bible, some objected by claiming that the practice would be innovative and "injurious; but he justly said, 'It is the old custom. Call to mind the homilies of Chrysostom on Matthew, and of Augustine on John.'"[242] Furthermore, as opposed to Luther, Zwingli and Calvin more thoroughly rejected the allegorical tendency and returned to a more sound exegetical method. Overall, "the expository sermons of the Reformers, while in general free, are yet

---

[240]Ibid., 142-43.
[241]Philip, "Preaching in History," 302.
[242]Broadus, *History of Preaching*, 115.

much more orderly than those of the Fathers," and "in general, it may be said that the best specimens of expository preaching are to be found in Chrysostom" and "in the Reformers, especially Luther and Calvin."[243]

The preaching of these three reformers, among others, in conjunction with the *sola scriptura* cry of the Reformation unleashed a torrent of biblical preaching that primarily manifested itself as exposition. Other rhetorical forces, however, were also forging their influence on preaching. The humanists of the Renaissance were rediscovering classical rhetoric along with the other elements of the "humanities." The medieval preaching manuals or *artes praedicandi* continued their influence to a certain degree. Yet, in 1535, when Erasmus published his preaching text *Ecclesiasticus*, which reintroduced classical oratory to homiletics, he appears to have announced a "death knell" to thematic preaching.[244]

The real rhetorical gargantuan of this era, however, whose thinking produced a watershed effect on preaching and oratory in general, was a French logician by the name of Peter Ramus (1515-1572). Reacting to Aristotelian scholasticism, Ramus' *Dialectic* relegated rhetoric to style and delivery. He eliminated invention, arrangement, and memory from the five classic canons of rhetoric, leaving only style and delivery.[245] This line of thought triumphed in England, especially at Cambridge and in early America, and came to one of its fullest homiletical expressions through William Perkins (1558-1602), an English Puritan, in his *The Art of Prophesying*.[246]

The Art of Prophesying "may be the first homiletics book in English."[247] Much more certain is the status it maintains as "the normative statement of Puritan homiletical method in England," which structured a sermon

---

[243] Ibid., 116.
[244] Edwards, *A History of Preaching*, 278. He argues, "In his huge textbook, Erasmus was the first to attempt to teach the entire discipline of classical rhetoric as an element in preparing readers to preach" and therefore "represents a watershed in textbooks on preaching" (278-79).
[245] See Kennedy, *Classical Rhetoric*, 249-52.
[246] Larsen, *The Company of the Preachers*, 206. See Perkins, *The Art of Prophesying* in *The Works of William Perkins*, vol. 3, 325-49.
[247] Larsen, *The Company of the Preachers*, 206.

according to text, doctrine, and uses.²⁴⁸ This sermonic approach embodied Ramist logic and produced sermons more concerned with logical demonstration than oral persuasion. Ramus' "humbling of rhetoric" also assisted in producing this "new Reformed method" because it aligned with the Puritan sentiment that the preacher should avoid all types of emotional persuasion in order to leave the results of the sermon "entirely in the hands of God."²⁴⁹ If the scholastic university sermon took Aristotelian logic to the extreme during the Middle Ages, then the Puritan sermon form took the extreme thought of Ramus and applied it to preaching. The problem is that both sermon forms subject the text to a type of rhetorical development that is foreign to the text. True expository preaching that unveils the content, structure, and spirit of the text becomes impossible.²⁵⁰

The "new Reformed method" codified by Perkins, however, was not ubiquitous in its influence. It appears to have held a level of dominance in the Puritan preaching of England and New England. However, another line of preaching identified as the modified modern form also appeared. This form of preaching is most often traced to "the father of the later Reformation preaching," a Belgian-born man by the name of Andrew Hyperius (1511-1564).²⁵¹

Hyperius authored two volumes on preaching. His second volume, *On the Making of Sacred Discourses*, has been called "the first really scientific treatise on the theory of preaching."²⁵² It effectively bridged the gap between the homily as practiced by the church Fathers and the scholastic university sermon of the Middle Ages by following the order of the text while also dividing it structurally for exposition. In other words,

---

[248] Edwards, *A History of Preaching*, 362.
[249] Ibid., 364.
[250] Larsen argues that the Puritan sermon form "is not classical exposition, in which the sermon is shaped by the very development within the text itself" because the text is subordinated "to the doctrinal theme suggested within it." In short, he claims that in this sermon form, "the text is not king!" (*The Company of the Preachers*, 256-57).
[251] Ibid., 202.
[252] Ibid. Larsen reports that the book was eventually "titled *The Practice of Preaching* when it was 'Englished' by John Ludham in 1577." See Andreas Hyperius, *The Practice of Preaching*, trans. John Ludham (London: Thomas East, 1975).

this modified version of the modern or scholastic sermon form gave far more freedom for the text to drive the development of the sermon while preserving the benefits of a unified rhetorical structure. Thus, expository preaching that prioritized the text received a new sermon form through which it could flourish. According to Larsen, "Since neither Luther nor Calvin bequeathed their followers any systematic statement of principles for preaching, this volume loomed large as an influence both on the Continent and in Britain."[253]

The Modern Era of Christian Preaching (A.D. 1648-1990)

In the wake of the biblical preaching spawned by the Reformation, France experienced the "Golden Age of the French Pulpit" during the 17th century.[254] According to Broadus, "The most famous Protestant preacher of the time was Jean Claude" (1619-1687), a French parish pastor.[255] "His early preaching tended to be like the ancient homilies," yet he "made the transition" to "the modified modern approach."[256] Most importantly, Claude published his perspective on this form of preaching as his *Essay on the Composition of a Sermon*, which Broadus calls "the favorite Protestant text-book ... for a century and a half."[257]

The effects of Claude and his text on homiletics proved immense and are well summarized by Old. He writes:

> Although Claude left us very few actual sermons, he did leave us a manual for the composition of sermons. It is a presentation of the Protestant plain style of preaching. ... He assumes that a sermon should be an exposition of a text of Scripture. ... The Word of God has sufficient authority in itself, and the minister's task is to present that Word with clarity. ... While Claude still assumes expository preaching, he becomes the advocate of preaching on texts

---

[253]Ibid.
[254]Broadus, *History of Preaching*, 136.
[255]Ibid., 172.
[256]Larsen, *The Company of the Preachers*, 209.
[257]Broadus, *History of Preaching*, 174.

rather than passages. Whereas the expository preaching of the sixteenth century tended to treat paragraphs, much Protestant preaching in the seventeenth century tended to preach on single sentences. ... Alexander Vinet, the great French Protestant preacher of the nineteenth century, tells us that from the time of Claude on, the preacher treated a subject rather than a text. ... The effect of Claude's approach was to make the amount of Scripture covered in a single sermon rather small. More and more sermons treated single verses of Scripture rather than pericopes or paragraphs.[258]

In short, Claude's desire for one central thought to drive the sermon led him to treat a subject addressed in a text. This approach broke with the traditional expository method of treating as many subjects as a textual unit surfaced. No one accepted and propagated this modification to the practice of expository preaching more than an Englishman named Charles Simeon (1759-1836).

Simeon is perhaps best known for pastoring Holy Trinity Church of Cambridge for 54 years until his death in 1836.[259] Handley Moule describes Simeon's influence when he writes, "If you knew what his authority and influence were, and how they extended from Cambridge to the most remote corners of England, you would allow that his real

---

[258] Old, *The Age of the Reformation*, 445-46.

[259] At the time of Simeon's appointment, the Church of England was in a period of spiritual darkness. Most Anglican divines would have been labeled "latitudinarian," as they "attached relatively little importance to dogmatic truth" and believed "reason rather than revelation was the 'candle of the Lord'" according to G.C.B. Davies, "Simeon in the Setting of the Evangelical Revival" in *Charles Simeon*, ed. Michael Hennel and Arthur Pollard (London: S.P.C.K., 1959), 12-13. In contrast, Simeon belonged to the Evangelical party "within the Established Church ... who had emerged in the middle of the eighteenth century" and "held a high view of the duty of saving individuals by preaching the gospel of Christ Crucified" as exemplified by John Wesley. See J.F. Clayton, "The Centenary of Charles Simeon," *Modern Churchman* 26, no. 9 (1936): 501. Alexander C. Zabriskie argues that Simeon was not just a member of the Evangelicals, but actually "the most important figure in the Evangelical movement in the Church of England" in "Charles Simeon: Anglican Evangelical," *Church History* 9, no. 2 (1940): 119.

sway over the Church was far greater than that of any Primate."[260] Furthermore, Larsen argues that "Simeon can rightly be called the father of modern evangelical homiletics."[261]

Ironically, Simeon never received homiletical training. He had no books on the subject, and he "did not know the head from the tail of a sermon" for the first seven years of his ministry.[262] Simeon, however, discovered Jean Claude's *Essay on the Composition of a Sermon* about "ten or twelve years after" he "had entered into the ministry."[263] Expressing his thoughts on this essay, Simeon writes:

> I was perfectly surprised to find that all the chief rules, which he prescribes for the composition of a sermon, had not only been laid down by myself, but practiced for some years. This shows that his rules are founded in nature; for it was from nature only (so to speak) that I learned them; I labored only to conceive clearly, and to state perspicuously the subjects that I handled; and in doing so, I formed the habit which he recommends. From seeing my own views thus reduced to system, I was led to adopt the resolution of endeavoring to impart to others the little knowledge I possessed in that species of composition; and to adopt Claude as the ground-work of my private lectures; correcting what I thought wrong in him, and supplying what I thought deficient; though in

---

[260]Handley C.G. Moule, *Charles Simeon* (London: The Inter-Varsity Fellowship, 1948), 148.
[261]Larsen, *The Company of the Preachers*, 404.
[262]Hugh Evan Hopkins, *Charles Simeon of Cambridge* (Grand Rapids: Eerdmans, 1977), 221.
[263]Charles Simeon and William Carus, *Memoirs of the Life of the Rev. Charles Simeon: With a Selection from His Writings and Correspondence* (New York: Robert Carter and Brothers, 1852), 35. Concerning Simeon, James M. Houston goes so far as to claim that "what saved his ministry was the discovery of Jean Claude's [essay]," which "was like a gift from heaven to the young preacher, having a system of preaching outlined by this seventeenth-century Huguenot," in "Editor's Note About Charles Simeon (1758-1836) and the Principles of Homiletics Exemplified in this Anthology of His Sermons" in *Evangelical Preaching*, xvi.

truth in his rules there is little either wrong or deficient; but in his illustration of them there is much, which I have endeavored to amend, and which I think is amended in my Skeletons.[264]

The version of Claude's essay that Simeon discovered was a translation completed by Robert Robinson, a Baptist pastor in Cambridge. In 1796, Simeon republished his own version of Robinson's translation, "omitting the opprobrious foot-notes, and in some places revising or omitting passages in the original text" in order to "simplify the theory, and set it in a practical light … to shew [sic] how texts may be treated in a natural manner."[265] Because this essay represents the ancestral artifact of the modified modern sermon that would be advanced by John Broadus and which would be accepted by Southern Baptists in general, it is necessary to overview its content as translated by Simeon.[266]

---

[264] Simeon and Carus, *Memoirs of the Life of the Rev. Charles Simeon*, 36-37.

[265] Smyth, *The Art of Preaching*, 181. Smyth adds, "Thus, by the enterprise of Charles Simeon, and with a view to the training of Evangelical clergy in the art of sermon composition, the tradition of the mediaeval *Artes Praedicandi* came back to the Church of England by way of the French Huguenot preachers of the seventeenth century, among whom it had been preserved with considerable modifications and developments. … So far as I have been able to discover, this was the first direct and significant impact of the French upon the English pulpit."

[266] See Larsen's taxonomy of sermonic form through church history in *The Company of the Preachers*, 857. Dargan adds that "in England, during the early part of the nineteenth century … the translations of Claude's *Essay on the Composition of a Sermon* were still widely read. In 1838 there appeared what Kidder calls 'a voluminous expansion of Claude's *Essay*' in *The Preacher's Manual*, by Rev. S.T. Sturtevant. The book was later published in this country. It consists of more than six hundred closely printed pages, based somewhat on the teachings of Claude…," in *The Art of Preaching in the Light of its History*, 201. Dargan goes on to claim that "after the publication of Cotton Mather's" *Manuductio ad Ministerium; Directions for a Candidate of the Ministry* "…there does not seem to have been in this country any homiletical work worth speaking of during the whole eighteenth century; but early in the nineteenth a start was made, both in teaching Homiletics and in writing books on the subject. … No doubt the translations of Claude's *Essay*, together with other English publications, were used by some American divines … this at least laid a foundation for the fine developments which have followed" (Ibid., 214-15).

Excursus: Jean Claude's Essay on the Composition of a Sermon[267]

In chapter one, Claude claims, "There are in general five parts of a sermon; the exordium, the connexion, the division, the discussion, and the application."[268] Yet, due to the extreme brevity of the connexion and division, "we can properly reckon only three parts: exordium, discussion, and application."[269] According to Smyth, this tri-partite sermon structure was "Simeon's most noteworthy achievement" homiletically speaking, as he revived "one of the two major characteristics of medieval preaching, namely, the formal sermon-scheme."[270]

Concerning the topic of text selection, Claude advises along the following lines. First, one should never choose a text that does not consist of a complete idea. Second, he should choose a text that includes the complete idea of the author. With these two rules, Claude is trying to warn against the two extremes of too much or too little text for preaching. Furthermore, although the text is primary, it must be considered in light of the audience.

In chapter two, Claude addresses general rules for sermons. Two of his six rules apply to the nature of exposition he endorsed:

1. A sermon should clearly and purely explain a text, make the sense easy to be comprehended, and place things

---

[267] Claude, "An Essay on the Composition of a Sermon," in Simeon, *Expository Outlines on the Whole Bible*, vol. 21, 287-427.
[268] Ibid., 287.
[269] Ibid. These five parts of a sermon are perhaps more commonly known today as introduction, context, outline, explanation, and conclusion. Simeon considers the conclusion as the primary point of application. When simplified, the sermon consists of an introduction, body, and conclusion.
[270] Smyth, *The Art of Preaching*, 178. Edwards, in *A History of Preaching*, 453, contends that Claude and Simeon have been given far too much credit for the origin of this sermon scheme. He understands the "Claude-Simeon method" to be the result of Roman Catholic influence upon the developing Protestant homiletic juxtaposed with the effect of applying "the insights of Greco-Roman rhetoricians to homiletics." However, Edwards agrees with Smyth's assessment that "the basic principle" championed by Claude and Simeon "that the sermon ought to have an outline, and the notion that it ought normally to be divided into three parts sandwiched between an introduction and an application, persisted throughout the nineteenth century, and are still persistent." See Smyth, *The Art of Preaching*, 208.

before the peoples' eyes, so that they may be understood without difficulty.

2. A sermon must give the entire sense of the whole text, in order to which it must be considered in every view.[271]

Collectively, these six rules paint the picture of a disciplined and prepared preacher, removing all distractions in order to explain a text of Scripture in a way that informs the mind and moves the heart.

Chapters three and four deal with the sermon components of connexion and division more closely. The connexion "is the relation of your text to the foregoing or following verses," and to find it, one must examine the discourse unit, apply common sense, and perhaps consult commentators.[272] Here, Simeon provides his own additional comments in brackets:

> The text should always be taken according to the precise sense which it bears in connexion with the context; and be always treated in the precise view. For, in addition to this being far more satisfactory to the audience, it will give an inexhaustible variety to the subjects, and infuse into every one of them a force and a spirit, which nothing else could impart.[273]

Simeon leaves little room to doubt that the hermeneutical key for accurate interpretation is context.

Claude says the number of divisions should never exceed four or five, and "the more admired sermons have only two or three parts."[274] He further contends that the majority of texts should be divided and that the key to establishing natural divisions is to "reduce the text to a categorical proposition, beginning with the subject, passing to the attribute."[275]

---

[271] Simeon, *Expository Outlines*, 297-98.
[272] Ibid.
[273] Ibid., 301.
[274] Ibid.
[275] Ibid., 307.

Simeon inserts, "This is, in fact, the great secret, (so to speak,) of all composition for the pulpit. Every text, whether long or short, must be reduced to a categorical proposition."[276] As will be shown, Simeon's secret of reducing a text to a subject to be developed soon became a standard-like homiletical practice even among Southern Baptists.

At this point in the translation, Simeon takes the opportunity to enumerate his additional rules for the composition of a sermon:

1. Take for your subject that which you believe to be the mind of God in the passage before you.
2. Mark the character of the passage.
3. Mark the spirit of the passage. As God's ambassadors, we should speak all that he speaks; and as he speaks it.[277]

The similarities these rules bear with "text-driven preaching" as advocated today by David Allen and others are striking.[278]

Over the course of the next four chapters, Claude discusses the four methods of treating a text. Treating a text by explication, observation, continuous application, or proposition based on a three-part sermon structure of introduction, body, and conclusion constitutes the hallmark of the Claude-Simeon homiletical method.[279] One of these four methods

---

[276] Ibid. Simeon further writes, "If the passage contains a great diversity of matter, the simple proposition should declare its main scope only; and the other points which are contained in the text, should be no further noticed, than as they elucidate the one great point which is intended to be considered" (Ibid.).

[277] Ibid., 307-09. Simeon asserts, "If these few hints be thoroughly understood and duly attended to, the composition of a sermon, which is supposed to be so difficult, will become extremely easy" if the student is careful "to seize the sense, the character, and the spirit of his text."

[278] David L. Allen writes, "A text-driven sermon is a sermon that develops a text by explaining, illustrating, and applying its meaning. Text-driven preaching stays true to the substance of the text, the structure of the text, and the spirit of the text," in "Introduction" to *Text-Driven Preaching*, 8. Smith, in *Dying to Preach*, writes, "Text-driven preaching ... is preaching where the text determines not only the subject of the sermon but its structure and spirit as well" (64-65).

[279] Edwards writes that "what is most distinctive about their method is the four methods they have of developing the sermon so that it succeeds in giving the entire sense of the text," in *A History of Preaching*, 454. However, Smyth suggests that "Simeon's system, although ingenious and indeed suggestive, is one which it would

is chosen based upon the nature of the text in order to compose the sermon only after the text has been understood, reduced to a categorical proposition, and properly divided.

A.W. Brown explains these four methods of sermon composition that Simeon taught:

> Explication "unfolds the text"; observation "draws out its substance in remarks ranging all the illustrations under a few leading remarks"; proposition "proves the truth in (a text) from other Scriptures"; and perpetual application "through reasoning ... makes the statements or example in the text press constantly upon actions and habits."[280]

According to Simeon, Claude did not intend for these four methods always to operate in isolation, though they certainly may. In fact, Simeon argues that "there are a great many texts in which it will be necessary to make use of two, or three, and sometimes even of all the four ways."[281] In general, explication proves most valuable when dealing with a point of doctrine. Observation matches historical or narrative texts.[282] Continued application operates best on texts exhorting to holiness and repentance. Finally, proposition is best suited for a topical treatment on a text with multiple subjects.

---

be difficult to master and to operate without a Simeon at your elbow to expound and illustrate it. In consequence ... Anglican preachers of a later generation forsook the formal intricacies of the Claudian system in favour [sic] of a simpler method which had developed naturally under the influence of Tillotson, and which had never been abandoned. This method consisted in the division, not of the text, but of the sermon, into two or three, or at most into four or five, main heads," in *The Art of Preaching*, 201. Therefore, Simeon's abiding influence rests more in his ideas concerning sermon structure than in his methods of sermon composition.

[280] Arthur Pollard, citing A.W. Brown in *Let Wisdom Judge: University Addresses and Sermon Outlines by Charles Simeon*, edited by Arthur Pollard (London: Inter-Varsity Fellowship, 1959), 17.

[281] Simeon, *Expository Outlines*, 396.

[282] Ibid., 351-90. Under observation, Claude provides a list of 27 topics or methods of observation that help facilitate invention. Examples include, "rise from species to genus ... reflect on the person speaking or acting ... contrast words and actions." These topics operate similarly to Aristotle's *topoi*.

Because Simeon begins the sermon process with a text of Scripture in order to preach its content, he is rightly labeled an expository preacher. Yet, what species of expository preaching is he advocating? He seems to be championing textual content developed through specific rhetorical methods. His method crystalizes with his own words. Simeon writes:

> Most men preach their text; see that you avoid this. Preach not your text, but the subject of the text. Take the subject of the text; illustrate it by the words of the text, but preach always the subject of it. Let your sermon come naturally out of your text, *'totus, teres, atque rotundus,'* like the kernel out of a hazel-nut; and not piecemeal. ... Take hold of some point in a text which will give you a handle for the whole. Do not thrust in a handle, but find that which is already in the text.[283]

More succinctly, he writes:

> I take a single text, and consider the main subject to which it relates as the warp. The peculiar language in which it is couched supplies me with the woof. The series of cross-thread with which I weave the subject may be handled in various ways.[284]

In other words, with text in one hand and a method of rhetorical development in the other, Simeon knits his sermons to express a specific categorical proposition. This line of expository preaching is the result of crossing the subject of the text with rhetorical modes of invention and is perhaps best identified as subject-driven, rhetorically designed expository preaching.

The final two chapters of Claude's essay speak to the nature of effective introductions and conclusions. The exordium or introduction

---

[283] Smyth, *The Art of Preaching*, 176.
[284] Moule, *Charles Simeon*, 156.

is necessary because simply reading the text before the sermon does not sufficiently prepare the audience to hear and understand the text's subject. Conclusions, he writes, "Ought to be lively and animating, full of great and beautiful figures, aiming to move Christian affections."[285] In general, Claude sees the preacher having "three principal ends … to instruct, to please, and to affect."[286]

The Modern Era of Christian Preaching (A.D. 1648-1990) *Continued*

In the history of preaching, Simeon is often acknowledged as the father of modern evangelical homiletics because he personifies a time of great transition. The 18th century, the century of Simeon's birth, witnessed the Enlightenment and a great spiritual malaise that tended to syphon the life out of strong biblical preaching.[287] However, in addition to Simeon, a remnant of preachers faithful to the Gospel persisted during these years. This remnant did not necessarily offer innovative sermon structure. Yet, their evangelistic preaching led to revival in England under John Wesley and George Whitefield and the Great Awakenings in America.[288] These revivals preceded and crossed into the greatest century of all for preaching.[289]

---

[285] Ibid., 408.

[286] Ibid., 403. These principle ends are parallel with Augustine's three functions of eloquence, which he lists as "to teach, to delight, and to sway." See Augustine, *Teaching Christianity*, 215. Augustine credits these functions to Cicero. Therefore, here is an instance of Greco-Roman rhetoric via a Roman Catholic preacher influencing both French and English Protestant preaching through Jean Claude and Charles Simeon.

[287] Dargan argues, "Deism and latitudinarianism in England, philosophic skepticism and rationalistic criticism in Germany, combined to make the eighteenth century the 'dark age of Protestantism,'" in *A History of Preaching*, 187.

[288] According to Larsen, Wesley's preaching "was more textual than expository," and Whitefield generally employed "a modified Puritan pattern" (*The Company of the Preachers*, 365-72). Among the faithful expository preachers of the time stands Andrew Fuller. As an English pastor and one of the founders of the Baptist Missionary Society, "he gained a wide reputation as preacher-theologian" and "was best known for his Sunday morning expository preaching" (Ibid., 410).

[289] Regarding the 19th century, Dargan claims, "This era marks one of the four great culminating points in the history of the Christian pulpit after the apostles. The three preceding culminations were those of the fourth, the thirteenth, and

Europe and England in particular witnessed the greatest preaching of the 19th century.[290] This era produced "the prince of preachers," Charles Haddon Spurgeon, along with other notables such as Robert Hall, Thomas Binney, Joseph Parker, John Henry Newman, F.W. Robertson, R.W. Dale, Alexandre Vinet, John Henry Jowett, F.B. Meyer, and G. Campbell Morgan.[291] However, it was Alexander Maclaren, the Scot, who became known as "the prince of expositors" and was described as "the supreme example, the perfect type, of the classic Protestant tradition of expository preaching."[292]

Across the Atlantic in America, preaching had taken its cues from trends in Europe. According to Ralph Turnbull, "The tradition of the Puritan and the stimulus of the evangelical movements in revival were still felt across the fast-growing nation."[293] According to Larsen, however, "in all the preaching by American-trained preachers at this time we see a marked move away from the Puritan style, influenced by the more classical rhetorical instruction, back to the modified form espoused by Hyperius and Henry Smith."[294] Furthermore, the combination of revival preaching in America with the geographic expansion of the frontier greatly influenced the preaching of growing denominations, including the Baptist one.

---

the sixteenth centuries. While the preaching of the nineteenth century was not marked by any one or two outstanding characteristics, but rather exemplifies the heightening of power in all directions, it is perhaps on that very account to be regarded as the greatest of the four epochs mentioned" (*A History of Preaching*, 350-51).

[290]Thomas Trotter, in "The Baptist Pulpit of the Nineteenth Century: British," claims, "The nineteenth century is the golden age of the British Baptist pulpit," in A.H. Newman, ed., *A Century of Baptist Achievement* (Philadelphia: American Baptist Publication Society, 1901), 373.

[291]Horton Davies notes that Victorian British preachers primarily preached topical sermons in response to the issues of their day. See his *Worship and Theology in England, From Watts and Wesley to Martineau, 1690-1900*, vol. 4 (Princeton: Princeton University Press, 1962), 288.

[292]Larsen, *The Company of the Preachers*, 580.

[293]Ralph G. Turnbull, *A History of Preaching*, vol. III (Grand Rapids: Baker, 1974), 83.

[294]Larsen, *The Company of the Preachers*, 445.

Southern Baptists and the Practice of Expository Preaching

a. Baptist Preaching Prior to 1800

In *With a Bible in Their Hands*, Al Fasol traces the roots of the Southern Baptist denomination and its preaching back to the English Baptists and French Huguenots who arrived on the "Carolina" coast in the late 1670s.[295] From this time until the mid-18th century, Baptist churches in America were relatively few and small in strength. In fact, "many New England colonists considered Baptists to be religious radicals of the most dangerous type."[296] Yet, around 1740, the First Great Awakening triggered an influx of new members. Revival spread across the land, and "Baptists multiplied ten times in the three decades following the revolution."[297]

The Awakenings, revivals, and camp meetings not only contributed to the Baptist denomination numerically, but also to its practices homiletically. McKibbens argues that although "the influence of English Baptists on Baptists in America must not be discounted … the preaching which has most shaped the character of the denomination has its foundations in the first Great Awakening, the Separate Baptist movement, and the subsequent westward migration."[298] These factors, coupled with rapid numerical growth, produced preaching so eclectic among Baptists that "anything like general characterization is well-nigh impossible."[299]

However, from their beginning, Baptists have taken preaching seriously, and therefore, even in the years prior to the 19th century, certain characteristics of Baptist preaching emerged. Perhaps the two most prominent aspects of Baptist preaching at this time were evangelism and controversy. The catalytic growth among Baptists sprung from

---

[295] Fasol, *With a Bible in Their Hands*, 11.
[296] McKibbens, "The Role of Preaching in Southern Baptist History," 30.
[297] Larsen, *The Company of the Preachers*, 435.
[298] McKibbens, "The Role of Preaching in Southern Baptist History," 31.
[299] Newman, *A Century of Baptist Achievement*, 388.

evangelistic preaching. Yet, this growth guaranteed diversity, which led Baptist preaching to become mainly "issue-centered."[300] Fasol remarks:

> Oliver Hart and John Leland exemplified this type of preaching. For Hart, Leland, and others like them, issue-centered sermons were initially the only kind they cared to preach. To them, expository sermons were superficial and beside the point. They were not concerned with biblical details, but biblical principle, especially the biblical principle that the state would not control the church.[301]

However, many Baptists, such as Richard Furman, utilized their engagement in dissent to preach doctrinal sermons that, though not expository, were at least Bible-centered.

b. Baptist Preaching from 1800-1845

According to Dargan, the history of Southern Baptist preaching before 1900 "easily falls into three obvious and clearly marked periods of varying length."[302] Period one coincides with the turn of the 19th century and concludes in 1845, the year Southern Baptists officially organized as a separate denomination. By this time, Baptists had garnered much respect as a people. Their denominational numbers dominated much of the South, and their preaching grew in influence.

The bulk of Southern Baptist preachers, however, lacked a formal education. Not only did the opportunity for education evade most Southern Baptists, but also, as a group, they held a certain level of prejudice against the very idea of ministers receiving formal education. For example, Old names Richard Furman, pastor of the First Baptist Church of Charleston from 1787 to 1825, as "the most important leader

---

[300]Fasol, *With a Bible in Their Hands*, 44.
[301]Ibid.
[302]E.C. Dargan, "The Baptist Pulpit of the Nineteenth Century: Southern" in Newman, *A Century of Baptist Achievement*, 388.

of Baptists in the South."[303] Furman, like many other Southern Baptist preachers, lacked a formal education but possessed a natural gift of popular oratory. Furman's case was common among the more influential Southern Baptist preachers who offset their lack of academic training with preaching that was full of energy, emotion, pathos, spirituality, and sentiment. It was preaching designed to strike the heart. On Southern Baptist preaching, Judson Allen notes:

> It is for this reason that Baptist sermons are frequently not logical discourses. They are usually more doctrinal than theological, more affirmative than explanatory. Congregations generally prefer preaching that seems to be the overflow of a full heart—spontaneous and fervent. This, they feel, is more spiritual—more in keeping with what they believe about the source and inspiration of the message.[304]

Theological debate among Southern Baptists continued into the 19th century. According to Fasol, "One of the key issues of the day—Landmarkism—seemed to have dictated a topical approach to preaching, especially since most preachers were more interested in 'proving' a point rather than preaching an exposition of Scripture text."[305] Therefore, Landmarkism, missions, slavery, soteriology, and the other major topics of debate continued to draw preachers toward a polemical versus an expository homiletical approach. Yet, preachers such as Basil Manly Sr., William Bullein Johnson, and others did temper this topical homiletic with rich doctrinal preaching that was Bible-centered.

During these years, the First Baptist Church of Charleston may have been the most influential Southern Baptist church in the South, but the strength of the denomination and its most prominent preaching

---

[303] Old, *The Modern Age*, vol. 6 of *The Reading and Preaching of the Scriptures in the Worship of the Christian Church* (Grand Rapids: Eerdmans, 2007), 718.
[304] Judson Boyce Allen, "Southern Baptist Preaching," *Encyclopedia of Southern Baptists*, vol. 2, ed. Norman Cox (Nashville: Broadman Press, 1958), 1109.
[305] Fasol, *With a Bible in Their Hands*, 46.

rested in the rural southern churches. Fervent evangelistic preaching continued. Strong doctrinal preaching existed. Yet, issue-centered preaching dominated.

c. Southern Baptist Preaching from 1845-1865

The official formation of the Southern Baptist Convention in May of 1845 produced a renewed energy in Southern Baptist preaching. There continued to be a great variety of homiletical types and approaches among Southern Baptists, but a greater denominational unity was solidifying around the missionary cause. The leaders of the newborn convention were men of energy and great character who enjoyed a level of popular respect previously unknown to Baptists in America. Rural churches continued to be the heartbeat of the convention, but a transition to the cities had begun. Overall, "it was a period of great preaching among the Baptists of the South."[306]

Three of the better-known Southern Baptist preachers of this era were Richard Fuller, James P. Boyce, and J.M. Pendleton. All of these men received formal education, signaling a transition in the Baptist attitude toward education. Fasol claims, "Richard Fuller was the epitome of a good Baptist preacher" who "combined devotion to Scripture, zeal for missions and evangelism, and clarity in his homiletics."[307] In terms of exposition, Fuller's sermons normally possess a strong relationship to the text and avoid polemical overtones.[308] Dargan claims Fuller "was one of the greatest preachers who have ever spoken on American soil."[309]

---

[306] Dargan, "The Baptist Pulpit of the Nineteenth Century: Southern," in *A Century of Baptist Achievement*, 395.
[307] Fasol, *With a Bible in Their Hands*, 54.
[308] Farrar Patterson provides further insight by arguing that "Fuller's preaching was developed logically rather than biblically. ... That is, his basic point of departure was the presentation of logical thoughts supported by scripture rather than starting with passages and exegeting them as the basis of the sermon. ... In spite of his absolute trust in the word of God, this shows in a subtle way that he started with his thoughts. Instead of going first to the Bible, he was concerned that the scriptures 'bear me out,' in "A History of Representative Southern Baptist Preaching from 1845 to 1895" (Th.D. diss., Southwestern Baptist Theological Seminary, 1966), 62-63.
[309] Dargan, "The Baptist Pulpit of the Nineteenth Century: Southern," in *A Century of Baptist Achievement*, 396.

Boyce's name is synonymous with the advancement in education and theological training for Southern Baptist preachers due to his leadership in founding Southern Baptist Theological Seminary in 1859. Even more critical to the practice of expository preaching is the fact that Boyce's sermons tended to major on the explanation of a text of Scripture. Fasol comments:

> The chief significance of Boyce for preaching, however, is that he popularized the practice of centering the sermon on its biblical text. Boyce was uncomfortable with the topical preaching in Southern Baptist preaching. Southern Baptists needed someone like Boyce to demonstrate a stronger use of the Bible in preaching. He became a role model. As a result, the acceptance of a textually based sermon eventually became the norm. Topical preaching was still done, but not with the frequency of previous times.[310]

However, the mainstay of most Southern Baptist preaching during this time reflected the homiletical practice of J.M. Pendleton. He preached biblical and doctrinal sermons. He "always used a one-verse text. The theme was drawn from this verse and developed logically. The points in the body did not necessarily come from the verse or its context. The subject was developed instead of the 'text' expounded."[311] His sermons could be called "biblical subject expositions."[312] The genetic linkage between this homiletical technique and that of Jean Claude, Robert Robinson, and Charles Simeon is almost unmistakable. Here is evidence for the influence of the French Protestant pulpit on the Southern Baptist pulpit via British Baptists.

It was this strand of preaching that most characterized Southern Baptist preaching between 1845 and 1865. Fundamentally, Southern

---

[310]Fasol, *With a Bible in Their Hands*, 77.
[311]Patterson, "A History of Representative Southern Baptist Preaching from 1845 to 1895," 93.
[312]Ibid., 94.

Baptists held to the inspiration and authority of the Bible. They displayed a wide variety of homiletical styles but collectively affirmed the cry of the Reformation, *sola scriptura*. Controversies continued, but evangelistic efforts remained high. In short, the Bible was central, but sermons tended more often than not to develop biblical content topically from short texts in the form of doctrines or principles.

d. Southern Baptist Preaching from 1865-1900

The timing of the onset of the Civil War collided with Southern Baptists experiencing new levels of growth and hope as a denomination. The darkness of war, however, soon overshadowed life as a whole. Nevertheless, Dargan asserts that during "this dark time the preachers stood to their posts at home, encouraged the people, set the example of self-sacrifice, buried the dead … comforted the bereaved … and conducted many glorious revivals."[313] When the war finally closed in 1865, a "New South" emerged. Along with other colleges, Southern Seminary reopened, and educational methods in general were enhanced. Town life also grew in significance while the rural heritage of the South remained strong.

Among the giants of the Southern Baptist pulpit of this era were John Broadus, J.B. Hawthorne, and B.H. Carroll. Broadus stands homiletically as the tallest of the three. He was both a preacher and a teacher. However, Broadus made his greatest contribution to homiletics by publishing his famous volume *On the Preparation and Delivery of Sermons* in 1870.[314] Fasol argues for the extent of the book's influence as follows:

> Broadus wrote the oldest, most continuously used book on homiletics in the history of Christendom. While Boyce

---

[313] Dargan, "The Baptist Pulpit of the Nineteenth Century: Southern," in *A Century of Baptist Achievement*, 395. According to McKibbens, "Baptist preaching walked calmly from the battlefields of the war to the pulpits of churches both North and South and delivered a message of hope and challenge to live the gospel in a war-weary land," in *The Forgotten Heritage*, 187.
[314] See Broadus, *On the Preparation and Delivery of Sermons*.

popularized the idea of centering the sermon on a biblical text, Broadus gave practical suggestions for actually doing so. ... When the seminary reopened on November 1, 1865, seven students enrolled. Broadus had only one student in his homiletics class. This student was blind. Broadus carefully detailed his lectures so that the blind student could conceptualize them. Those lectures were the basis of Broadus' watershed book.[315]

Broadus' practical suggestions for centering the sermon on the biblical text primarily surface through his advocacy of the functional elements of preaching, which include explanation, argumentation, illustration, and application. By introducing these elements to preaching, Broadus "gave the Baptist sermon a distinctive shape" by articulating an imitable *via media* between the informal homily and the abstrusely structured rhetorical sermon.[316]

Broadus is regarded by many as the "prince of expositors" of the 19th century.[317] However, an examination of his homiletical technique reveals that he was not primarily an expository preacher, if exposition means treating a passage (versus a short text) of Scripture in its natural literary context.[318] Old's account of Broadus' approach, along with its apparent source and influence, bears repeating:

---

[315] Fasol, *With a Bible in Their Hands*, 78. McKibbens adds, "The simple fact is that for seventy-five years or more every work on preaching was merely supplemental to that of Broadus. Even today, over a century after he first published it, the work of Broadus stands ghostlike behind many a modern approach to preaching," in *The Forgotten Heritage*, 188.
[316] McKibbens, *The Forgotten Heritage*, 195.
[317] Nolan Howington, "Expository Preaching," *Review & Expositor* 56, no. 1 (1959): 60.
[318] Broadus' definition of expository preaching is quite broad. He argues that a sermon is expository as long as it is "occupied mainly" or "very largely with the exposition of Scripture," and that it "may be devoted to a long passage, or to a very short one, even a part of a sentence." See Broadus, *On the Preparation and Delivery of Sermons*, 303. This definition differs from a more strict definition, which argues that expository preaching treats the thought units of Scripture in a natural fashion whether they be a paragraph, chapter, whole book, or the entire Bible. See Knott,

By far the most significant principle of the preaching of this master was his concern that it be the Bible that is preached. He was not, however, an expository preacher in the formal sense in which John Chrysostom and John Calvin were expository preachers. ... Broadus was a preacher of texts rather than passages. ... [H]e believed the best texts for preaching were short statements that incorporated the revealed truths of Holy Scripture. ... A good number of nineteenth century-preachers preached this way. One of the greatest textual preachers was Spurgeon. ... Among Baptists this was an especially popular approach to expository preaching. To be sure, plenty of Congregationalists, Methodists, and Presbyterians took this approach as well, but Baptists particularly favored it. The reason for this seems to be that Robert Robinson (1735-1790), a prominent eighteenth-century English Baptist, had advocated this method. Interestingly enough, Robinson got the idea from the French Huguenot preacher Jean Claude, who had written a work on the art of preaching that Robinson had translated into English and commented on extensively. It apparently became a favorite homiletical guide among Baptists.[319]

Patterson's evaluation of Broadus' homiletic provides further insight. He argues that the points of Broadus' sermons "were usually stated as a logical development of the subject" of the sermon rather than the meaning of the text.[320] Patterson argues that Broadus could have "on

---

How to Prepare an Expository Sermon; Blackwood, *The Preparation of Sermons*; Steward, *Heralds of God*; and Montgomery, *Expository Preaching*.

[319] Old, *The Modern Age*, vol. 6 of *The Reading and Preaching of the Scriptures*, 729-30. Further enlightening is Old's footnote. He writes, "As my research progresses, I am discovering that Jean Claude and Robinson's translation and commentary are very important. I regret not having given them more attention in my earlier studies" (730).

[320] Patterson, "A History of Representative Southern Baptist Preaching from 1845 to 1895," 140.

occasion … made a stronger use of scripture," as "most of the explanation sections … were not explanations of the scripture but of the points of the sermon. There was very little real interpretation of scripture in his preaching."[321]

An evaluation of Broadus' textbook appears to support Patterson's findings. Out of his approximately 500-page volume, Broadus dedicates a mere 20 pages to preaching expository sermons. Furthermore, instead of trumpeting the superiority of exposition, Broadus classifies the expository sermon as merely an "important variety" among other legitimate forms, such as subject-sermons and text-sermons.[322] Through Broadus' comments, the reader also gets the sense of just how infrequently Southern Baptists practiced exposition. He remarks:

> Almost every preacher one meets, if asked whether he often makes expository discourses, will answer, "No, I have long believed there ought to be more preaching of that kind, but the attempts I formerly made in that direction were quite unsuccessful, and it seems I have no talent for it." But how few men have ever fairly tried to develop such a habit.[323]

If Broadus' assessment is correct, how weak in exposition the Southern Baptist pulpit of the late 19th century must have been, especially in light of Broadus' definition of an expository sermon, "one which is occupied mainly, or at any rate very largely, with the exposition of Scripture."[324]

Therefore, it comes as no surprise that J.B. Hawthorne, one of the other popular Southern Baptist preachers between 1865 and 1900, was primarily a topical preacher. "Hawthorne generally used one verse or less" for his sermons, and he ranged "from preaching the direct ideas of the text on a few occasions" to "secondary ideas of the text

---

[321] Ibid., 144-45.
[322] Broadus, *A Treatise on the Preparation and Delivery of Sermons*, 299.
[323] Ibid.
[324] Ibid., 303.

frequently, and minor ideas in the text much of the time."[325] In short, if Broadus was "the homiletician" of Southern Baptists, then Hawthorne "for many years was the acknowledged orator of the Southern Baptist Convention."[326] Unfortunately, Southern Baptists lacked a man to call "the expositor." For this reason, Patterson claims that the preaching between 1865 and 1879 displayed "a slight decline of quality in terms of biblical content, as compared to the preaching of the earlier period."[327]

During these years, it would have been impossible for one man to fill the vacuum of strong Bible exposition within Southern Baptist preaching. B.H. Carroll, however, made a strong attempt. Although born in Mississippi, Carroll became known as "the patriarch of Texas Baptists."[328] The First Baptist Church of Waco called him as pastor in 1871, and he quickly earned a reputation for his "admirable powers as a preacher of the word of God."[329]

Carroll held such a high view of preaching because he had such a high view of Scripture. Robert J. Robinson studied the 241 available sermons of Carroll's and reported that 157 of his sermons were expository, 55 were topical, and 24 were textual.[330] Fasol claims, "Carroll preached primarily expository sermons which were often based on multiple-passage texts."[331] Carroll did not have the advantage of a formal theological education or a working knowledge of Greek or Hebrew. Perhaps this explains why he primarily exposited multiple texts in a sermon versus a single literary unit or paragraph. Regardless, Carroll utilized the actual text of Scripture as the content of his sermons to a greater degree than the majority of other Southern Baptist preachers at the time. According to Patterson, "B.H. Carroll must be accorded a place in history as one

---

[325] Fasol, *With a Bible in Their Hands*, 83.
[326] Patterson, "A History of Representative Southern Baptist Preaching from 1845 to 1895," 160 and 169.
[327] Ibid., 170.
[328] Old, *The Modern Age*, vol. 6 of *The Reading and Preaching of the Scriptures*, 737.
[329] Dargan, "The Baptist Pulpit of the Nineteenth Century: Southern," in *A Century of Baptist Achievement*, 403.
[330] Robert J. Robinson, "The Homiletical Method of Benajah Harvey Carroll" (Th.D. diss., Southwestern Baptist Theological Seminary, 1956), 147-51.
[331] Fasol, *With a Bible in Their Hands*, 86.

of Christianity's most outstanding biblical preachers."[332] Much of the fruit of Carroll's study of Scripture can be found in his *An Interpretation of the English Bible*.[333]

Overall, Carroll resisted the trend among Southern Baptists toward topical preaching during the late 19th century. Almost all Southern Baptist preachers were biblical preachers. The majority, however, chose to communicate biblical truth from the pulpit in a topical rather than expository manner. Yet, due to the influence of Broadus and Carroll, expository preaching increased, and more churches began to desire it. Dargan attributes this trend to Broadus. He writes, "The influence of Broadus, alike by his book on preaching, his teaching, and his example, has been felt against the tendency to spiritualize the Scriptures, and largely to induce more expository preaching."[334] Fasol, on the other hand, ascribes the increase in exposition to Carroll and R.C. Burleson. He claims:

> The evangelistic preaching of Carroll and Burleson would combine their exegetical skills with a strong sensitivity to the capabilities of their congregations. Thus expository preaching became more appealing to Southern Baptists during this time period.[335]

On balance, both Broadus and Carroll played a critical role in the increase of exposition. Broadus contributed through his book, which elevated Scripture and presented effective practices for actually performing exposition. Carroll wielded his influence in perhaps a more pure form by actually practicing expository preaching the best way he knew.

---

[332]Patterson, "A History of Representative Southern Baptist Preaching from 1845 to 1895," 197.
[333]Benajah Harvey Carroll, *An Interpretation of the English Bible*, ed. James Britton Cranfill and J.W. Crowder, 17 vols. (Nashville: Broadman, 1947-48).
[334]Dargan, "The Baptist Pulpit of the Nineteenth Century: Southern," in *A Century of Baptist Achievement*, 404.
[335]Fasol, *With a Bible in Their Hands*, 91.

e. Jeff Ray and Southern Baptist Preaching from 1900-1945

Concerning the early years of the 20th century, Edmund Lacey reports that Southern Baptists held their theological ground in the face of liberalism and that the Bible continued to be at the center of Southern Baptist preaching. This age, however, "witnessed a decline in expository preaching on biblical texts and observed the increase in topical and textual preaching on 'living' issues."[336] This homiletical focus on "living" issues directly corresponds with the desire of preachers to be "intensely practical."[337] It appears, therefore, that Southern Baptists as a whole did not believe expository preaching was relevant or capable of meeting people's spiritual needs. Lavonn Brown describes the preaching of Southern Baptists during this time:

> During the first two decades of the twentieth century, the central place of preaching began to yield to a new emphasis on pastoral duties. ... Preachers began to rely on "sermon seeds" and "sermon starters" to aid them in preparation. This in turn encouraged preaching which developed topics rather than texts. Most of the biblical preaching of the period was done by educators. Occasionally a pastor distinguished himself as a biblical preacher. The majority of the preachers developed ideas or topics rather than texts. Expository preachers were few. The first quarter of the twentieth century was an age of topical preaching.[338]

One might be tempted to conclude that Southern Baptists wavered in their stance on the Bible. Yet, that was the farthest thing from the truth. Almost every Southern Baptist pulpit announced and read a biblical text each week. However, according to Brown, "All too often

---

[336] Edmund Lacey, "A History of Representative Southern Baptist Preaching from 1895 to the First World War" (Th.D. diss., Southwestern Baptist Theological Seminary, 1960), 210.
[337] Ibid., 212.
[338] Lavonn D. Brown, "A History of Representative Southern Baptist Preaching from the First World War to the Depression, 1914-1929" (Th.D. diss., Southwestern Baptist Theological Seminary, 1964), 3-4.

... the announced text was not used in the sermon development. ... The practice of developing the title primarily and the text secondarily was characteristic of this age."[339] W.O. Carver, long-time professor of education at Southern Seminary, laments this reality in his memoirs. He writes:

> The truly able Southern Baptist expository preachers are very few. Such preaching is difficult and requires equipment and hard study, but it is most rewarding if faithfully done. Our churches and our denomination are in great need of it.[340]

Concerning individual preachers of this era, no other Southern Baptist pastor surpassed George W. Truett in notoriety or influence. Truett pastored First Baptist Church of Dallas from 1897 until his death in 1944. According to Old, "No one typifies the best of the Southern Baptist tradition quite as well as George Truett."[341] He was considered "the brightest star in the galaxy of sermonic geniuses among the Baptists."[342] Truett possessed a natural gift for oratory, and his preaching was both pastoral and evangelistic. Furthermore, "his sermons were closely tied to a biblical text"; however, "he was not an expository preacher. He used the central idea of the text and built a textual or topical sermon around the idea."[343] Expository preaching

---

[339] Ibid., 213-14.
[340] William O. Carver, *Out of His Treasure: Unfinished Memoirs* (Nashville: Broadman Press, 1956), 48. Carver penned these words in the context of expressing what great results he had when preaching expository sermons through the book of Romans during a set of evangelistic meetings in 1905. Due to the meetings being a tremendous success, he records, "I was able to confirm my strong conviction that expository preaching can be made popular as well as profitable in the building of churches and individuals. It is deplorable that we have so little of it" (48).
[341] Old, *The Modern Age*, vol. 6 of *The Reading and Preaching of the Scriptures*, 740.
[342] Brown, "A History of Representative Southern Baptist Preaching from the First World War to the Depression," 143.
[343] Fasol, *With a Bible in Their Hands*, 97. Concerning Truett, Old claims, "What he may have lacked as an expository preacher he more than made up for as an evangelist," in *The Modern Age*, vol. 6 of *The Reading and Preaching of the Scriptures*, 748.

was not unknown among Southern Baptists. It was simply not a part of their mainstream homiletical tradition.

Brown points out that educators rather than pastors performed most of the biblical or expository preaching of the day among Southern Baptists. Specifically, Brown mentions W.O. Carver, E.Y. Mullins, and Jeff Ray. Both Carver and Mullins were educators at Southern Seminary and practiced exposition to a great degree. Yet, neither of them actually served as a professor of homiletics. Ray, on the other hand, not only practiced exposition but also taught it for 37 years to more than 5,000 men at Southwestern Seminary.

Interestingly enough, Ray was a contemporary and close friend of George Truett. Both men were supremely influenced by their role model and father figure in the ministry, B.H. Carroll. The two of them even resided at the Carroll residence during their years at Baylor. Afterwards, Truett gave himself to the task of pastoral ministry and preaching. Ray began with pastoral ministry but eventually answered the call to dedicate himself to the training of the next generation of Southern Baptist preachers.

Rhetorically speaking, Ray did not possess any extraordinary qualities. He was neither the gifted orator nor the evangelist that Truett was, and he never occupied a pulpit of great notoriety. Furthermore, Ray never completed his theological training to earn his master's degree. He was also a product of his own time and, for most of his early years, failed to practice expository preaching. However, much like the 16th-century Reformers, Ray held a certain theological conviction concerning the nature of Scripture that demanded a specific philosophy of preaching—expository preaching. Southern Baptists as a whole had always stood upon the inspiration and authority of Scripture and yet, for one reason or another, had generally failed to allow this conviction to drive their homiletical practice. In this matter, Ray was different to a large degree. Ray realized that the nature of Scripture warranted a singular homiletical approach. Therefore, he championed expository preaching in a day and a denomination that had largely dismissed it.

According to Wheeless, Ray simply "carried on the homiletical training methods employed by Broadus before him."[344] However, this is not entirely accurate. Ray did employ Broadus' book as the main text of study for his introductory homiletics course at Southwestern. Yet for course two, which covered the practice of developing sermon outlines, Ray utilized his own text, *Expository Preaching*.[345] This textbook transition is significant because it displays that, through *Expository Preaching*, Ray sought to supply something that Broadus did not provide—practical instructions on how to compose an expository sermon. Ironically, this missing element is exactly what Broadus accuses almost every other homiletical author of his day of omitting.[346]

Broadus allocates a concentrated section of his text to "practical suggestions as to the proper management of expository preaching," which he labels "hints ... derived from some experience and observation, from conversation with other ministers, and from the study of the best specimens within reach."[347] These "hints," however, constitute a mere 16 pages of his approximately 500-page volume. Moreover, while some of his suggestions are very practical, the majority of them remain at the level of theory rather than practice.[348]

Earlier in his volume, Broadus writes, "To explain the Scripture would seem to be among the primary functions of the preacher."[349] Such

---

[344]Wheeless, "The Life and Work of Jefferson Davis Ray," 165.
[345]Charles Koller studied under Ray at Southwestern, and during the time of his tenure as president of Northern Baptist Theological Seminary, he wrote Ray a personal letter concerning *Expository Preaching* that said, "It is fully in line with the splendid teaching that you gave us years ago, and I am glad that your ministry is to have a wider field which your book will give it. I am sure that every man who reads the book will be strengthened as a preacher. Mrs. Koller and I often recall, and with great pleasure, the happy days at Seminary, and your instruction in particular." See Charles W. Koller to Jeff D. Ray, 20 October 1941, Ray Collection.
[346]Broadus writes, "The treatises of Homiletics, while never failing to urge that the method has great advantages, seldom furnish the student with any directions for his guidance in attempting it," in *A Treatise on the Preparation and Delivery of Sermons*, 302-03.
[347]Ibid.
[348]Ibid., 304-05. For example, Broadus' first suggestion is that, in order to succeed in exposition, the preacher must aim for unity and structure. However, he does not provide specific instructions or examples on how to do so.
[349]Ibid., 146.

a statement appears to hold up expository preaching as the superior homiletical approach. However, by hedging this statement and omitting a clear emphasis on exposition in his book as a whole, Broadus left a textual gap that needed to be filled in order for Southern Baptists to embrace expository preaching.

Ray recognized this gap and sought to fill it with *Expository Preaching*. Fasol claims the following regarding Ray:

> Ray was trying to make Broadus readable and available to a broader audience, especially those unable to receive seminary training. He also perhaps wanted to use his book as a primer to point people back to Broadus' book.[350]

In relationship to the other homiletical texts of the day, Broadus perhaps took the next step to articulate some practical instructions for preachers concerning expository preaching. Yet, according to Ray, it appears that Broadus did not go far enough. Otherwise, Ray would not have sensed the need to produce a volume for either the uneducated preachers outside his classroom or the young preachers in his classroom who needed to be instructed in how to construct an expository sermon outline. Fasol's words once again crystalize Ray's role.

> Ray filled a gap. He filled a gap when expository preaching was not held in high esteem, and he held the mantle for it for many years here at Southwestern. In fact, he may be getting more reward in heaven now for his contributions than he did on earth. I would add this about Ray … the thing that he really caught onto and allowed to influence his philosophy of preaching was biblical authority. Broadus implied it, but Ray made it explicit. … Ray differed from Broadus in that he was trying to state clearly that all of the Bible is authoritative and proper for preaching material.[351]

---

[350] Al Fasol, Interview with Author, Fort Worth, January 23, 2014.
[351] Ibid.

Gripped by biblical authority, Ray sought to fill the gap Broadus left in expository preaching by authoring the very first volume by a Southern Baptist that exclusively advocated for expository preaching. As an advocate for expository preaching in the first half of the 20th century, Ray found himself in an extreme minority. No other element establishes the truth of this reality more than the fact that in the history of Southern Baptists, Ray appears to be one of only two authors to publish a work advocating exclusively for expository preaching until Jerry Vines published *A Practical Guide to Sermon Preparation* in 1985.[352]

From a fragile, newborn seminary on the Texas prairie, Ray called out in the homiletical desert for preachers to dedicate themselves to expository preaching. He then prepared the way for later generations to do so by instructing them in the classrooms of Southwestern Seminary and publishing *Expository Preaching*. In short, Ray planted a seed for biblical exposition among Southern Baptists that laid the groundwork for a later homiletical paradigm shift. The homiletical seed Ray planted would eventually grow, mature, and serve as the foundation upon which Southwestern Seminary now stands as an advocate for text-driven preaching.

Ray's version of expository preaching, of course, was far from ideal. It was severely flawed, in fact. The flaws in Ray's version of expository preaching stem primarily from the fact that he did not account for the meaning of a Scriptural text contained at the level of genre and semantic structure.[353] Yet, his advocacy of exposition as a philosophical approach to preaching was right and far more consistent with the Southern Baptist view of Scripture. Ray may not have supplied the

---

[352] The following year, Jerry Vines published a companion volume, *A Guide to Effective Sermon Delivery* (Chicago: Moody Press, 1986). After Ray published *Expository Preaching*, Douglas M. White published *He Expounded: A Guide to Expository Preaching* in 1952, later published as *The Excellence of Exposition* (Neptune, NJ: Loizeaux Brothers, 1977).

[353] Ray argues that a sermon can be expository without possessing an expository structure. He claims, "A sermon is often expository in its nature even though it may not be technically so in its homiletical structure," in *Expository Preaching*, 46. As a result, what Ray often labeled as expository preaching jettisoned the meaning of a text at the structural level, producing sermons that failed to exposit the full meaning of the text.

ideal methods for expository preaching. He did everything in his power, however, to win over the hearts of a generation of young preachers to the idea of exposition. As a result, Ray assisted in changing the status of expository preaching among Southern Baptists as he instructed those in his classroom and wrote for those outside his classroom.

Conclusion

Over the course of their history, Southern Baptists have become known as people of the book.[354] Indicative of such a reality is the very title of one of the works most dedicated to chronicling the history of Southern Baptist preaching, *With a Bible in Their Hands*. Fortunately, Southern Baptists as a whole have preached almost entirely with a Bible in their hands. Unfortunate, however, is the fact that most Southern Baptist preachers have historically not sought primarily to preach the message of the Bible Sunday by Sunday in an expository manner. Therefore, while Southern Baptist preaching as a whole has been biblical preaching, it has not been expository preaching.

The roots of Southern Baptist preaching grow out of the Protestant Reformation, which demanded a return to the authority of Scripture.[355] Baptists eventually formed as a denomination because they believed the Bible and held to it as their highest authority. According to William H. Willimon and Richard Lischer, "The central principle for expository preaching is the authority of scripture in the pulpit."[356] However, this chapter has shown that the influence of biblical authority on Southern Baptist preaching has been both helped and hindered by the influence

---

[354] See Bush and Nettles, *Baptists and the Bible*. In the forward to the first edition, W.A. Criswell writes, "Baptists and the Bible naturally go together. It would be unthinkable to find Baptists apart from the Bible. As in our day, so in our past, there has been a strong trust and acceptance on the part of Baptist people for God's book" (xi).

[355] McKibbens notes that "Baptist preaching emerged on the heels of the turbulent sixteenth century, when the Christian world was shaken by a movement sparked by an Augustinian monk named Martin Luther" in *The Forgotten Heritage*, 3.

[356] See "Expository Preaching" in William H. Willimon and Richard Lischer, eds., *Concise Encyclopedia of Preaching* (Louisville: Westminster John Knox Press, 1995), 131.

of the homiletical methodologies of men like Andrew Hyperius, Jean Claude, Robert Robinson, Charles Simeon, and John Broadus.

Most if not all of these preachers believed in the authority and sufficiency of Scripture. Yet, for one reason or another, they failed to practice a homiletical strategy that remained fully consistent with their theological convictions concerning the Scriptures. Instead of expositing natural units of Scripture in a manner that honored the substance, structure, and spirit of the text, they would generally take a short text and reduce it to a categorical proposition or subject to amplify with rhetorical methods of invention. In fact, Charles Simeon's sermon outlines were often so foreign to the text and rhetorically idiosyncratic that Smyth labeled them inimitable.[357] In general, this subject-driven, rhetorically developed homiletical practice became standard procedure for Southern Baptist preachers primarily through the influence of John Broadus.

Among Southern Baptists, however, Jeff Ray was an anomaly. Ray held to biblical authority to such a degree that he realized it held overarching ramifications for one's homiletical philosophy. Therefore, expository preaching became for him the only acceptable homiletical practice because it demanded that the preacher treat a passage of Scripture. Ray's definition of expository preaching reflects this fact. However, Ray's varieties of expository preaching also reveal that his conception of exposition was broad and flexible. In the end, Ray filled a gap in Southern Baptist preaching not by presenting new homiletical practices, but by championing the philosophy of expository preaching as the primary homiletical ramification of biblical authority.

Many immediate effects ensued as a result of Ray's call for expository preaching among Southern Baptists. Most, however, would come in the years following Ray's tenure. Moreover, a widespread homiletical paradigm shift within Southern Baptist life would require more than championing a homiletical philosophy. It would require a deeper change at the level of theological conviction. Ray fought for his conviction concerning biblical authority within his classroom at Southwestern

---

[357]Smyth, *The Art of Preaching*, 201.

Seminary. Less than 30 years after his death, conservative Southern Baptists would fight a battle for the Bible on the largest scale the denomination had to offer. As a result, the denominational soil would soon soften, allowing the homiletical seed Ray planted at Southwestern Seminary to sprout and grow to maturity.

CHAPTER 7

JEFF RAY'S INFLUENCE ON EXPOSITORY PREACHING AMONG SOUTHERN BAPTISTS

In the history of Southern Baptist preaching, Ray filled a gap not by presenting innovative methods, but by championing the philosophy of expository preaching based on the authority of Scripture in a way that was accessible to the average preacher. Ray's contribution to the legacy of expository preaching among Southern Baptists did not take the form of his own preaching or persona. Rather, Ray's contribution solidified over the course of 37 years in the form of thousands of men upon whom he impressed the conviction to preach the Word. Ray made his most lasting contribution to the legacy of expository preaching among Southern Baptists by establishing the homiletical foundation upon which Southwestern Seminary stands as an advocate for text-driven preaching today.

Ray's Place in the Preaching Legacy of Southwestern Seminary

Fasol reports that "topical preaching remained popular" among Southern Baptists "from 1945 to 1979, but a vast majority of preachers, in theory, if not in practice, extolled expository preaching."[358] Southern Baptist preachers continued to maintain their evangelistic emphasis, but a shift began from the traditional oratorical style to a more conversational one. Unlike any other previous era of Southern Baptist preaching, topical and expository preaching seemed to flourish simultaneously.[359]

Perhaps the two most famous Southern Baptist expositors of the mid- to late-20th century were W.A. Criswell and Herschel Hobbs. Criswell followed George Truett as pastor of First Baptist Church of Dallas, where he became widely known for his expository preaching.[360] Criswell wrote to Ray on multiple occasions and expressed the following words:

> I have known you all my life and needless to say your example and service as a minister of Christ have been an inspiration to me. ... You tell that wife of yours to take good care of you, for we believe you are about the most essential man we have in the country, and this is said with full cognizance of the talk about the indispensability of our President! The laurels go to you and not to him.[361]

Hobbs served as pastor of multiple Southern Baptist churches and as a denominational leader at large.[362] Expository preaching did flourish through men who championed it like Criswell, Hobbs, and others.

---

[358] Fasol, *With a Bible in Their Hands*, 182.
[359] Ibid.
[360] W.A. Criswell is the only Southern Baptist preacher listed by Stitzinger who qualifies as one of the few "significant biblical expositors" of the 20th century. See Stitzinger, "The History of Expository Preaching," 27. Joel Gregory claims that "expository" preaching was not a predominant term in Southern Baptist life until Criswell (Joel Gregory, Interview with Author, Waco, February 5, 2014). Vines argues in *A Practical Guide to Sermon Preparation* that "Dr. W.A. Criswell broke the ground for all the preachers in my particular denomination" in regard to expository preaching (xiv).
[361] W.A Criswell to Jeff D. Ray, 18 October 1944, Ray Collection; and W.A. Criswell to Jeff D. Ray, 4 December 1944, Ray Collection.
[362] H. Leon McBeth names Herschel Hobbs and W.A. Criswell as the two "pastor-theologians" who "have greatly influenced Southern Baptists through their preaching" in the 20th century, in *The Baptist Heritage: Four Centuries of Baptist Witness* (Nashville: Broadman Press, 1987), 676.

However, in his article "Expository Preaching," Nolan Howington made it clear in 1959 that "even within the Bible belt, among Southern Baptists who claim the Scriptures as their basic authority in matters of faith and practice, there are few expository preachers."[363]

The majority of the Southern Baptist homiletical landscape, therefore, continued in darkness regarding expository preaching. Yet, a few bright lights pierced this darkness by adopting the practice of expository preaching. Ray had already shed light for Southern Baptists on the path to exposition by publishing *Expository Preaching* in 1940. Evidence that his light continued to shine surfaces as Howington first quotes Ray's definition of expository preaching before mentioning the definition of a few other authors, none of whom were Southern Baptists.[364] Howington served as a professor of preaching at Southern Seminary, but the ripple effects of Ray's contributions to expository preaching among Southern Baptists emanated from Southwestern.

Southwestern Homiletics: The Jesse Northcutt Era

After Ray retired in 1944, the mantle of teaching preaching at Southwestern Seminary transferred primarily to one of Ray's former students, Jesse Northcutt. Northcutt's teaching career began in 1939 and extended until 1987, being interrupted only briefly by a pastoral assignment from 1948 to 1950.[365] Fasol argues, "As a professor of preaching at Southwestern Seminary, Northcutt taught preaching to more students than anyone else in the history of Christendom."[366] In total, he "taught approximately ten thousand preachers among Southern

---

[363] Howington, "Expository Preaching," 56.
[364] Ibid., 57. Howington also cites Ray's *Expository Preaching* a second time in reference to Ray's claim that expository preaching involves the making of a message, but also the making of the man. Finally, Howington utilizes one of Ray's metaphors for expository preaching when he paraphrases Ray, explaining that "an exegete is like a diver bringing up pearls from the ocean bed; an expositor is like the jeweler who arranges them in orderly fashion and in proper relation to each other" (62).
[365] Fasol, *With a Bible in Their Hands*, 178.
[366] Ibid., 179.

Baptists."[367] According to Scott Tatum, Ray had given "his students a solid foundation in expository preaching," and Northcutt exemplified that foundation by preaching sermons that were biblical expositions.[368] In fact, Northcutt attributed his teaching and practice of expository preaching almost entirely to Ray. In a personal letter to Ray dated November 16, 1948, Northcutt writes:

> Dr. Gardner of the Baptist Standard has asked me to prepare a series of articles on "Expository Preaching." About all I know on the subject is what I have learned in your classes or through your books. I know that in the preparation of the articles I will have to lean heavily upon both your published and unpublished works.[369]

As Southwestern grew, H.C. Brown Jr. and Gordon Clinard joined as faculty members in the preaching department.[370] "The three men in the department—Brown, Clinard, and Northcutt—collaborated in the writing of what has been one of the most widely used texts on homiletics. They titled it *Steps to the Sermon*."[371] After it was published in 1963, "this book was the most popular homiletics textbook in Southern Baptist schools" for the next 25 years.[372] In the preface to the book, the three co-authors mention the primary scholars who influenced the formation of *Steps to the Sermon*. Furthermore, they mention "the men who were classroom teachers of the authors," including Ray, who "teach again on almost every page."[373]

---

[367] Tatum, "The Contribution of Jesse James Northcutt to Southern Baptist Preaching," 46.
[368] Ibid., 44.
[369] Jesse Northcutt to Jeff D. Ray, 16 November 1948, Ray Collection.
[370] Tatum, "The Contribution of Jesse James Northcutt to Southern Baptist Preaching," 46.
[371] Ibid., 47.
[372] Fasol, *With a Bible in Their Hands*, 179.
[373] H.C. Brown Jr., H. Gordon Clinard, and Jesse J. Northcutt, *Steps to the Sermon: A Plan for Sermon Preparation* (Nashville: Broadman Press, 1963), ix.

Jeff Ray's Influence on Expository Preaching

As mentioned above, Ray's conviction regarding biblical authority drove him to champion expository preaching. He advocated that the ideas of the sermon should ideally be directly contained in the text. Ray, however, did leave room in *Expository Preaching* for a preacher to draw his sermon theme from the text in a less than direct way. That room seems to expand in *Steps to the Sermon*. The authors write, "God speaks through a *prepared man* by giving to him a *sermon idea*. This prepared man studies his idea and relates it to a text, a thesis, and a purpose."[374] Furthermore, Brown, Clinard, and Northcutt address "Discovering the Idea of the Sermon" before they deal with "Interpreting the Text."[375] They then argue that a sermon idea may originate from "the experience of the people, the Scriptures, a planned program of preaching, the experience of the preacher, and flashes of inspiration."[376]

The authors never discount the authority or sufficiency of Scripture. However, they never seem to emphasize it, especially when arguing that "the beginning of a sermon is the conception of the idea of the message in the mind and heart of the preacher," which may or may not find its origin in Scripture.[377] The remnant of Ray's emphasis on the sermon displaying direct biblical authority appears somewhat lost until Brown, Clinard, and Northcutt dedicate a section to the relationship of the text to the idea of the sermon. They write:

> When the preacher has interpreted his passage, he is ready to begin to phrase the final form of the idea of the sermon. If it is to be a biblical message, the idea of the sermon must be found in and based on the passage of Scripture. The idea of the sermon may be directly contained in the text.[378]

Brown, Clinard, and Northcutt footnote the last sentence to Ray's *Expository Preaching* and argue that, when the sermon idea is

---

[374]Ibid., viii.
[375]Ibid., xi.
[376]Ibid., 30.
[377]Ibid.
[378]Ibid., 63.

directly contained in the text, it constitutes "the truest kind of biblical preaching."[379] The thought in seed form of a sermon re-presenting a text was still germinating and budding in Southern Baptist homiletic theory.

Following *Steps to the Sermon*, H.C. Brown Jr. published *A Quest for Reformation in Preaching* in 1968, which appears to be a further maturation of Ray's ideas concerning biblical authority. In reaction to the paucity of true biblical preaching of his day, Brown writes, "Is not today's pulpit characterized by a pathetic poverty of content?"[380] According to Brown, the dire condition of the pulpit called for a reformation, and through this work, he suggested it could come through four avenues. Brown focuses in this volume, however, only on the fourth, "the homiletical or preaching fitness of the men for the ministry," which embraces five convictions that, "if understood and practiced by preachers, will aid the quest for reformation in preaching."[381] The second of these five convictions Brown articulates as "an understanding of the true nature of the text of the sermon as the fabric of the sermon."[382]

Brown makes this second conviction explicit by arguing the following:

> Since the only authentic document for authoritative content about God in personal revelation is the Bible, the task of the preacher is to use the Bible correctly in sermon preparation and delivery. ... Biblical authority and preaching should be correlates. Preaching should be an extension of God's revelation from the Bible to the sermon to the people. When this ideal is achieved, the minister preaches with authentic Biblical authority.[383]

---

[379]Ibid., 64. According to Joel Gregory, chapter three of *Steps to the Sermon*, titled "Interpreting the Text," which contains the portion referring to the text and the idea of the sermon, was written exclusively by Jesse Northcutt. See Gregory, "Interpretation in Preaching," 14.
[380]H.C. Brown Jr., *A Quest for Reformation in Preaching* (Waco: Word Books, 1968), 16.
[381]Ibid., 5.
[382]Ibid., 6.
[383]Ibid., 35.

Preaching with biblical authority is paramount according to Brown, and he claims that the strongest type of biblical authority a sermon can possess is "direct" biblical authority achieved when the "sermon uses Scripture in the message with the same sense as it has in the text."[384] Brown, Clinard, and Northcutt allocate a single section of *Steps to the Sermon* to the idea that a sermon idea can be directly contained in the text. Furthermore, the co-authors footnote this concept to Ray. However, in *A Quest for Reformation in Preaching*, Brown argues that true expository preaching demands direct biblical authority.

The only problem is that Brown continues to validate a spectrum for the level of biblical authority a sermon may possess. In addition to direct biblical authority, Brown identifies indirect biblical authority, the casual biblical sermon, the combination biblical sermon, and the corrupted biblical sermon.[385] Brown claims that, most likely, more casual biblical sermons "have been preached during the twentieth century than all other types combined."[386] In the spirit of the age, Brown labels only the corrupted biblical sermon as "a perversion of Biblical truth."[387]

If Ray could have known that chapter seven of his *Expository Preaching*, which legitimizes a variety of ways a preacher may get his theme from the text, would be influential in subsequent authors legitimizing sermons with less than direct biblical authority, perhaps he would have revised it. The reality, however, is that this chapter might articulate the acceptable homiletical practice of most Southern Baptist preachers at the time. Unfortunately, the development of descriptions distinguishing levels of biblical authority in a sermon did not continue as observations only. The descriptions, instead, became approved homiletical options for preachers.

Southwestern Homiletics: The Al Fasol Era

As a Southwestern Seminary student, Fasol sat under the homiletical instruction of Jesse Northcutt, Gordon Clinard, and Clyde Fant. He studied homiletics "most directly," however, from H.C. Brown Jr., who

---

[384]Ibid., 36.
[385]Ibid., 87-133.
[386]Ibid., 105.
[387]Ibid., 87.

supervised his Ph.D. studies.[388] Fasol taught his first homiletics course at Southwestern in the summer of 1971, which initiated a tenure that lasted until 2005. During these years, *Steps to the Sermon* served as his primary textbook of choice. In 1989, however, Fasol authored *Essentials for Biblical Preaching: An Introduction to Basic Sermon Preparation*, which contains a chapter dedicated to "checking for biblical authority."[389] Here, he argues, "A sermon may reflect one of three different kinds of biblical authority: direct, secondary, or casual. Or it may call on a combination of these approaches."[390]

In fairness to Fasol, the homiletical variety Ray's version of exposition had previously allowed proved problematic. Perhaps Ray's variety prevented Brown, Clinard, and Northcutt from ever agreeing on a definition of expository preaching.[391] Such lack of clarity concerning a definition of exposition is perhaps why Fasol, after compiling six different definitions of expository preaching, finally just decided to use the term "biblical preaching" for his homiletical approach.[392] Regardless, it appears that the emphasis on expository preaching rooted in biblical

---

[388] Al Fasol, Interview with Author, Fort Worth, January 23, 2014.

[389] Al Fasol, *Essentials for Biblical Preaching: An Introduction to Basic Sermon Preparation* (Grand Rapids: Baker, 1989), 89.

[390] Ibid., 90. Fasol footnotes Brown's *A Quest for Reformation in Preaching* and writes, "Many of these concepts were developed by Brown in conjunction with several homiletic students, of which I was one. Brown acknowledged our assistance in his preface" (165). Other homiletics professors at Southwestern during Fasol's tenure appear more concerned that a sermon display direct biblical authority only. Joel Gregory, who studied at Southwestern under Jesse Northcutt and taught at Southwestern from 1982-1985, argues that when a preacher applies proper hermeneutics to the text, "he may stand with confidence that every movement in the sermon finds direct biblical authority" (in "Interpretation in Preaching," 15). Scott L. Tatum, who taught homiletics at Southwestern from 1976-1988, argues that a preacher should "never use as a major point an idea which is not clearly taught in the scripture. There should be positive biblical authority for everything contained in the sermon. For that reason, major points need to come from the mind of the preacher as he has discovered them for himself in scripture," in "Preaching from 1 Peter," *Southwestern Journal of Theology* 25, no. 1 (Fall 1982): 54.

[391] Al Fasol, Interview with Author, Fort Worth, January 23, 2014. Fasol recalled that Brown, Clinard, and Northcutt could all agree that they advocated "biblical preaching," although exactly what that meant remained ambiguous.

[392] Ibid.

authority that Ray championed began to wane over the course of the following generations.

Fasol does claim in his book that "the Bible is authoritative for preaching," and that one of the book's aims "is to lead preachers to base their sermons on a biblical text and not to use the text only as a springboard to launch into diatribes of personal opinion without authentic exposition of divine revelation."[393] Yet, one cannot help but wonder if Fasol expressed a slightly different view of Scripture than Northcutt and Ray. The following statements by Fasol produce the possible discrepancy:

> The Bible is the record of God's revelation of himself to humanity. ... Since these stories are based in fact, the Bible has a message for life today. ... The Bible can serve as a source for sermon ideas in several ways, the most common of which is to let the biblical text directly suggest an idea. ... On rare occasions a sermon will not have a particular biblical text. Although such a sermon should allude to biblical principles or even use specific verses for explanatory purposes, a biblical text *per se* is not an absolute requirement.[394]

Here, Fasol's convictions concerning Scripture appear incongruent with Ray's. What appears to be a minor theological difference eventually bears massive homiletical implications that Ray would have not supported.

Southwestern Homiletics: The David Allen Era

The effects of Ray championing expository preaching for 37 years at Southwestern seemed to be lost. However, David Allen arrived as a new professor of preaching at Southwestern in 2004. Previously, Allen had attended Southwestern as a student from 1978 to 1981, during which

---

[393] Fasol, *Essentials for Biblical Preaching*, 10.
[394] Ibid., 27-38.

time he studied preaching with Al Fasol and Farrar Patterson.[395] When Allen came as a professor, he articulated a term that expressed his philosophy of preaching that was unique from what was being taught.

Allen called it "text-driven preaching." Allen does not claim to have coined the term, but he began using it in the late 1980s and early 1990s as a professor of preaching at Criswell College.[396] Between 1975 and 1978, Allen completed his undergraduate degree at Criswell and studied homiletics under Paige Patterson. The textbooks for his homiletics course with Patterson included Broadus' famous volume and a lesser-known text, *Expository Preaching without Notes* by Charles W. Koller. Allen claims that his academic training in expository preaching began at Criswell and proved more thorough than the training he received later at Southwestern. Interestingly enough, years earlier, Ray had instructed Paige Patterson's father, T.A. Patterson, and Charles Koller in expository preaching when they were students at Southwestern Seminary.[397] Ray certainly did not exercise direct influence on Allen. However, in order to understand Ray's role in the establishment of the foundation upon which Southwestern Seminary teaches text-driven preaching today, it is necessary to articulate the roots of Allen's homiletical convictions.

In 1968, Allen was a young boy who attended West Rome Baptist Church of Rome, Georgia. During the summer of the same year, West Rome Baptist Church called Jerry Vines to be their next pastor.[398] Years earlier, however, Vines had made a change in his preaching. The change occurred after Vines attended a Bible conference at Tennessee Temple University, where he heard Warren Wiersbe preach for the very first time.[399] Vines recounts the experience:

> My life and ministry were changed when I decided to devote myself to expository preaching. The first ten years of

---

[395]David Allen, Interview with Author, Fort Worth, September 19, 2014.
[396]Ibid.
[397]See McBeth, *Texas Baptist*, 286. See also Charles W. Koller to Jeff D. Ray, 20 October 1941, Ray Collection.
[398]Jerry Vines, *My Life and Ministry* (Nashville: B&H Publishing, 2014), 84.
[399]Ibid., 79.

ministry, my sermons were generally topical in nature. ... Then I actually stumbled upon the method of expository preaching. At a Bible conference I had the opportunity to hear Dr. Warren Wiersbe teach the Word. Although I was a seminary graduate and had been preaching for several years, I had never heard anyone take the Bible and expound it as did Dr. Wiersbe. ... My approach to preaching completely changed. I determined to begin using the expository method. All I had to go by was Dr. Wiersbe's example. I had never studied the expository method, I was aware of no books on the subject, and I had heard very little preaching of that kind. I just had the conviction in my heart that that was the kind of preaching the Lord wanted me to do. So I started.[400]

Vines joined an extreme minority among Southern Baptists when he adopted the expository method. Allen did not realize at the time how rare exposition had become and how blessed he was to hear it as a young boy. Vines agrees with Merrill Unger's assessment in 1955 that "to an alarming extent the glory is departing from the pulpit of the twentieth century."[401] According to Vines, "probably even in the 1980s there [was] still a famine of good, solid Bible preaching throughout the land."[402] However, in 1985, Vines published *A Practical Guide to Sermon Preparation* and apparently became only the third Southern Baptist to compose a volume that advocated exclusively for expository preaching.[403] The publication of his book was one sign among others that indicated that expository preaching was on the rise. Vines writes:

---

[400] Vines, *A Practical Guide to Sermon Preparation*, xi-xii.
[401] See Merrill F. Unger, *Principles of Expository Preaching* (Grand Rapids: Zondervan, 1955), 11.
[402] Vines, *A Practical Guide to Sermon Preparation*, 2.
[403] As mentioned previously, Douglas M. White appears to be the second Southern Baptist in this list between Ray and Vines.

> But we are experiencing at present a resurgence of interest in and practice of good preaching. That is certainly true in my own Southern Baptist denomination. When I first began preaching in the 1950s, expository preaching was rare. Today many pastors are seriously pursuing the expository method. That may be one of the reasons our churches are experiencing solid, substantial growth. The time is right for a renewed emphasis on the expository method.[404]

Concerning the book, Vines admits it may have never been written if Paige Patterson had not "urged me to begin and drove me to completion."[405] Patterson, one of the chief architects of the Conservative Resurgence within the Southern Baptist Convention, had a sense of how great the need was for a Southern Baptist to author a text that taught a homiletical philosophy consistent with biblical inerrancy.[406] Once available, Allen began to utilize Vines' text along with its companion volume, *A Guide to Effective Sermon Delivery*, in his preaching courses at Criswell.

Allen may not have sensed the presence of Ray's influence in his classroom in the late 1980s. However, the remnant of Ray's call for expository preaching could be heard in the early pages of his textbook of

---

[404] Ibid. Old concurs with Vines' assessment in *Our Own Time*, vol. 7 of *The Reading and Preaching of the Scriptures in the Worship of the Christian Church*, xvii. He writes, "It seems to be that a new age of preaching began in the closing decades of the twentieth century. ... By the late eighties it had become a popular refrain, 'Where have all the preachers gone?' By the nineties, however, there began to be rumors that some very strong young preachers could be heard. ... It was preaching with a somewhat different ring ... but most of all it had a strong expository structure. Preaching through the Bible was regaining in popularity."
[405] Vines, *A Practical Guide to Sermon Preparation*, vii.
[406] Allen argues that, in general, the average Southern Baptist pastor was not taught how to do expository preaching during the gap years between Jeff Ray and the Conservative Resurgence (David Allen, Interview with Author, Fort Worth, September 19, 2014). Paige Patterson notes one of the reasons for the success of the conservatives "was the decision to focus primarily on one issue: the reliability of the Bible," in *Anatomy of a Reformation: The Southern Baptist Convention 1978-2004* (Fort Worth: Seminary Hill Press, 2004), 7.

choice. In the opening chapter of *A Practical Guide to Sermon Preparation*, Vines cites the definitions of expository preaching provided by several notable expositors, none of whom are Southern Baptists. Just before he provides his own definition, however, Vines writes, "Jeff Ray summarizes the expository method well when he says: 'In preaching, exposition is the detailed interpretation, logical amplification, and practical application of Scripture.'"[407]

By 1985, the year Vines published *A Practical Guide to Sermon Preparation*, the Conservative Resurgence among Southern Baptists was well underway.[408] In fact, James C. Hefley labels 1980-1988 "eight years of resurgence," as conservatives proclaimed their "belief that every word of the Bible is true."[409] Looking back at the results of the resurgence, Patterson writes:

> What are the results? At the end of 25 years of conservative advance, new executives committed to the resurgence and to the inerrancy of Scripture have been installed in all the agencies and institutions. Every board of trustees is decidedly conservative. Giving has reached all-time highs in recent years. The six seminaries have ballooned from 10,000 to 15,000 students. ... Dozens of new evangelically-minded professors have taken their places on seminary faculties.[410]

---

[407]Vines, *A Practical Guide to Sermon Preparation*, 7, citing Ray, *Expository Preaching*, 71.

[408]The Conservative Resurgence refers to a conservative movement for theological renewal among Southern Baptists. It was led primarily by Paige Patterson, who then served as the president of The Criswell College, and Judge Paul Pressler of Houston. The movement officially began in the fall of 1978 when a group of conservative Southern Baptists met in Atlanta, Georgia. The movement first found success in 1979 with the election of Adrian Rogers as president of the Southern Baptist Convention. See Patterson, *Anatomy of a Reformation*, 3-6.

[409]James C. Hefley, *The Conservative Resurgence in the Southern Baptist Convention* (Hannibal, MO: Hannibal Books, 1991), 45.

[410]Patterson, *Anatomy of a Reformation*, 13.

Furthermore, in 2000, the 1963 edition of *The Baptist Faith and Message*, with its neo-orthodox language in reference to Scripture, was revised. In 1963, the confession read, "The Holy Bible was written by men divinely inspired and is the record of God's revelation of Himself to man."[411] The revisions in 2000 read as follows: "The Holy Bible was written by men divinely inspired and is God's revelation of Himself to man. ... Therefore, all Scripture is totally true and trustworthy. ... All Scripture is a testimony to Christ, who is Himself the focus of divine revelation."[412] The changes to *The Baptist Faith and Message* contributed to bringing closure to the Conservative Resurgence and establishing six seminaries that would employ professors committed to inerrancy.

Therefore, when Patterson hired Allen in 2004 to teach preaching at Southwestern Seminary, the theological foundations for "text-driven preaching" had been established. Although Allen did not share any direct connections with Ray, he found himself positioned at Southwestern Seminary to champion the philosophy of preaching demanded by the nature of Scripture. Ray had sought to blaze this trail almost 100 years earlier. He had lacked, however, the widespread support supplied by a denomination explicitly postured toward biblical inerrancy.

The trajectory of homiletical instruction following Ray at Southwestern may not have progressively climbed toward text-driven preaching. However, Allen's advocacy for text-driven preaching placed him in the footsteps of Ray, who sought to allow biblical authority to drive his homiletical approach. In this way, Ray made his most lasting contribution to the legacy of expository preaching by establishing biblical authority as a homiletical foundation upon which Southwestern Seminary now stands as an advocate for text-driven preaching today.[413]

In short, Allen followed a homiletical trail that Ray had begun to blaze by taking biblical authority seriously. Ray stood in the minority

---

[411] Ibid., 16.
[412] Ibid.
[413] When asked, "How would you describe Southwestern's legacy of training preachers and its contribution to Southern Baptist preaching?" Joel Gregory answered, "The influence of direct biblical authority through the method of expository preaching was primarily seated at Southwestern" (Joel Gregory, Interview with Author, Waco, February 5, 2014).

of his denomination as he called for preachers to practice exposition. In recent years, men like David Allen, Steven Smith, Calvin Pearson, Matthew McKellar, Vern Charette, Denny Autrey, Deron Biles, Barry McCarty, and others at Southwestern Seminary have stood in a denomination committed to the authority of Scripture and called for the practice of text-driven preaching.[414]

Ray is responsible in large part for Southwestern being a place where preaching has always been primary.[415] Specifically, Ray planted a homiletical seed among Southern Baptists at Southwestern Seminary for expository preaching. The conditions for growth, however, were not ideal and continued not to be so until the late 1980s. Multiple forces converged to produce the fertile ground needed for expository preaching to grow. None proved more crucial than the Conservative Resurgence, Criswell and Vines adopting expository preaching, and Allen forming his convictions and perhaps coining the term "text-driven" preaching. Ultimately, the recent homiletical shift toward expository preaching among Southern Baptists became possible due to a prior theological shift supplied by the Conservative Resurgence. Ray chose to become a Baptist because he read his Bible. Ray advocated for expository preaching because he believed the Bible. Southern Baptists have shifted closer

---

[414] See David Allen et al., *A Pastor's Guide to Text-Driven Preaching* (Fort Worth: Seminary Hill Press, 2016); Smith, *Dying to Preach*; and Akin, Allen, and Matthews, eds., *Text-Driven Preaching*.

[415] H.C. Brown Jr., ed., writes, "Southwestern has been a seminary where preaching is primary, even as it is primary in God's Book," in *Southwestern Sermons* (Nashville: Broadman Press, 1960), vi. Brown claims that between 1914 and 1929, "The central place of preaching began to yield to a new emphasis on pastoral duties," and that "this trend towards increased organizational activities eventually weakened the influence of the Southern Baptist pulpit and robbed the preachers of an opportunity to be powerful biblical interpreters," in "A History of Representative Southern Baptist Preaching from the First World War to the Depression," 212. Ray emphatically resisted this trend. He argued, "The right sort of church is not built by managerial skill—by diplomacy and engineering and wire-pulling and gum-shoeing and pussy-footing. The right sort of church is built by an open, frank, outright, thorough, impartial feeding of the people out of the Holy Scriptures—rightly dividing the Word of God. ... If a preacher once gets his people in the habit of yielding to a 'thus saith the Lord' he will find church management greatly simplified," in *The Highest Office*, 54-55.

toward expository preaching than ever before because they have returned to the Bible as God's inerrant Word.

Establishing Jeff Ray's Impact upon Expository Preaching

Depth instead of breadth summarizes Ray's entire approach to homiletical instruction and seminary training. The heart of seminary education for Ray was more than the impartation of information. The primary business was rather the formation of character. He agreed with Dr. Grenfell, a medical missionary, who said the work was "not filling a bucket with information, but lighting a lamp that will go out and shine through all the world."[416] Ray responded, "Let the theological teachers be men who can fill the bucket, but above everything else let them be men who can light the lamp."[417] Ray filled the bucket and lit the lamp of thousands of preachers. Elliott estimates that Ray taught approximately 5,000 students at Southwestern Seminary, and "the results of his instruction can be seen in hundreds of cultivated pulpits across the land."[418]

Ray's impact on preaching and preachers was intensely personal. Across the campus of Southwestern, students affectionately referred to him as "Uncle Jeff" and revered him as a spiritual father and "the sage of Seminary Hill."[419] One of these spiritual sons of Ray, Jesse Northcutt, wrote the following concerning Ray and his influence:

---

[416] Jeff Ray, "The Big Business of Making Preachers," *The Southwestern Evangel* 11 (March 1927): 229.
[417] Ibid.
[418] Evidence that Ray wielded influence on preachers and the teaching of preachers beyond Texas is revealed by a letter written from J.L.H. Hawkins, asking what textbooks Ray used in his homiletics classes at Southwestern. Hawkins was taking over the chair of evangelism and homiletics at Golden Gate Baptist Theological Seminary at the time. See J.L.H. Hawkins to Jeff D. Ray, 30 April 1944, Ray Collection.
[419] Ray, "Give Attention to the Public Reading of the Scripture," audiocassette.

Jeff Ray's Influence on Expository Preaching

> Hundreds, no doubt, even thousands of students, have been inspired by his faithful and forceful teaching. His compassionate heart, his ready wit, his incisive use of the English language, his forceful preaching presented to students a living example of what a preacher and pastor should be for his people. ... For such a man who has accomplished so much good for young preachers through the years, we should pause to give heartfelt thanks to Almighty God.[420]

Additionally, R.T. Daniel, another of Ray's former students, wrote him as follows:

> You said one day in the Evangelism class that you had dreamed of preaching to great crowds and influencing the lives of many people; of being a great orator, swaying the emotions of masses of people. Dear Uncle Jeff, more than any other man I know you are doing just that. Your boys, whom you have trained, are preaching around the world today. Who else is doing so much as that? Only God can measure the influence of a single life, but may I testify to you that you have helped me to know God better, and to properly evaluate the privilege of holding one of "The Highest Offices" in the world.[421]

When addressing his homiletics class on his 32nd anniversary of teaching at Southwestern Seminary, Ray stated:

> There are many positions with more of the éclat that would appeal to my human ambition and there are many places of wider influence and usefulness for the man who is able to fill them. But from the beginning I have had a

---

[420] Jesse Northcutt to Jeff D. Ray, 26 October 1944, Ray Collection.
[421] R.T. Daniel to Jeff D. Ray, 6 July 1936, Ray Collection.

> never-varying conviction that for a man of my turn of mind and limited ability there is not a position in the gift of our people where a more genuine, a more permanent, or more far-reaching service could be rendered. I have, therefore, always been, and am now, satisfied with and happy in the task which in the over-ruling providence of God my brethren have assigned me.[422]

Ray concluded the address by telling his students that he was "overcome with a keen desire to contribute some small part to your effectiveness as preachers of the gospel."[423]

No statement could more clearly articulate exactly what Ray accomplished as a teacher of preachers for 37 years at Southwestern Seminary. Ray took the first 5,000-plus men who ever studied at Southwestern Seminary and grounded them in the truth that the Bible is authoritative and sufficient for every sermon they would ever preach. Furthermore, Ray provided his students with practical methods to perform expository preaching, and, in this way, he contributed to the legacy of expository preaching among Southern Baptists by laying the foundation for text-driven preaching at Southwestern Seminary.

In his two-volume set on the history of biblical preaching, David Larsen writes of Ray:

> Following Carroll and shaping Southern Baptist preaching in Texas and west-ward was Jefferson Davis Ray (1860-1951), who served as professor of preaching at Southwestern from 1907 to 1944. He was known especially for his powerful reading of the Scripture, and he epitomizes the preaching Carroll modeled for his students. In arguing for expository preaching, Ray pleaded for preachers to probe the text for "the juicy inner substratum meaning of the Word of God." He was clearly an advocate

---

[422] Jeff D. Ray, "Address to Homiletics Class on Ray's 32nd Year of Teaching," Ray Collection, Box 7, Folder 594.
[423] Ibid.

Jeff Ray's Influence on Expository Preaching

of what he called the classical expository sermon, with unity and orderly structure. ... He helped fulfill the vision of B.H. Carroll in the founding of Southwestern.[424]

Ray's contributions to the legacy of expository preaching at Southwestern Seminary loom even larger when surveying the individual men he influenced.[425] A full discussion of these men would be impossible. Yet, a short summary of their responses to Ray's homiletical instruction and influence in their lives is appropriate.

J. Carl Wright, pastor of First Baptist Church Newcastle, Texas, wrote the following to Mrs. Ray after hearing of Ray's death:

> Dr. Ray made a great contribution to my personal life. While in his class of Homiletics I learned many things about the Bible, and sermon building. I bless God that it was my privilege to sit at his feet. I think Dr. Ray was the greatest professor of Homiletics in the south-land. His was a long and useful life. Few men have made as great a contribution to the world as did he. ... Today there are perhaps thousands of pastors of those country site churches who will bless God for the timely counsel and instruction of such a noble soul.[426]

Identifying himself with the "class of '38," Max Stanfield, pastor of Immanuel Baptist Church of Oklahoma City, Oklahoma, wrote Ray upon hearing of his retirement:

> The announcement of your plans to retire caused me to want to express my deepest appreciation to you for your

---

[424] Larsen, *The Company of the Preachers*, 556-57.
[425] In regard to Ray's personal influence on Southwestern, it is worth mentioning that Southwestern's eighth president, Paige Patterson, was born to two Southwestern students whom Ray affectionately nicknamed "Pat" and "Pet." See McBeth, *Texas Baptist*, 286.
[426] J. Carl Wright to Georgia Ray, 28 June 1951, Ray Collection.

contribution to my personal ministry as well as to that of thousands of preachers all over the world. Seldom do I prepare a sermon or review my delivery of a sermon without thinking of the man who taught me homiletics.[427]

Over the course of his life, Ray received hundreds of letters from his former students who expressed their gratitude for Ray's influence in their life and ministry. The following statements serve as further samples of what these students expressed to Ray. J.D. Grey, writing to Miss Georgia, claimed that Ray "was truly one of the greatest men we young preachers ever knew. His influence is being felt now in the lives of all of us who were his students in the years gone by."[428] B.J. Martin, pastor of First Baptist Church, Ballinger, Texas, wrote, "May you rest assured that we are thankful for you and your wife and the impact you had upon the lives of Texas Baptist preachers."[429] E.W. Cofer, pastor of First Baptist Church of Sugarland, Texas, penned the following to Ray: "You inspired me a lot to try to be a true preacher of the Gospel. No one can take your place in the Seminary and in the hearts of the Baptists of Texas or the world so far as that goes."[430]

In the eyes of many of his students, Ray "was the seminary."[431] Stewart Newman, a younger colleague of Ray's at Southwestern, perhaps describes Ray's role best with the following words of appreciation:

> May I take this means of recognizing the deep debt that I owe to you. As a younger member of the firm, I am mindful of the inheritance which has come to me from you as one of the foundation stones on which this Seminary was built. I am grateful for the fact that your life investment is not confined to the past, but with such remarkable spirit you are living in the present to make

---

[427] Max Stanfield to Jeff D. Ray, 10 May 1944, Ray Collection.
[428] J.D. Grey to Georgia Ray, 14 July 1951, Ray Collection.
[429] B.J. Martin to Jeff D. Ray, 29 July 1948, Ray Collection.
[430] E.W. Cofer to Jeff D. Ray, 22 May 1944, Ray Collection.
[431] D.D. Seger to Jeff D. Ray, 4 July 1951, Ray Collection.

Jeff Ray's Influence on Expository Preaching

your contribution the more valuable. I trust we younger men shall somehow be able to live up to the expectations which are made and at the same time prove to be not altogether untrue to the legacy which is ours.[432]

Newman could not have more accurately described Ray and his role when he labeled him a "foundation stone" of the seminary. The foundation stones of any edifice rarely receive the attention given to the outer and more visible architectural components. Yet, they play the greatest role in supplying support and strength for the entire structure.

In the same way, Ray poured his life into building the foundation of Southwestern Seminary by investing himself in the lives of thousands of young preachers. These young preachers dispersed from Fort Worth to locations all over the world and influenced hundreds of thousands through their preaching and ministry. The majority of those influenced by these preachers never knew Jeff Ray. However, as Wm. D. Wyatt claimed after Ray's death, "The old soldier has not faded away—he will continue to shine with true glory in the lives of those whom he taught and to whom he ministered. I am sure that he has a great reward in the glory land."[433]

A former student of Ray's and pastor of Memorial Baptist Church of Temple, Texas, Guy Moore, was right when he wrote Ray the following words:

> There is no way of knowing how much good you have rendered to ministers in your work there as teacher, but I for one want to thank you for the many things you gave us during my brief stay in the class.[434]

---

[432] Stewart A. Newman to Jeff D. Ray, 2 January 1941, Ray Collection.
[433] Wm. D. Wyatt to Georgia Ray, 5 July 1951, Ray Collection. E.D. Head, Southwestern's third president, also wrote Ray and acknowledged his influence that emanated through the young preachers he instructed. Head wrote, "May blessing continue to go to countless others ... through your own life and through the life of these thousands whom you have influenced ... more and more, and through yet many years" (E.D. Head to Jeff D. Ray, 20 November 1939, Ray Collection).
[434] Guy Newman to Jeff D. Ray, 29 May 1942, Ray Collection.

Ray humbly accepted the fact that God had chained him to a desk grading the sermons of immature preachers at a young and struggling school. Yet, according to George Truett, from that desk, Ray became "a far larger blessing to" his "fellow preachers than" he would "have ever dreamed."[435] According to L.R. Scarborough, Southwestern's second president, Ray put his life for many years into Southwestern Seminary and "helped thousands to preach better and live better."[436] Ray never lost his desire to pastor and occupy a prominent pulpit from which he could preach God's Word. He knew, however, that "after all is said, faithful service is the highest mark of success," and that though "we do not always see it that way ... God does."[437]

Conclusion

Homiletically speaking, Southern Baptists have not been an expository people. Rather, the majority of Southern Baptist preaching has been textual-topical in nature and rhetorically driven in structure. The homiletical methodologies producing such preaching trace back to Jean Claude and the 16th century, and Ray was not exempt from their influence. Ray advocated for expository preaching by instructing students in these methods that both helped and hindered true biblical exposition. However, Ray distinguished himself among Southern Baptist preachers by allowing the authority of Scripture to dictate his philosophy of preaching. Despite his methodological inconsistencies, Ray established the philosophical foundation required for text-driven preaching to be taught at Southwestern today. Through his role at Southwestern Seminary, Ray was largely responsible for preserving and nurturing an endangered philosophy of preaching among Southern Baptists during his generation.

Ray preserved and nurtured expository preaching at Southwestern Seminary by ingraining into 5,000-plus men both why they should embrace exposition theologically and how they should perform exposition

---

[435]George W. Truett to Jeff D. Ray, 8 February 1938, Ray Collection.
[436]L.R. Scarborough to Jeff D. Ray, 23 November 1937, Ray Collection.
[437]Jeff D. Ray to J. Wesley Smith, 4 June 1945, Ray Collection.

Jeff Ray's Influence on Expository Preaching

practically. These men embodied the trajectory of Southwestern's preaching legacy and became the foundation upon which students at Southwestern learn text-driven preaching today. Young preachers at Southwestern today deserve to know in whose footsteps they walk, upon whose shoulders they stand, and whose homiletical blood courses through their veins.

The difference between the expository preaching taught by Ray and the text-driven preaching taught at Southwestern today is not theological but methodological in nature. Text-driven preaching simply supplies a more robust methodology for the preacher to honor the authority of Scripture by allowing the text to drive more fully the sermon's substance, spirit, and structure. The trajectory of Southwestern's homiletical instruction has not always been completely consistent with the direction Ray established. Yet, by returning exclusively to the philosophy of expository preaching and the advocacy of text-driven preaching as a methodology, Southwestern now stands upon the homiletical foundation that Ray laid.

When W.W. Barnes delivered the address at Ray's funeral on June 20, 1951, he did not comment on Ray's broad reputation. Rather, he paid tribute "to a remarkable life … for its length of years, to be sure, but remarkable more for its depth of living."[438] In the same way, Ray's mark on expository preaching may not have been wide, but it was deep. Deep in the sense that he invested in the lives of men. One of Ray's former students wrote Ray the following:

> Here is the thing I have discovered about you, it is your utter self-forgetfulness and throwing of caution to the four winds in your desire to build for the future, strong men, who shall lift high the torch and carry it on across the years in the courage which you have done.[439]

---

[438] W.W. Barnes, "Address Delivered by Dr. W.W. Barnes at Broadway Baptist Church in Connection with the Funeral Services of Jeff D. Ray," Ray Collection, Box 7, Folder 593.
[439] Leon McHill to Jeff D. Ray, undated, Ray Collection.

Northcutt responded to Ray's contributions by arguing, "For such a man who has accomplished so much good for young preachers through the years, we should pause to give heartfelt thanks to Almighty God."[440] Ray's legacy prompted another student to write to Ray and say, "The good you've done and the inspiration you've given could never be measured."[441] Ray is, perhaps, a forgotten man in the matter of preaching. His mark on expository preaching at Southwestern Seminary, however, lives on.

---

[440]Jessie Northcutt to Jeff D. Ray, 26 October 1944, Ray Collection.
[441]Gabriella Day to Jeff D. Ray, 9 May 1944, Ray Collection.

BIBLIOGRAPHY

Books

Adam, Peter. *Speaking God's Words: A Practical Theology of Preaching.* Vancouver: Regent College Publishing, 1996.

Akin, Daniel L., David L. Allen, and Ned L. Mathews, eds. *Text-Driven Preaching: God's Word at the Heart of Every Sermon.* Nashville: B&H Academic, 2010.

Alexander, James W. *Thoughts on Preaching.* New York: Charles Scribner, 1864.

Allen, David L. *Preaching Tools: An Annotated Survey of Commentaries and Preaching Resources for Every Book of the Bible.* Fort Worth: Seminary Hill Press, 2016.

Allen, David, Steven Smith, Matthew McKellar, and Paige Patterson. *A Pastor's Guide to Text-Driven Preaching.* Fort Worth: Seminary Hill Press, 2016.

Allen, R. Earl and Joel Gregory. *Southern Baptist Preaching Today.* Nashville: Broadman Press, 1987.

_____. *Southern Baptist Preaching Yesterday.* Nashville: Broadman Press, 1991.

Aristotle. *Rhetoric and the Poetics*. Translated by W. Rhys Roberts and Ingram Bywater. New York: Random House, 1984.

Armitage, Thomas. *Preaching: It's Ideal and Inner Life*. Philadelphia: American Baptist Publication Society, 1880.

Arthurs, Jeffrey D. *Devote Yourself to the Public Reading of Scripture: The Transforming Power of the Well-Spoken Word*. Grand Rapids: Kregel, 2012.

_____. *Preaching with Variety: How to Re-create the Dynamics of Biblical Genres*. Grand Rapids: Kregel, 2007.

Augustine. *Teaching Christianity*. Translated by Edmund Hill. Hyde Park, NY: New City Press, 1996.

Baker, Robert A. *Tell the Generations Following: A History of Southwestern Baptist Theological Seminary, 1908-1983*. Nashville: Broadman Press, 1983.

_____. *The Blossoming Desert: A Concise History of Texas Baptists*. Waco: Word Books, 1970.

_____. *The Southern Baptist Convention and Its People, 1607-1972*. Nashville: Broadman Press, 1974.

Bainton, George. *The Art of Authorship*. New York: D. Appleton and Company, 1890.

Barnes, William Wright. *The Southern Baptist Convention, 1845-1953*. Nashville: Broadman Press, 1954.

Basden, Paul A., ed. *Has Our Theology Changed? Southern Baptist Thought Since 1845*. Nashville: Broadman and Holman, 1994.

Beecher, Henry Ward. *Yale Lectures on Preaching.* London: James Clark & Co., 1874.

Beekman, J., J. Callow, and M. Kopesec, *The Semantic Structure of Written Communication.* Dallas, TX: Summer Institute of Linguistics, 1981.

Begg, Alistair. *Preaching for God's Glory.* Wheaton: Crossway, 2010.

Blackwood, Andrew W. *The Preparation of Sermons.* New York: Abingdon-Cokesbury Press, 1948.

Brastow, Lewis O. *The Work of the Preacher: A Study of Homiletic Principles and Methods.* Boston: The Pilgrim Press, 1914.

Breed, David R. *Preparing to Preach.* New York: Hodder & Stoughton, 1911.

Broadus, John Albert. *A Treatise on the Preparation and Delivery of Sermons*, 18th Edition. New York: A.C. Armstrong & Son, 1892.

_____. *On the Preparation and Delivery of Sermons.* Edited by J.B. Weatherspoon. New York: Harper & Row, 1944.

_____. *Paramount and Permanent Authority of the Bible.* Philadelphia: American Baptist Publication Society, 1887.

_____. *The History of Preaching.* New York: A.C. Armstrong and Son, 1907.

Brooks, Phillips. *On Preaching.* New York: The Seabury Press, 1964.

Brown, H.C., Jr. *A Quest for Reformation in Preaching.* Waco: Word Books, 1968.

Brown, H.C., Jr., ed. *More Southern Baptist Preaching.* Nashville: Broadman Press, 1964.

_____. *Southern Baptist Preaching.* Nashville: Broadman Press, 1959.

_____. *Southwestern Sermons.* Nashville: Broadman Press, 1960.

Brown, H.C., Jr., H. Gordon Clinard, and Jesse J. Northcutt. *Steps to the Sermon: A Plan for Sermon Preparation.* Nashville: Broadman Press, 1963.

Browne, P.D. *The Seventh and James Street Baptist Church of Waco, Texas, 1898-1948.* Waco: Baylor University Press, 1948.

Bush, Russ L. and Tom J. Nettles. *Baptists and the Bible.* Nashville: Broadman and Holman, 1999.

Buttrick, George A. *Jesus Came Preaching.* Grand Rapids: Baker, 1970.

Carroll, Benajah Harvey. *An Interpretation of the English Bible,* ed. James Britton Cranfill and J.W. Crowder. 17 vols. Nashville: Broadman, 1947-48.

_____. *Inspiration of the Bible.* New York: Fleming H. Revell, 1930.

Carroll, J.M. *A History of Texas Baptists.* Dallas: Baptist Standard Publishing Co., 1923.

_____. *Texas Baptist Statistics.* Houston: J.J. Pastoriza Printing and Litho. Co., 1895.

Carson, D.A. *Exegetical Fallacies,* 2nd Edition. Grand Rapids: Baker Academic, 1996.

Bibliography

―――――. *New Testament Commentary Survey*, 6th ed. Grand Rapids: Baker Academic, 2007.

Carter, James E. *Cowboys, Cowtown, & Crosses: A Centennial History of the Tarrant Baptist Association*. Fort Worth: Tarrant Baptist Association, 1986.

Carver, William O. *Out of His Treasure: Unfinished Memoirs*. Nashville: Broadman Press, 1956.

Chapel, Bryan. *Christ-Centered Preaching: Redeeming the Expository Sermon*. Grand Rapids: Baker Academic, 2005.

Cox, James W., ed. *Biblical Preaching: An Expositor's Treasury*. Philadelphia: The Westminster Press, 1983.

Dargan, Edwin Charles. *A History of Preaching,* vol. I. Grand Rapids: Baker, 1954.

―――――. *A History of Preaching,* vol. II. Grand Rapids: Baker, 1954.

―――――. *The Art of Preaching in the Light of Its History*. New York: George H. Doran Company, 1922.

―――――. *The Doctrines of Our Faith*. Nashville: Sunday School Board Southern Baptist Convention, 1899.

Davies, Horton. *Worship and Theology in England, From Watts and Wesley to Martineau, 1690-1900*, vol. 4. Princeton: Princeton University Press, 1962.

Davis, H. Grady. *Design for Preaching*. Philadelphia: Fortress Press, 1958.

Dawson, Jerry F. and John W. Storey, eds. *Teaching Them: A Sesquicentennial Celebration of Texas Baptist Education*. Dallas: Baptist General Convention of Texas, 1996.

Doriani, Daniel M. *Putting the Truth to Work: The Theory and Practice of Biblical Application*. Phillipsburg, NJ: P&R Publishing, 2001.

Edwards, O.C., Jr. *A History of Preaching*. Nashville: Abingdon Press, 2004.

Elliott, L.R. *Centennial Story of Texas Baptists*. Dallas: Baptist General Convention of Texas, 1936.

Ellison, Robert H. *The Victorian Pulpit: Spoken and Written Sermons in Nineteenth-Century Britain*. Selinsgrove: Susquehanna University Press, 1998.

Ellison, Ronald C. *Texas and Baptist Sunday Schools, 1829-1996*. Dallas: Baptist General Convention of Texas, 1997.

Fant, Clyde E. *Bonhoeffer: Worldly Preaching*. Nashville: Thomas Nelson Inc., 1975.

Fasol, Al. *A Complete Guide to Sermon Delivery*. Nashville: Broadman & Holman, 1996.

_____. *Essentials for Biblical Preaching: An Introduction to Basic Sermon Preparation*. Grand Rapids: Baker, 1989.

_____. *With a Bible in Their Hands: Baptist Preaching in the South, 1679-1979*. Nashville: Broadman and Holman, 1994.

Fee, Gordon D. and Douglas Stuart. *How to Read the Bible for All Its Worth*. 3rd Edition. Grand Rapids: Zondervan, 2003.

BIBLIOGRAPHY

Fletcher, Jesse C. *The Southern Baptist Convention: A Sesquicentennial History*. Nashville: Broadman & Holman, 1994.

Gardner, Charles S. *Psychology and Preaching*. New York: The Macmillan Company, 1918.

Garrett, James Leo, Jr. *Baptist Theology: A Four-Century Study*. Macon: Mercer University Press, 2009.

_____. *Live Stones: The Centennial History of Broadway Baptist Church, Fort Worth, Texas, 1882-1982*. Fort Worth: Broadway Baptist Church, 1984.

Garrett, James Leo, Jr., ed. *The Legacy of Southwestern: Writings that Shaped a Tradition*. North Richland Hills, Smithfield Press, 2002.

Greidanus, Sidney. *Preaching Christ from the Old Testament: A Contemporary Hermeneutical Method*. Grand Rapids: Eerdmans, 1999.

_____. *The Modern Preacher and the Ancient Text: Interpreting and Preaching Biblical Literature*. Grand Rapids: Eerdmans, 1988.

Hefley, James C. *The Conservative Resurgence in the Southern Baptist Convention*. Hannibal, MO: Hannibal, 1991.

Hiscox, Edward T. *The Standard Manual for Baptist Churches*. Philadelphia: American Baptist Publication Society, 1890.

Holifield, E. Brooks. *The Gentlemen Theologians: American Theology in Southern Culture, 1795-1860*. Durham: Duke University Press, 1978.

Hopkins, Hugh Evan. *Charles Simeon of Cambridge*. Grand Rapids: Eerdmans, 1977.

Hyperius, Andreas. *The Practice of Preaching*. Translated by John Ludham. London: Thomas East, 1975.

Jeffs, Harry. *The Art of Exposition*. London: Pilgrim Press, 1910.

Johnson, Charles D. *Higher Education of Southern Baptists: An Institutional History 1826-1954*. Waco: The Baylor University Press, 1955.

Jones, Linda K. *Theme in English Expository Discourse*. Edward Sapir Monograph Series in Language, Culture, and Cognition, no. 2. Lake Bluff: IL: Jupiter Press, 1977.

Jowett, J.H. *The Preacher: His Life and Work*. New York: Hodder & Stoughton, 1912.

Kaiser, Walter C. *Toward an Exegetical Theology: Biblical Exegesis for Preaching and Teaching*. Grand Rapids: Baker Academic, 1981.

Kennard, J. Spencer. *Psychic Power in Preaching*. Philadelphia: G.W. Jacobs, 1901.

Kennedy, George A. *Classical Rhetoric and Its Christian and Secular Tradition from Ancient to Modern Times,* 2nd ed. Chapel Hill: The University of North Carolina Press, 1999.

Knott, Harold E. *How to Prepare an Expository Sermon*. Cincinnati: The Standard Publishing Company, 1930.

Koller, Charles W. *Expository Preaching without Notes*. Grand Rapids: Baker, 1962.

Kuruvilla, Abraham. *Privilege the Text! A Theological Hermeneutic for Preaching*. Chicago: Moody, 2013.

Bibliography

Larsen, David L. *The Company of the Preachers*. 2 Vols. Grand Rapids: Kregel, 1998.

Lefever, Alan J. *Fighting the Good Fight: The Life and Work of Benajah Harvey Carroll*. Austin: Eakin Press, 1994.

Longman, Tremper, III. *Old Testament Commentary Survey*, 4th ed. Grand Rapids: Baker Academic, 2007.

MacArthur, John, Jr. *Rediscovering Expository Preaching*. Dallas: Word, 1992.

Masters, Victor I. *Making America Christian*. Atlanta: Home Mission Board of the Southern Baptist Convention, 1921.

Mathewson, Steven D. *The Art of Preaching Old Testament Narrative*. Grand Rapids: Baker Academic, 2002.

McBeth, Harry Leon. *Texas Baptist: A Sesquicentennial History*. Dallas: Baptistway Press, 1998.

_____. *The Baptist Heritage: Four Centuries of Baptist Witness*. Nashville: Broadman Press, 1987.

McCartney, Dan and Charles Clayton. *Let the Reader Understand: A Guide to Interpreting and Applying the Bible*, 2nd Edition. Phillipsburg, NJ: P&R, 2002.

McConnell, F.M. *McConnell's Manual for Baptist Churches*. Philadelphia: The Judson Press, 1926.

McDill, Wayne. *12 Essential Skills for Great Preaching*, 2nd ed. Nashville: B&H Academic, 2006.

McKibbens, Thomas R., Jr. *The Forgotten Heritage: A Lineage of Great Baptist Preaching*. Macon: Mercer University Press, 1986.

Merida, Tony. *Faithful Preaching: Declaring Scripture with Responsibility, Passion, and Authenticity*. Nashville: B&H Academic, 2009.

Meyer, F.B. *Expository Preaching Plans and Methods*. New York: Hodder and Stoughton, 1910.

Montgomery, R. Ames. *Expository Preaching*. New York: Fleming H. Revell, 1939.

Morgan, G. Campbell. *Preaching*. New York: Fleming H. Revell, 1937.

Moule, Handley C.G. *Charles Simeon*. London: The Inter-Varsity Fellowship, 1948.

Mueller, William. *A History of Southern Baptist Theological Seminary*. Nashville: Broadman, 1959.

Newman, A.H., ed. *A Century of Baptist Achievement*. Philadelphia: American Baptist Publication Society, 1901.

Old, Hughes Oliphant. *Our Own Time*. Vol. 7 of *The Reading and Preaching of the Scriptures in the Worship of the Christian Church*. Grand Rapids: Eerdmans, 2010.

_____. *The Age of the Reformation*. Vol. 4 of *The Reading and Preaching of the Scriptures in the Worship of the Christian Church*. Grand Rapids: Eerdmans, 2002.

_____. *The Modern Age*. Vol. 6 of *The Reading and Preaching of the Scriptures in the Worship of the Christian Church*. Grand Rapids: Eerdmans, 2007.

Bibliography

Osborne, Grant R. *The Hermeneutical Spiral: A Comprehensive Introduction to Biblical Interpretation*. Downers Grove: IVP, 2006.

Overdorf, Daniel. *Applying the Sermon: How to Balance Biblical Integrity and Cultural Relevance*. Grand Rapids: Kregel, 2009.

Patterson, Paige. *Anatomy of a Reformation: The Southern Baptist Convention 1978-2004*. Fort Worth: Seminary Hill Press, 2004.

Pendleton, J.M. *Baptist Church Manual*. Nashville: Broadman & Holman, 1966.

Perkins, William. *The Works of William Perkins*. Edited by Ian Breward. Appleford, England: The Sutton Courtenay Press, 1970.

Plummer, Robert. *40 Questions About Interpreting the Bible*. Grand Rapids: Kregel, 2010.

Price, J.M., ed. *Southwestern Men and Messages*. Kansas City: Central Seminary Press, 1948.

Ray, Georgia Miller. *The Jeff Ray I Knew: Pioneer Preacher in Texas*. San Antonio: The Naylor Company, 1952.

Ray, Jeff D. *B.H. Carroll*. Nashville: Baptist Sunday School Board, 1927.

_____. *Expository Preaching*. Grand Rapids: Zondervan, 1940.

_____. "Introduction." *Modern School of the Prophets*. Nashville: Broadman Press, 1939.

_____. *Meant for Men*. Nashville: Broadman Press, 1939.

_____. *The Country Preacher.* Nashville: Sunday School Board of the Southern Baptist Convention, 1925.

_____. *The Highest Office.* New York: Fleming H. Revell, 1923.

_____. *The Scarlet Sin.* Nashville: Broadman Press, 1942.

_____. *Trouble.* Philadelphia: Judson Press, 1929.

Riley, B.F. *History of the Baptists of Texas.* Dallas: B.F. Riley, 1907.

Robertson, A.T. *The Glory of the Ministry: Paul's Exultation in Preaching.* New York: Fleming H. Revell, 1911.

Robinson, Haddon W. *Biblical Preaching: The Development and Delivery of Expository Messages.* 3rd Edition. Baker Academic: Grand Rapids, 2014.

Rummage, Stephen Nelson. *Planning Your Preaching: A Step-by-Step Guide for Developing a One-Year Preaching Calendar.* Grand Rapids: Kregel, 2002.

Ryken, Leland. *How to Read the Bible as Literature ... and Get More Out of It.* Grand Rapids: Zondervan, 1984.

_____. *Words of Delight: A Literary Introduction to the Bible.* Grand Rapids: Baker, 1987.

Scarborough, L.R. *A Modern School of the Prophets.* Nashville: Broadman Press, 1939.

Simeon, Charles. *Evangelical Preaching: An Anthology of Sermons by Charles Simeon.* Edited by James M. Houston. Portland, OR: Multnomah Press, 1986.

Bibliography

―――――. *Expository Outlines on the Whole Bible*, 21 vols. Grand Rapids: Zondervan, 1956.

―――――. *Let Wisdom Judge: University Addresses and Sermon Outlines by Charles Simeon*. Edited by Arthur Pollard. London: Inter-Varsity Fellowship, 1959.

Simeon, Charles and William Carus. *Memoirs of the Life of the Rev. Charles Simeon: With a Selection from His Writings and Correspondence*. New York: Robert Carter and Brothers, 1852.

Smith, Steven W. *Dying to Preach: Embracing the Cross in the Pulpit*. Grand Rapids: Kregel, 2009.

―――――. *Recapturing the Voice of God: Shaping Sermons like Scripture*. Nashville: B&H Academic, 2015.

Smyth, Charles. *The Art of Preaching: A Practical Survey of Preaching in the Church of England 747-1939*. London: SPCK, 1953.

Spurgeon, Charles. *Lectures to My Students*. Grand Rapids: Zondervan, 1954.

Stanley, Andy and Lane Jones. *Communicating for a Change*. Sisters, OR: Multnomah, 2006.

Stenger, Werner. *Introduction to New Testament Exegesis*. Grand Rapids: Eerdmans, 1993.

Stewart, James S. *Heralds of God*. London: Hodder & Stoughton, 1946.

Streett, R. Alan. *The Effective Invitation*. Old Tappan, NJ: Fleming H. Revell, 1984.

Tidwell, Josiah B. *Concerning Preachers.* New York: Fleming H. Revell, 1936.

Torbet, Robert G. *History of the Baptists*, rev. ed. Valley Forge, PA: Judson, 1963.

Turnbull, Ralph G. *A History of Preaching,* vol. III. Grand Rapids: Baker, 1974.

Unger, Merrill F. *Principles of Expository Preaching.* Grand Rapids: Zondervan, 1955.

Vines, Jerry. *A Guide to Effective Sermon Delivery.* Chicago: Moody, 1986.

_____. *A Practical Guide to Sermon Preparation.* Chicago: Moody, 1985.

_____. *My Life and Ministry.* Nashville: B&H, 2014.

Vines, Jerry and Jim Shaddix. *Power in the Pulpit: How to Prepare and Deliver Expository Sermons,* rev. ed. Chicago: Moody, 2017.

_____. *Progress in the Pulpit: How to Grow in your Preaching.* Chicago: Moody, 2017.

Wayland, Francis. *Letters on the Ministry of the Gospel.* Boston: Gould and Lincoln, 1863.

White, Douglas M. *He Expounded: A Guide to Expository Preaching.* Chicago: Moody, 1952.

_____. *The Excellence of Exposition.* Neptune, NJ: Loizeaux Brothers, 1977.

Whitesell, Faris D. *The Art of Biblical Preaching.* Grand Rapids: Zondervan, 1950.

Wingren, Gustaf. *The Living Word.* London: SCM, 1960.

Wood, Presnall H. and Floyd W. Thatcher. *Prophets with Pens.* Dallas: Baptist Standard Publishing, 1969.

Articles

Chatfield, Donald F. "Textbooks Used by Teachers of Preaching." *Homiletic* 9, no. 2 (1984): 1-5.

Clayton, J.F. "The Centenary of Charles Simeon." *Modern Churchman* 26, no. 9 (1936): 500-04.

Craig, Kevin. "Is the 'Sermon' Concept Biblical?" *Searching Together* 15 (Spring/Summer 1968): 22-29.

Criswell, W.A. "Prince of Preachers." *Baptist Standard* (July 8, 1954): 11.

Davies, G.C.B. "Simeon in the Setting of the Evangelical Revival." In *Charles Simeon,* ed. Michael Hennel and Arthur Pollard, 12-13. London: S.P.C.K., 1959.

"Dr. Ray's Funeral to be Wednesday." *Fort-Worth Star-Telegram* 71 (June 19, 1951): 2.

Edwards, Rex D. "The Art of Expository Preaching." *Ministry Magazine,* 12 December 1994, 5-7.

Elliott, L.R. "Jeff D. Ray." In *Southwestern Men and Messages,* ed. J.M. Price, 99-101. Kansas City: Central Seminary Press, 1948.

Gregory, Joel C. "Interpretation in Preaching." *Southwestern Journal of Theology* 27, no. 2 (Spring 1985): 8-18.

Howington, Nolan. "Expository Preaching." *Review & Expositor* 56, no. 1 (1959): 56-65.

Maston, T.B. "Jeff D. Ray and Southwestern Seminary." *Southwestern Journal of Theology* 10 (Fall 1967): 71-83.

Matthews, Harlan Julius. "Preaching and Preachers." In *Centennial Story of Texas Baptists,* ed. L.R. Elliot, 73-124. Dallas: Baptist General Convention of Texas, 1936.

McKibbens, Thomas R., Jr. "The Role of Preaching in Southern Baptist History." *Baptist History and Heritage* 15 (January 1980): 30-36.

Philip, James. "Preaching in History." *Evangelical Review of Theology* 8, no. 2 (October 1984): 298-307.

Ray, Jeff D. "On Closing Theological Seminaries." *Baptist Standard* 45 (March 23, 1933): 2.

_____. "The Big Business of Making Preachers." *The Southwestern Evangel* 11 (March 1927): 229.

_____. "The Preacher and the Man in Overalls." *The Southwestern Evangel* 14 (February 1930): 161.

_____. "The Preacher and the Ordinances." *The Southwestern Journal of Theology* 4 (January 1920): 8-14.

_____. "The Preaching of John the Baptist." *Baptist Standard* 17 (March 23, 1905): 6.

_____. "The Preaching Schleiermacher." *The Southwestern Evangel* 10 (February 1926): 5-6.

_____. "The Redemption that is in Christ Jesus." In *Southwestern Men and Their Messages,* ed. J.M. Price, 102-108. Kansas City: Central Seminary Press, 1948.

_____. "The Studious Preacher." *The Southwestern Evangel* 13 (October 1928): 11.

_____. "The Tonic Value of Conscious Co-Operation with God." *The Southwestern Evangel* 9 (July 1925): 40-42.

Robinson, Haddon. "Better Big Ideas: Five Qualities of the Strongest Preaching Ideas." In *The Art and Craft of Biblical Preaching: A Comprehensive Resource for Today's Communicators,* eds. Haddon Robinson and Craig Brian Larsen, 355-57. Grand Rapids: Zondervan, 2005.

_____. "The Heresy of Application." In *The Art and Craft of Biblical Preaching: A Comprehensive Resource for Today's Communicators,* eds. Haddon Robinson and Craig Brian Larsen, 306-11. Grand Rapids: Zondervan, 2005.

Stitzinger, James F. "The History of Expository Preaching." *TMSJ* 3.1 (Spring 1992): 5-32.

Tatum, Scott L. "Preaching from 1 Peter." *Southwestern Journal of Theology* 25, no. 1 (Fall 1982): 46-57.

_____. "The Contribution of Jesse James Northcutt to Southern Baptist Preaching." *Southwestern Journal of Theology* 27 (Spring 1985): 38-48.

Shurden, Walter B. "Documents on the Ministry in Southern Baptist History." *Baptist History and Heritage* 15 (January 1980): 45-54.

Wills, Lawrence. "The Form of the Sermon in Hellenistic Judaism and Early Christianity." *HTR* 77 (1984): 296-99.

Zabriskie, Alexander C. "Charles Simeon: Anglican Evangelical." *Church History* 9, no. 2 (1940): 103-19.

Collections

Ray, Jeff D. *Jeff D. Ray Collection*. Archives, A. Webb Roberts Library, Southwestern Baptist Theological Seminary, Fort Worth, Texas.

Dissertations

Brown, Lavonn D. "A History of Representative Southern Baptist Preaching from the First World War to the Depression, 1914-1929." Th.D. diss., Southwestern Baptist Theological Seminary, 1964.

Fasol, Al. "A History of Representative Southern Baptist Preaching, 1930-1945." Th.D. diss., Southwestern Baptist Theological Seminary, 1975.

Lacey, Edmund. "A History of Representative Southern Baptist Preaching from 1895 to the First World War." Th.D. diss., Southwestern Baptist Theological Seminary, 1960.

Lake, Judson S. "An Evaluation of Haddon Robinson's Homiletical Method: An Evangelical Perspective." Th.D. diss., University of South Africa, 2003.

Patterson, T. Farrar. "A History of Representative Southern Baptist Preaching from 1845-1895." Th.D. diss., Southwestern Baptist Theological Seminary, 1966.

Robinson, Robert J. "The Homiletical Method of Benajah Harvey Carroll." Th.D. diss., Southwestern Baptist Theological Seminary, 1956.

Rose, Lucy Atkinson. "Preaching in the Round-Table Church." Ph.D. diss., Emory University, 1994.

Wheeless, Derek Dwayne. "The Life and Work of Jefferson Davis Ray." Ph.D. diss., Southwestern Baptist Theological Seminary, 2001.

Interviews

Allen, David. Interview with Author. Fort Worth, September 16, 2014.

Fasol, Al. Interview with Author. Fort Worth. January 23, 2014.

Garrett, James Leo. Interview with Author. Fort Worth. February 18, 2014.

Gregory, Joel. Interview with Author. Waco. February 5, 2014.

Lovejoy, Grant. Interview with Author. Telephone Interview. Fort Worth. April 3, 2014.

Tatum, Scott L. Interview with Author. Telephone Interview. Fort Worth. February 15, 2013.

Pamphlets

Ray, Jeff D. *The Preacher and His Books*. Fort Worth: Southwestern Baptist Theological Seminary, 1943.

Sound Recordings

Ray, Jeff D. "Give Attention to the Public Reading of the Scripture." TC1884. Southwestern Baptist Theological Seminary, 1950. Audiocassette.

_____. "Revival Sermon on Paul's Letter to Rome." TC2855. Southwestern Baptist Theological Seminary, 1949. Audiocassette.

Reference Works

Concise Encyclopedia of Preaching. Edited by William H. Willimon and Richard Lischer. Louisville: Westminster John Knox Press, 1995.

Encyclopedia of Southern Baptists. 2 Vols. Edited by Norman Cox. Nashville: Broadman Press, 1958.

Tarrant County Historic Resources Survey. Fort Worth: Historic Preservation Council for Tarrant County, 1989.

Unpublished

Ray, Jeff D. *The First Faculty of the Seminary.* Fortieth Anniversary—The Southwestern Baptist Theological Seminary. March 8, 1948.

Smith, Steven W. "Building an Expository Sermon." Classroom lecture notes, PRCHG 3313—Introduction to Expository Preaching, Spring 2009, Author's personal notes.

Southwestern Baptist Theological Seminary. Catalogue, 1908-2015.

Taylor, Alva. *History of the First Baptist Church, Corsicana, Texas.* Corsicana: First Baptist Church, 1952.

APPENDIX

An Excursus on Understanding the Structure of the Text

The Semantic Structure of Written Communication[442]

Preachers deal in words. Words are the building blocks of language. Language is the primary means of communication. Therefore, in order for preachers to handle God's words accurately and faithfully communicate what God has said in whatever language they speak, they must understand how language works.

The Nature of Language: Form and Meaning

What is language? "Language is a means of communication through a system of verbal signs" (6). A sign is a composite of form and meaning. First, a sign has form (object, sound, graphic representation, etc.), and that form is assigned a certain meaning. "The types of signs used in language are known as symbols" (6). These symbols structure into phonemes (the sounds associated with individual letters), syllables (a unit of pronunciation containing one vowel sound with or without

---

[442]This short volume by Beekman, Callow, and Kopesec is an introduction to how language works. One would do well to read it entirely. However, what follows is a summary and paraphrase of their work. It presents a primer for preachers seeking to divide rightly the Word of truth. Unless otherwise noted, all quotes are from Beekman, Callow, and Kopesec, *The Semantic Structure of Written Communication* (page numbers in parentheses).

surrounding consonants), words, and larger groupings of words to form clauses, phrases, sentences, paragraphs, and discourse units.

The Form of Language is Structured: Surface Structure

Not only are signs a composite of form and meaning, but so also is language a composite of form and meaning. Grammar (or surface structure) names the way the forms of language (phonemes, words, phrases, clauses, sentences, etc.) are arranged or structured for the sake of communication. In fact, "thought can only be shared with others by giving it perceptual shape" (8). It takes a combination of structural units to produce language, and for that language to communicate ideas (cognitive notions), it must be arranged/structured a certain way. Unstructured sounds, words, and sentences constitute a meaningless amorphous, linguistic mass incapable of communicating. Structure (grammar/surface structure), however, provides the sophistication necessary for communication to occur.

To summarize, "sounds are used to form grammatical units that, in turn, 'encode,' 'represent,' or 'realize' ideas" (32). Simply put, language is a composite of form and meaning, and the form is structured. Therefore, in order to do text-driven preaching, a preacher must determine the structure of the text, starting with its grammatical structure.

Diagramming Surface Structure

Diagramming the grammatical structure of the text is particularly critical when preparing to preach a paragraph unit of epistolary literature. Each paragraph unit consists of a set of sentences. The grammatical arrangement of these sentences and the arrangement of their internal components contributes to the meaning of the text.

Diagramming narrative and poetic literature looks a little different. For narrative literature, the preacher should arrange the individual episodes (perhaps consisting of one or more paragraphs) of the story along the timeline of the plot narrative in order to visualize how each episode relates to the ones surrounding it. This arrangement visualizes the movement and development of the story.

Poetic literature requires even more flexibility when diagramming. Traditional diagramming of sentence structure is possible and necessary. However, also pay attention to the larger structure of the strophe built by the following possible devices: repetition, parallelism, chiasm, narration, lyrical rhythm, an acrostic, etc. Individual sentence structure is meaningful but subordinate to the structural arrangement of the sentences constituting the poetic unit as a whole. (Note that examples of grammatical diagramming applied to different kinds of literature have been included in Chapter 2 under "Constructing an Exegetical Outline of the Text.")

The Meaning of Language is Multidimensional

Language is a composite of form and meaning. The form portion of language naturally possesses structure. We call this structure "grammar" or "surface structure." The other component of language is meaning. Meaning, like form, is also multidimensional. Specifically, three aspects contribute to meaning: referential meaning, situational meaning, and structural meaning. Referential meaning refers to the subject matter at hand. Situational meaning arises from the context and circumstances of the communication situation. Some circumstance(s) has called for the author to communicate. Structural meaning deals with how the author chose to package the information. "Bill hit the ball" does not mean the exact same thing as "The ball was hit by Bill." The first sentence is about Bill. The second is about the ball. The nuanced difference in meaning results from a packaging variance.

Text-driven preaching seeks to re-present the substance, structure, and spirit of the text in a sermon. Though an oversimplification in one sense, the three dimensions of meaning (referential, situational, and structural) are summarized by the terms substance (referential meaning), structure (structural meaning), and spirit (situational meaning.) Text-driven preaching demands re-presenting all three of these elements of the text because each element contributes to the meaning of the text.

The Meaning of Language is Structured: Semantic Structure

Meaning is multi-dimensional, but is it also structured? The form side of language certainly is structured. Therefore, is meaning also structured? The meaning of written discourse is either "an inaccessible, amorphous mass," or it is structured and "amenable to linguistic analysis and theory" (14). The good news is that meaning is also structured, and the phenomenal news is that this structure, called "semantic structure," is "near universal, its features, relations, and functions being essentially the same in all languages" (14). In other words, surface or grammatical structure is language-specific (English, German, French, Spanish, etc.). Semantic structure, however, is a set of packaging principles shared by all languages.

Inherent categories or packaging principles of the mind exist because "the human mind cannot handle large quantities of information unless it applies the 'packaging' principle" (14). Memory and comprehension demand that the mind break down incoming information into units. These units are created and distinguished one from another according to three basic principles: unity, coherence, and prominence. These principles operate almost ubiquitously. From a single tree leaf in nature to man-made artifacts such as art, music, sculpture, speech, and language; unity, coherence, and prominence appear and guide information creation and processing. Therefore, a unit of information of any kind, including language, is a unit because it possesses unity, coherence, and prominence.

The Units of Semantic Structure

There are three basic types of units that constitute semantic structure: the concept, the proposition, and the propositional cluster. A concept (single word or group of words) names a grouping or isolated segment of the world that "may be categorized into four universal classes" (things, events, attributes, and relations) (16). The proposition is "a combination of concepts that communicates an action, experience, process, or state using one of the illocutionary functions" (statement, command, or question) (17). A propositional cluster forms when additional propositions join to explain the first.

Appendix

Language in the form of written discourse consists of these propositional clusters. In non-narrative discourse, propositional clusters form a paragraph. Paragraphs form a section. Sections form divisions. In narrative discourse, propositional clusters form a paragraph. Paragraphs form an episode. Episodes form a scene. Scenes form a story. Therefore, the units of semantic structure combine to form a hierarchy that starts with a simple concept and builds to an entire body of written discourse.

When interpreting written language, it is critical to keep in mind that each semantic unit, from the concept to a discourse as a whole, will possess unity, coherence, and prominence. Therefore, each semantic unit can be studied from two perspectives: internally and externally. Internal examination focuses on the semantic unit itself—the analytical features of unity, internal coherence, and prominence. External examination focuses on the function of the semantic unit within the larger context—the holistic features of class, external coherence, and thematic content.

For example, a paragraph is a combination of propositional clusters united around a central concept or topic. Details that further develop the central proposition in a coherent fashion are supplied by subordinate propositions. Furthermore, a paragraph will relate to surrounding paragraphs based on the class of information referred to, the part it plays to produce coherence among multiple paragraphs, and the overall theme of the discourse at large. The reality of these internal and external semantic structure features reinforce the exegetical necessity of zooming in and zooming out when studying a passage of Scripture. The divine and human authors of Scripture have "packaged" the meaning of the text with a specific semantic structure. Text-driven preaching, therefore, seeks to take a natural thought unit of text, unpack it, and re-package it into a sermon that captures the substance, structure, and spirit of the text.

The Relationship between Surface and Semantic Structure

Language is a form-meaning composite where both form and meaning possess structure. The structure of form is called "grammatical" or "surface structure." The structure of meaning is called "semantic structure." Both types of structure serve to convey the meaning of the text, but how do they relate? In short, semantic structure is the "master" structure served by the subordinate role of surface structure (32). More often than not, the two work in tandem to mark content as more or less prominent. However, there is not a "direct and simple one-to-one representation" between surface and semantic structure (33). Rather, "both direct matching" between the two types of structure and "skewing (mismatching) can occur" (33). In other words, what surface structure might mark as prominent in a paragraph, semantic structure could override and mark as subordinate, and vice versa.

For example, in the last paragraph unit in Paul's letter to Philemon, verse 21 places "I write" in the grammatically prominent position (finite verb of the sentence). However, Paul's point is not the act of his physical writing. His point is that he is confident of Philemon's obedience, communicated via two perfect, active participles (being confident and knowing). The first participle fronts the sentence, and the two together sandwich the finite verb. Thus, by position and function, these two participles override as more prominent the content placed in the grammatically prominent position. Remember, the purpose of determining the structure of a text is to understand how it is packaged. One cannot unpack and repack the text for a sermon until the packaging is discerned. Ultimately, the packaging (structure) of a text is all about how the information it contains is related internally (unity, coherence, prominence) and externally (class, external coherence, theme).

The Role of Prominence in Language

Of all the internal and external features, perhaps prominence is the most critical for preachers to determine. According to Linda Jones:

> The human mind is incapable of assigning equal importance to all the data it receives from its sensory sources, probably because it is incapable of paying equal attention to all the data at once. When we look at a picture, we never perceive all its details simultaneously. There are certain parts of the

picture that we notice immediately, while the rest we do not. Always in human perception there are foreground and background, figure against ground, important and not important, theme and not-theme (or background).[443]

Beekman, Callow, and Kopesec extrapolate:

> Prominence is simply making one or more parts of a unit more important than the other parts. Any well-formed discourse will do this. Otherwise, it just goes on monotonously and nothing is highlighted. The difference between a politician and a good teacher is probably along this line. The politician may not want to make any promise or pledge stand out, in order that he not be held accountable for it. So he may talk very fluently for half an hour without ever highlighting anything. You then go home and talk to someone else, and he asks, "Well, what did he say?" You reply, "Well, he spoke fluently, and it was very impressive, and he really carried people with him." "But what did he actually say?" You cannot remember because nothing was made prominent. ... Some sermons are like that, too. You get a very rosy impression, but you cannot actually remember what was said. That is usually because prominence features are either deliberately or inadvertently omitted so that the point was not put across.[444]

A lack of proper prominence is the reason why Haddon Robinson claims, "Sermons seldom fail because they have too many ideas; more often they fail because they deal with too many unrelated ideas."[445]

---

[443]Linda K. Jones, *Theme in English Expository Discourse*, Edward Sapir Monograph Series in Language, Culture, and Cognition, no. 2 (Lake Bluff, IL: Jupiter Press, 1977), 2-3.
[444]Beekman, Callow, and Kopesec, *Semantic Structure*, 24.
[445]Robinson, *Biblical Preaching*, 16.

Preachers often fail to mark information (the main idea) as prominent in their sermons. This omission results in all information being presented as equally prominent. The audience, therefore, receives no organizing principle with which to process the information. Thus, the message is lost because it was not properly unpacked and repacked for maximum communication and comprehension.

Regarding prominence, think of every paragraph (or natural thought unit of Scripture) as a wagon wheel. As every wagon wheel has a hub, so too does every paragraph. This hub is the organizational center made naturally prominent by surface and semantic structure. Every semantic unit will have natural prominence, but the author may choose to override what is naturally prominent with marked prominence. By using devices specific to each language, an author may highlight as prominent content that would otherwise not be naturally prominent in the paragraph, as the above example from Philemon displays. Some of the devices utilized in the Greek New Testament for marked prominence include: fronting (ordered first in the sentence), cataphora (a reference to something ahead in the text), rhetorical questions, repetition, direct speech, inclusio, and chiasm. Of course, complex and compound paragraphs do exist.[446] However, most paragraphs will be "simple" and feature a single theme or hub.

The Structure of Language and Preaching

Determining the structure of a text allows the preacher to do two things. First, the structure of the text will reveal the main idea or hub of the paragraph. Second, the structure of the text will reveal the exact nature of the relationship that ties each piece of the paragraph together. Grasping these two elements is essential to text-driven preaching. Part of the wonder and adventure of preaching the Word of God is the fact that no two paragraphs (or natural thought units) of Scripture are exactly

---

[446] A complex paragraph may take various forms. For example, a paragraph might serve to support a portion of another paragraph and not the main idea of the overarching discourse unit, such as 1 Timothy 1:8-11. A compound paragraph essentially has more than one main hub or theme. Compound paragraphs are common to hortatory literature, where multiple commands are given.

Appendix

alike. Each one will have a unique main idea along with a unique set of relations that define how each of the parts relate to each other and the main idea. This means no two paragraphs in Scripture have the exact same structure. On the surface, this might appear daunting. However, the beauty of semantic structure alleviates the preacher's fear. Although no two paragraphs possess the exact same structure, each paragraph in Scripture depends on a finite set of communication relationships.

The Finite Set of Communication Relations and Preaching

Beekman, Callow, and Kopesec define and describe the communication relationships as follows:

> Every configuration of propositions consists of propositions related to one another by what are called the communication relations. Looked at from a different perspective, communication relations are those relations which relate propositions to each other in configurations. ... Without them, all discourses would consist of single propositions, unconnected with any other propositions. Further, the same set of relations is used regardless of whether it is two propositions that are being linked together, or two large units, such as divisions, parts, acts, etc. ... From the analytical perspective (internal), the relations are "links" between the various parts that make up a unit. From a holistic perspective, the role is the "functional contribution" that a particular unit gives to the structure of which it is a constituent—whether it is a proposition in a cluster, a cluster in a paragraph, a paragraph in a section, etc.[447]

Take Colossians 3:5-11 as an example. The sentence begins with a general statement, "Put to death therefore what is earthly in you" (ESV). The remainder of the sentence specifies what is earthly: "sexual

---

[447]Beekman, Callow, and Kopesec, *Semantic Structure*, 77.

immorality, impurity, passion, evil desire, and covetousness, which is idolatry." Therefore, the communication relation linking verse 5a with verse 5b is a Generic-Specific relation. Verses 6 and 7 follow, providing two grounds for putting to death whatever is earthly. This is a Head-Grounds relation. Verse 8 essentially restates the command given in verse 5, revealing by repetition the main idea of this paragraph. Verse 9a specifies an aspect of verse 8, another Generic-Specific relation. Finally, verses 9b-11 provide two additional grounds (Head-Grounds relation) for heeding the command in verse 9a. Recognizing these communication relationships unlocks how the paragraph works and is therefore key to proper interpretation.

Discerning the communication relations at work in each thought unit of Scripture occurs by studying the content of the unit to see how each part relates to the other. This skill operates intuitively to a large degree for most readers. However, text-driven preachers must consciously work at it. The Greek New Testament often provides clues to cue interpreters via conjunctions and prepositions that specify the relationship between paragraph constituents. All relevant data, however, must be analyzed, such as "overt relator words, the presence or absence of finite forms of the verb, mood, the content of the units, etc." (78). Overall, nothing trumps understanding the actual semantic content of the unit(s) under investigation in order to see how one piece relates to another.

Chart of the Finite Set of Communication Relations[448]

Review the chart of relations between communication units from Beekman, Callow, and Kopesec. At first glance, it might appear to be quite complicated. However, with a little explanation, it becomes much more user-friendly. The first division distinguishes between the relations of communication units and relations between a communication unit and a concept. Remember, a concept is one word or groups of words that name an element of the referential realm. Therefore, a communication unit such as the relative clause "who knew they were trespassing" might

---

[448]Beekman, Callow, and Kopesec, *Semantic Structure*, 112-13.

Appendix

THE SEMANTIC STRUCTURE OF WRITTEN COMMUNICATION

CHART OF RELATIONS INVOLVING COMUNICATION UNITS[1]

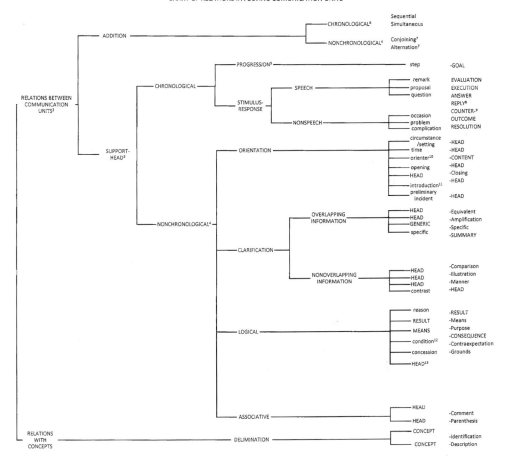

[1] A communication unit (CU) is a proposition or a configuration of propositions that functions as a unit.

[2] As a larger configuration is analyzed into its constituent CU's, each constituent will be found to be in some relation with at least one other constituent in that configuration, and each will have with respect to the other a role corresponding with that relationship.

Let the Text Talk

THE SEMANTIC STRUCTURE OF WRITTEN COMMUNICATION

[3] For a given pair of labels, the role of the CU having greater natural prominence is indicated in upper-case letters, and the role of the CU having lesser prominence is shown in lower case. The role labels for each pair are shown in the order in which the units more frequently occur in New Testament Greek texts.

[4] Nonchronological should to be taken to mean that there is no relative temporal relationship between the pair of CU's; rather, that the focus is not on the temporal notion.

[5] Often a sequence of events, usually performed by the same participant, lacks the feature of stimulus-response, yet involves a movement toward a more prominent event or goal. In such cases, this set of labels is needed.

[6] In a CU display, these labels will be used in conjunction with the label HEAD, e.g. sequential $HEAD_1$ – sequential $HEAD_2$, or simultaneous $HEAD_1$ – simultaneous $HEAD_2$.

[7] These labels will not normally be used in a CU display. Conjoining will be marked with subscript numbers following the head or support role label that the conjoined units have with respect to other units, e.g. $HEAD_1$ – $HEAD_2$ – etc. or $reason_1$ – $reason_2$ – etc. If alternation is involved, the units would be labeled as follows: alternate $HEAD_1$ – alternate $HEAD_2$ – etc. or alternate $reason_1$ – alternate $reason_2$ – etc.

[8] REPLY is a verbal response to any speech stimulus other than the response which naturally corresponds with that stimulus.

[9] For each speech stimulus, there is a corresponding counter-role response in which a different speaker, in response to a remark, proposal, question, etc., makes an alternative or substitute is labeled COUNTERREMARK, COUNTERPROPOSAL, COUNTERQUESTION, etc. Within the bracketed sets, any one stimulus may be paired with any of the responses.

[10] Types of orienteers are speech, perceptual, emotional, cognitive, volitional, evaluative, and prominence.

[11] Introduction includes topic orienter, preview (topic and part of the theme are stated), prologue (used in narrative genre). These more specific labels may be used at the discretion of the analyst.

[12] The condition element of this relation may be subdivided into three types: contrary to fact, potential fact:general, and potential fact:particular.

[13] The HEAD in this relation may be either an IMPLICATION/CONCLUSION (statement), an EXHORTATION (command), or a QUESTION. In relation to EXHORTATION, grounds will include motivation. Some analysts may prefer this more specific label.

be related to the concept "the boys." The communication unit identifies or describes the concept.

The remainder of the communication relations, however, fall under relations between units, distinguished first between relations that link units of equal importance (Addition or Coordinate) and relations that link units of unequal importance (Support/Head or Subordinate). The Addition relations have either a temporal focus, making them chronological, or a non-temporal focus, making then non-chronological.

The vast majority of the communication relations fall under the Support/Head division because they link communication units that are subordinate to a head unit(s). These, like the Addition relations, first divide according to time—is there a temporal focus or not? A temporal focus leads to the Chronological categories of Progression or Stimulus/Response. The Progression relations typically involve a single character taking actions or steps that lead to a goal. The Stimulus/Response relations, which are typical of narrative literature or dialogue, involve multiple characters and unfold along a cause-effect basis.

The Non-Chronological category of the Support/Head division is the realm of the vast majority of non-narrative communication relations. Four categories name the possible relation of a subordinate communication unit to the Head unit: orientation, clarification, logical, and associative. Orientation supports the Head unit with time, location, subject matter, etc. Clarification relates to the Head unit with explanation or restatement. Logical connects to the Head unit via argumentation by reason, grounds, etc. Associative departs from the main subject matter of the Head unit with some type of side comment or discussion.

The specific relations under each category are listed to the far right of the chart. These relations name how each piece of a paragraph or natural thought unit of text works. Although it might not be necessary to label every part of the text according to this nomenclature for preaching, preachers should work to understand how each part of the text relates to the other parts. This is how preachers harness the structure of the text, the semantic structure—that is, the master structure—so that it drives the development of sermon structure.